RETHINKING AUSTRALIAN CITIZENSHIP

EDITED BY

WAYNE HUDSON
Griffith University

JOHN KANE
Griffith University

PUBLISHED BY THE PRESS SYNDICATE OF THE UNIVERSITY OF CAMBRIDGE
The Pitt Building, Trumpington Street, Cambridge, United Kingdom

CAMBRIDGE UNIVERSITY PRESS
The Edinburgh Building, Cambridge CB2 2RU, UK   http://www.cup.cam.ac.uk
40 West 20th Street, New York, NY 10011–4211, USA   http://www.cup.org
10 Stamford Road, Oakleigh, Melbourne 3166, Australia   http://www.cup.edu.au
Ruiz de Alarcón 13, 28014, Madrid, Spain

© Cambridge University Press 2000

This book is in copyright. Subject to statutory exception
and to the provisions of relevant collective licensing agreements,
no reproduction of any part may take place without
the written permission of Cambridge University Press.

First published 2000

Printed in Australia by Brown Prior Anderson

Typeface New Baskerville (Adobe) 10/12 pt.   *System* QuarkXPress® [BC]

A catalogue record for this book is available from the British Library

National Library of Australia Cataloguing in Publication data
Rethinking Australian citizenship.
Bibliography.
Includes index.
ISBN 0 521 59337 9.
ISBN 0 521 59670 X (pbk.).
1. Citizenship – Australia. I. Hudson, Wayne. II. Kane, John, 1945– .
323.60994

ISBN 0 521 59337 9 hardback
ISBN 0 521 59670 X paperback

RETHINKING AUSTRALIAN CITIZENSHIP

The notion of citizenship has recently been taken up internationally as a way of rethinking questions of social cohesion and social justice. In Europe, the concept of national identity is under close scrutiny, while the pressures of globalising markets and the power of transnational corporations everywhere raise questions about the true place and meaning of citizenship in civil society. In Australia, a traditional view of citizens belonging to a single nation made up of one people with a special relationship to one land has been challenged from a range of differing perspectives. All contributors are leading analysts in their chosen field, and their complementary essays add up to a thorough and comprehensive examination of the many dimensions of contemporary citizenship. The result is a rich and coherent volume that shows the diverse ways in which Australian citizenship can be re-imagined.

Wayne Hudson is Professor of History and Philosophy, School of Humanities, Griffith University.

John Kane is a lecturer in Political Theory, School of Politics and Public Policy, Griffith University.

Powell's Rethinking Australian Citizenship (N

90.00/6.98   **NDJ**

Australia & the Pacific   56420

Contents

List of Contributors   vii

1 Rethinking Australian Citizenship   1
   WAYNE HUDSON AND JOHN KANE

Part I Theoretical Debates

2 Differential Citizenship   15
   WAYNE HUDSON

3 Republicanism and Citizenship   26
   PHILIP PETTIT

4 Postmodernism and Citizenship   37
   PETER BEILHARZ

5 Democracy and Citizenship   45
   ALASTAIR DAVIDSON

6 Feminism and Citizenship   56
   EVA COX

7 Limits to Citizenship   66
   BARRY HINDESS

Part II Different Citizenships

8 Political Citizenship   77
   MIKE SALVARIS

CONTENTS

9	Indigenous Citizenship TIM ROWSE	86
10	Multicultural Citizenship MARY KALANTZIS	99
11	Legal Citizenship MARGARET THORNTON	111
12	Economic Citizenship JOCELYN PIXLEY	121
13	Social Citizenship WINTON HIGGINS AND GABY RAMIA	136
14	Sexual Citizenship BARBARA SULLIVAN	150
15	Educational Citizenship DAVID HOGAN	158
16	Citizenship and Military Service APRIL CARTER	174
17	Media Citizenship ELIZABETH VAN ACKER	185
18	Environmental Citizenship PETER CHRISTOFF	200
19	Communitarianism and Citizenship JOHN KANE	215
20	Global Citizenship GEOFFREY STOKES	231

References   243
Index   266

Contributors

PETER BEILHARZ is Reader in Sociology at La Trobe University, Melbourne.

APRIL CARTER is Lecturer in the Department of Government, University of Queensland, Brisbane.

PETER CHRISTOFF is Lecturer in the Department of Geography and Environment at the University of Melbourne, Melbourne.

EVA COX is Senior Lecturer in the Department of Writing, Social and Cultural Studies at the University of Technology, Sydney.

ALASTAIR DAVIDSON is Professor of Citizenship Studies at Swinburne University of Technology, Melbourne.

WINTON HIGGINS is Associate Professor in the School of History, Philosophy and Politics, Macquarie University, Sydney.

BARRY HINDESS is Professor of Politics in the Research School of Social Sciences at the Australian National University, Canberra.

DAVID HOGAN is Professor of Education at the University of Tasmania, Hobart.

WAYNE HUDSON is Professor of History and Philosophy in the School of Humanities, at Griffith University, Brisbane.

MARY KALANTZIS is Professor in the Faculty of Education, Language and Community Services, Royal Melbourne Institute of Technology, Melbourne.

JOHN KANE is Lecturer in Political Theory, School of Politics and Public Policy, Griffith University, Brisbane.

PHILIP PETTIT is Professor of Philosophy in the Research School of Social Sciences, Australian National University, Canberra.

JOCELYN PIXLEY is Senior Lecturer in Sociology at the University of New South Wales, Sydney.

GABY RAMIA is a Lecturer in the Department of Management, Monash University, Melbourne.

TIM ROWSE is an ARC Fellow in the Department of Government, University of Sydney, Sydney.

MIKE SALVARIS is Senior Research Fellow in the Institute for Social Research at Swinburne University of Technology, Melbourne.

GEOFFREY STOKES is Associate Professor in the Department of Government and Director of the Centre for Democracy, University of Queensland, Brisbane.

BARBARA SULLIVAN is Senior Lecturer in the Department of Government, University of Queensland, Brisbane.

MARGARET THORNTON is Professor of Law and Legal Studies, La Trobe University, Melbourne.

ELIZABETH VAN ACKER is Lecturer, School of Politics and Public Policy, Griffith University, Brisbane.

CHAPTER 1

Rethinking Australian Citizenship

Wayne Hudson and John Kane

Across the world citizenship is being taken up as a way to rethink questions of political and social justice. Critics of economic rationalism turn to citizenship in order to present ethical social concerns to governments. Conservatives use the rhetoric of citizenship to insist on duties and community service. In the United States there has been a revival of republican and communitarian approaches to citizenship (Goodwin 1995; Dagger 1997). In Canada debates about citizenship have expanded to include multicultural citizenship and the rights of First Nations (Kymlicka 1995). Citizenship is also a contested concept in Africa and the Middle East (Mamdani 1996; Nielsen 1993). In Europe, European citizenship has been construed as a form which is neither cosmopolitan nor national (Hyland 1995; Meehan 1993a; Van Berkel and Roche 1997). At the same time, national citizenship is becoming more difficult to acquire as xenophobic nationalism revives in response to immigration (Barbieri 1998; Brubaker 1992; Einhorn, Kaldor and Kavan 1996; Cesarani and Fulbrook 1996; Jacobson 1997). In Australia citizenship has recently become central to debates about how to reinvent Australian national identity.

There are several reasons for this remarkable burst of interest in citizenship discourse. One is the collapse of the traditional left that occurred with the fall of the iron curtain. Justly or unjustly, the old socialist rhetoric no longer commands the respect and attention, nor incites the fears it once did. In times of waning solidarity, those who still cherish the dream of social justice look for a different rhetoric, one that will bite. Citizenship seems to answer because it is ready-to-hand in our traditions. It is an idea that elicits positive, if vague, response and its developmental possibilities may not yet be exhausted. In much recent work, citizenship discourse is clearly a new vehicle for pressing familiar demands for egalitarian social and economic goals. Citizenship discourse is also less immediately divisive than socialist discourse. By the same token, however, its neutrality means that it can be deployed for quite different and contradictory political purposes. This may be another reason for its appeal. It all depends on which citizenship values one emphasises – equal rights or equal responsibilities, citizen capacities and empowerment or citizen loyalty and obedience.

A further reason for the current focus on citizenship is simply that the world is changing. Europe provides a pertinent case. As it moves from economic to political union, the relationship of national citizens to the new, larger entity must necessarily be defined. Some reconceptualisation of citizenship needs to be evolved to fit the altered circumstances. Relationships between other nation-states might not be shifting as dramatically, but in the long run the changes may be no less profound. We are repeatedly assured, at least, that the nation-state, the focal point for citizenship discourse for several centuries, is inexorably mutating as a result of globalisation. It is in the context of these changes, both in the world itself and in theoretical perspectives upon it, that Australians are reconsidering their own citizenship traditions. This book is a contribution to that rethinking.

The Australian Context

What most Australians understand by citizenship is a mixture of legal and political citizenship. The history of legal and political citizenship in Australia, however, is problematic. No satisfactory or coherent conception of Australian citizenship was ever formulated in the colonial period, and no adequate debate or core notion of citizenship was ever widely accepted (Chesterman and Galligan 1997; Irving 1997). Instead, Australian citizenship was conceived largely in statist and passive terms. Immigration issues prevailed over any positive notion of citizenship, occluding questions of access to rights or even of the right to vote (Davidson 1996). This was partly the product of a delayed national development. Federation in 1901 did not make Australia a nation-state (this was achieved only retrospectively in 1939 in the passing of the *Statute of Westminster Adoption Act* of 1942), and there is no substantive mention of citizenship in the Constitution. Until 1948 Australians had the rights of 'Britons'. Even the *Nationality and Citizenship Act* of 1948 dealt only with how aliens could become citizens, and the distinction between Australian citizens and non-citizens was not legally enacted until the 1984 amendment to that Act. In the postwar period citizenship was overwhelmingly seen as an ingredient of nation-building, as a matter of turning 'New Australians' into real Australians (Jordens 1995).

On the other hand, from the nineteenth century onwards, citizenship existed as an administrative reality at a range of discrete levels. Often citizenship was associated with attempts to refine and police exclusionary categories.[1] For example, aliens could become British subjects in particular Australian colonies in the nineteenth century, but lost that status if they left the colony. Similarly, specific regulations were designed to exclude Asians, Africans and Pacific populations, while keeping Aborigines as British subjects but not full citizens. For most of our history, Aborigines were 'citizens without rights' (Chesterman and Galligan 1997), and the undifferentiated notion of citizenship eventually ascribed to them failed to take account of their diversity.[2] According to some scholars, all this amounts to an Australian tradition of *non-citizenship* (Chesterman and Galligan 1997; cf. Rowse 1998).

Over many decades positive government on behalf of disadvantaged individuals and groups was the real basis of Australian citizenship (Beilharz, Considine and Watts 1992; Galligan 1998).[3] A more positive notion of citizenship, however, was implicit in the colonial liberalism indebted to the British idealist philosopher T.H. Green, and in the ameliorist pursuit of citizenship through education associated with Meredith Atkinson and other Workers' Educational Association (WEA) intellectuals. Again, important strands of thought about citizenship can be found among Indigenous peoples (Stokes 1997) and in the work of early Australian feminists (Lake 1994). Substantive conceptions of citizenship were also promoted by Australian churches, both Protestant and Catholic. Nonetheless, our heritage in the area of citizenship leaves much work to be done.

Today there is a widely recognised need to invent new and stronger forms of Australian citizenship. Citizenship needs to be reconstructed, not just at the level of symbols and ideas, but also of practices if civil society is to be revitalised and the prevailing cynicism about politicians, parties and parliaments overcome. There is a lack of extensive training in political citizenship, the effective exercise of which requires the inculcation of appropriate competencies (van Steenbergen 1994, 2; van Gunsteren 1998, 19). This constitutes a *civics deficit* in Australia. There is also a need to consider contexts in which citizenship has been lost or eroded; for example, in education (Marginson 1997). Likewise, the commonality currently held to be central to Australian citizenship must be questioned. The *Australian Citizenship Act* (1948) refers to 'the common bond involving reciprocal rights and obligations uniting all Australians', and the current oath of loyalty stresses agreement with core attitudes: 'whose democratic beliefs I share' (*Oath of Australian Citizenship* 1994). Commonality assumes that Australian citizens should acquire *common* skills, knowledges and values. But what exactly is this commonality? What really follows from citizenship as membership of 'the community of the Commonwealth of Australia'? It will not do simply to appeal to 'the community', without knowing how the status of plural communities in Australia is to be determined. Donald Horne argues that citizenship in a contemporary context is about replacing culturally chauvinist and ethnic views of national identity with a civic definition of what it means to be Australian. It is, he says, a matter of a new civic patriotism – of a more effective way of talking about ourselves (Horne 1994). Others argue that a universal nationalism based on civil society needs to replace the older ethnic Australian nationalism (cf. Castles et al. 1990; Yeatman 1994). Certainly the role of nationalist notions in a postcolonial Australia needs to be clarified.

The federal character of Australian citizenship also needs to be addressed (Galligan 1995, 1998). It can be misleading to apply approaches to citizenship devised in Britain (which has no written constitution and only a nascent federalism) to Australia. Yet federalism is neglected in many discussions of citizenship (see Burgess and Gagnon 1993; Smith 1998; Painter 1998). Australians are citizens of their respective states as well as of the Commonwealth. There is also a major question about how far citizenship questions should be steered in a populist direction. Some Australians are attracted to doctrines of the sovereignty of 'the people'; they support citizen-initiated referenda and other forms of direct democracy, especially at the local government level. Others advocate representative democracy precisely because it excludes the people from political power except at elections, when diversely valued votes, oligarchic media ownership, and inequalities of information operate to minimise their influence. It may be that an explicitly republican approach to governance offers a way forward here (cf. Pettit 1998). In Australia, relatively few links are made between citizenship and republicanism, and in the course of the debate over the republic there has been little discussion of republican citizenship. This will need to change if Australia becomes an explicit republic.

Theoretical Issues

The need to rethink Australian citizenship becomes even more pressing in the light of contemporary international debates that have questioned the theoretical terms in which citizenship has been traditionally understood. In these debates the move away from older conceptions of citizenship has not yet led to the acceptance of a single alternative approach. Instead, a confusing plurality of different perspectives prevail. Feminists, for example, argue that citizenship must be embodied and gendered, republicans urge a stronger conception of civic freedom, and postmodernists challenge notions of identity and 'universal' rights. Controversies have arisen about whether citizenship is a creation of the modern state or derives from civil society, and about whether citizenship can be derived from a theory of human rights or should be understood as specific to particular legal regimes and their technologies. In the process, citizenship itself has become a highly contested concept, defined by different authors in different ways.

As a result, discussions of citizenship are now often makeshift and transitional to a new synthesis which has not yet appeared. In these discussions there are tensions between *citizenship as a moral and political philosophical idea, citizenship as a formal legal status,* and *citizenship as an administrative category.* Frequently citizenship is identified with *democratic political* citizenship (cf. Klusmeyer 1996), to the neglect of other forms of citizenship. There is also a tendency to overstate the distinction between *the liberal conception of citizenship,* which sees the citizen as a rational agent capable of giving consent to laws and *the civic republican conception of citizenship,* for which citizenship is a practice or activity that is good in itself.[4] Both characterisations are idealised simplifications of the historical record, and can be misleading in theoretical contexts.[5]

Disagreements have also arisen between *internationalists,* who emphasise the duty of human beings to be concerned for the whole human race and the situation of the planet, and *nationalists,* for whom the only realistic account of citizenship remains centred on the nation-state. Internationalists have trouble showing how their idealistic stances translate into enforceable arrangements, while nationalists are often theoretically conservative. Further, most of the literature on citizenship has *an urban bias.* Citizens seem to live in cities, and little attention is paid to the specific problems of rural citizenship, leaving the life situations of two-thirds of the world's people unaddressed. Similarly, many discussions of citizenship reveal a secularist bias, as if human beings *should* regard their civic identities as their most fundamental allegiance.

To understand the contemporary theoretical debates, it is essential to grasp that the account of citizenship which profoundly influenced recent Australian thinking, that of British sociologist T.H. Marshall, is now widely rejected. Marshall interpreted citizenship as a process through which citizens obtained civil, political, and finally social rights. Citizenship was a *status* allowing members of a nation-state equal access to critical rights and powers that could be used to modify economic, political and social inequalities (Marshall 1965). It was also *a set of social relationships between the individual and the state, and between citizens themselves.* Citizenship for Marshall is centred on the welfare state (Barbalet 1988, 1996; Twine 1994; Roche 1992). Today his work is widely criticised as being tied to obsolete notions of 'society' and 'class', as being characteristically British in construing citizens as passive recipients rather than actors in their own cause (Bulmer and Rees 1996), and as too centred on the nation-state. These criticisms do not reduce the importance of Marshall's insight into the ways in which changes of economic and social organisation, as well as of particular institutional regimes (for example, schooling), may gradually make possible new forms of civic competence. They do, however, reduce the value of his concept of citizenship as a normative ideal by which contemporary arrangements can be measured and towards which we can aspire (cf. Marshall 1950, 291). With the decline of Keynesianism and the emergence of the contractual state, other conceptions of citizenship are becoming important, including some which emphasise wider clusters of rights.[6] This is important in the context of states which deny their citizens effective rights or which 'ethnically cleanse' parts of their populations. Approaches which theorise citizens as reflexive, active beings rather than as passive subjects (Janoski 1998) are of great importance in polities which are not nation-states (such as Taiwan), in Latin America where the state may be oppressive (Jellin and Hershberg 1996), and with respect to Indigenous peoples whose rights have been denied or violated by nation-state regimes.

Marshall's classic work has not been the only target of criticism. Liberal conceptions of citizenship generally are also now seriously contested. Many question how far liberalism is, or ever was, an adequate approach to citizenship (Bridges 1994; Slawner and Denham 1998). Feminist scholars, influenced by Anglo-Saxon interpretations of postmodernism and poststructuralism, attack liberal citizenship and its alleged universality of rights on the grounds that it promotes the subordination of women (Vogel and Moran 1991; Walby 1994). Some argue that we need *a gendered citizenship* to do justice to the experiences and life paths of women, especially since women practise 'an ethic of care' and devote many hours of labour to domestic duties in the private sphere (Pateman 1988, 1992). Feminist scholars have also questioned *the formalism of masculinist citizenship*, and the extent to which women lack the empowering conditions of citizenship, including basic conditions such as freedom from interference with their bodies. Still other feminist scholars argue for *an institutionally embodied account of citizenship* which grasps its social reality, pointing to the crucial importance of material circumstances such as the availability of paid work (Pixley 1993), real networks, relationships and access to wealth and property (Cox 1995; Yeatman 1994). Anna Yeatman, for example, claims that *citizens are subjects who share a public life* and attempts to theorise the sociological individuation of the subject, instead of merely positing a given community of pre-existent subjects. Her work nicely emphasises the social reality of citizenship against models that treat citizens merely as products of the exercises of state power (Yeatman 1996, 1997, 1998).[7]

Another theoretical literature, influenced by German discussions, argues that *citizenship should be based on mutual recognition, as well as, or instead of, on a shared identity or membership of a single moral community*. On this view, citizens may be no less citizens because they differ in their identities and in their traditions. This implies that ethnic nationalism must be no longer crucial to citizenship at a time in which large numbers of people live and work as denizens in countries of which they are not citizens (Bauböck 1994, 1995; Hammar 1990). Some argue that denizens should be given citizen rights no matter where they happen to have been born (Carens in Beiner 1995). There are also fierce debates about the relationship between citizenship and multiculturalism (Gutmann 1992; Singh 1996; Kymlicka 1995; Cardozo and Musto 1997; Dunne and Bonazzi 1995; Glazer 1997). The Canadian theorist of citizenship Will Kymlicka, for example, argues for group as well as individual rights, and further alleges that group rights are consistent with rather than opposed to liberal principles (Kymlicka 1995).

There is also a tension between discussions of citizenship focused on passports granted by nation-states and discussions which do not involve clear exclusion rules; for example, discussions which characterise citizenship as the right to have rights. Here it is important to remember that citizenship was not linked with nationality until comparatively recent times, and did not always imply an association with a fixed territory (Habermas in Beiner 1995). Although the nation-state still provides the enabling conditions for many exercises of citizenship, and remains of overriding importance in the context of immigration and naturalisation, the role of nation-states today is less and less a completely sovereign one. Indeed, many scholars argue that the seventeenth-century western theory of absolute sovereignty should be rejected (Tully 1995; Camilleri and Falk 1992; Ferrajoli 1991). This means that modern notions of citizenship may have to be rethought in principle. Perhaps we should think of citizenship as multiple, complex and relational (Meehan 1993a; Yeatman 1994; Soysal 1994). David Heater (1990, ch. 9), for example, sets out 'a cube of citizenship', relating world, continental/regional, nation-state, and provisional/local citizenships.

Some scholars suggest that it would be better to take a more negative view of citizenship as merely a mark in a passport and a conspiracy against the world (Hindess 1993, 1996). Many of these critics dismiss participation as a myth (Minson 1993; Ignatieff in Beiner 1995), and insist that citizens are in fact not self-governing nor members of self-governing communities. They argue that both liberal and civic republican notions of citizenship are inappropriate to complex contemporary societies. Others question the overemphasis on egalitarianism in recent discussions, as well as the standard distinctions between active and passive citizenship, citizens and consumers, and between social rights and the economy. More technically articulated and domain-specific approaches to citizenship may be needed that take more account of mundane practical and administrative concerns if governmental and administrative regulation are to be effectively managed (Osborne and Gaebler 1993; Burchell 1995; Dean and Hindess 1998). It is also possible, however, to make a case for high ethical approaches to citizenship within some domains without supporting either communalist notions of citizenship (Walzer 1991), or versions of civil republicanism, which imply a form of civic religion (cf. Oldfield 1990a, b; Clarke 1994; Gutmann 1992). To do this, however, it may be necessary to defend forms of religious citizenship which go beyond notions of citizenship as *secular solidarity* (Turner 1986; Turner and Hamilton 1994).

Given such a wealth of positions, Australians are bound to take account of the new climate in the theory of citizenship and to position themselves in terms of them. The contributions to this volume do exactly that.

The Contributions

All the contributors to this volume agree that there is a need to engage with the new citizenship discourse in the Australian context, and that the standard approaches to Australian citizenship do not take adequate account of contemporary political, social, economic, and cultural conditions. Overall no clear consensus emerges about exactly how to rethink Australian citizenship. They also differ in the theoretical approaches they take and in the objects which they address. In practice, the contributions range over the *domain of citizenship*, the *subject of citizenship*, and the *object of citizenship*. By the *domain of citizenship* is meant the social, political or other field in which talk about the practice of citizenship makes sense. By the *subject of citizenship* is meant the person or entity that is the bearer of citizenship in any particular domain. By the *object of citizenship* is meant the purposes at which citizenship practice aims, the point of its existence, in particular domains. Though these categories *are* always relevant, they do not always receive the same degree of attention from an individual writer. Depending on the point of theoretical-political interest, the principal focus may be on only one, or two, of them.

Several contributions focus on a particular *domain of citizenship*, or on the theme of multiple domains. There is general agreement that citizenship can no longer be limited to legal-political citizenship in a nation-state, even if none on how plural citizenships in diverse domains are to be articulated. Wayne Hudson in particular emphasises this theme with his concept of differential citizenships across different fields of deployment. Peter Beilharz, too, argues that postmodern conditions raise the spectre of multiple identities – urban, local, regional – that do not map easily onto the nation state. Geoff Stokes, on the other hand, focuses on a single domain, albeit one that encompasses the whole world, and discusses the developing institutions that make that domain a real focus of global citizenship practice. Elizabeth van Acker investigates another potential new domain of citizenship in the technological web of communications that are increasingly encompassing the globe. Insofar as she speculates whether new identities may be created in the process of communication, she also enters the field of the *subject of citizenship* that other contributors take as their main focus.

Individual human beings are not the only possible *subjects of citizenship*. States themselves, corporations and other collectivities may also be citizens in particular domains (thus states are, as Stokes points out, the principal subjects of international citizenship). Tim Rowse, discussing the citizenship capacities of Indigenous Australians delineates as the real subjects of Indigenous citizenship an ensemble of corporations, councils, land trusts and representative bodies. Eva Cox emphasises the role of civil associations, and the social capital inherent in them, in creating the good society that current definitions of citizenship overlook. Even where individual citizens form the main focus, the question of how this individual subject is to be understood remains in serious question for other contributors. Thus Mary Kalantzis argues for a highly, multiculturally and individually differentiated citizen in her chapter on civic pluralism. Margaret Thornton takes issue with traditional liberal legal approaches to the citizen in Australia, arguing that it has been too masculinist and formalist, and that the subject of citizenship has to be rethought in both pluralist and gendered terms. Barbara Sullivan emphasises sexual heterogeneity among the subjects of citizenship, and argues for richer conceptions of equal citizenship to accommodate this.

Most of the other contributors are primarily concerned with the *objects of citizenship*, the things at which citizenship aims. Thus Alastair Davidson seeks a citizenship that promotes a more adequate form of democratic practice. Philip Pettit takes a republican approach that aims at a form of liberty he describes as non-domination. Mike Salvaris focuses on connecting citizenship more closely to the exercise of power in society, while Jocelyn Pixley would link it to the means of economic flourishing. David Hogan focuses on educating citizens for liberty and virtue, while April Carter argues a cogent case for citizen responsibility for bearing arms in defence of the polity. John Kane in a discussion of communitarian citizenship distinguishes two different objects commonly attaching to citizenship, namely a sense of belonging and the exercise of responsibility. Barry Hindess, in pessimistic mood, concludes that citizenship's only use now is as a rather thin rhetorical defence against powers too large to control. Two other contributions traverse the three categories equally. Thus Peter Christoff is concerned with the domain of ecological citizenship (the whole globe), the subjects (individuals or ecosystems?) and the object (preservation of humankind or preservation of natural systems for their own sake). Winton Higgins and Gaby Ramia encompass all categories when they argue that social citizenship should be conceived as a radically inclusive democratic project systematically linked to grassroots associational life, with less emphasis on statist enterprise and greater on diversity and individual agency.

Clearly many of the issues raised by these contributions will be debated by Australians in the years to come. At this point, what is crucial is that we open our minds to a wider range of possible approaches to citizenship than we have considered in the past, and seek to combine a willingness to make changes with political and economic realism. In the outcome, it is likely that we will find a distinctly Australian way of handling many of the issues raised in this volume.

Notes

1 Children, aliens, criminals, the sick, and the mad, are still excluded from citizenship for certain purposes, although there is now a literature on child citizenship (Meredyth and Tyler 1993; Funder 1996).
2 One possible response, as Mick Dodson (in Davis 1996) argues, would be to take Aboriginal sovereignty seriously (Reynolds 1996) and to recognise that Aborigines have specific group rights. For discussions of new possibilities for constructing Indigenous citizenship, see Peterson and Sanders (1998, pt III).
3 For citizenship in nineteenth-century Australia, see S. Macintyre (1991), Beilharz, Considine and Watts (1992), McKenna (1996) and Skates (1997). There was also a significant tradition of Australian civics education Thomas (1993, 1994). In Australia civics was often heavily historical, which meant that students were taught the history of the British Empire. For the very different American approach to civics education, see Callan (1997).
4 For accounts of civic republican citizenship, see Oldfield (1990a, b); cf. Clarke (1994, 1996). Oldfield refers to participation as 'the highest form of human living together most individuals can aspire to' (1990b, 6), a view few would now accept. For discussion of liberal citizenship, see Macedo (1991, ch. 5). Macedo argues that liberalism is morally committed, not neutral.

5 Literature on citizenship in English does not alert the reader to the complexity of citizenship, either in recent centuries in Europe or worldwide. Religious citizenship (e.g. medieval Christian citizenship) and Imperial citizenship (e.g. of the Austro-Hungarian Empire) are little discussed (see, however, Riesenberg 1992), and, outside of excellent specialist studies, little attention is paid to the Luso-Hispanic world or to the Middle East. Moreover, the standard stereotypes of Athenian and Roman citizenship are inaccurate and need to be revised (Manville 1991; Nicolet 1990). Even in the ancient world, citizenship based on membership of a community of shared or common law might extend beyond national and territorial boundaries (Pocock in Beiner 1995). On the history of citizenship, see J.G.A. Pocock's essay 'The Ideal of Citizenship Since Classical Times' in Beiner (1995); Heater (1996) and Riesenberg (1992). For the limitations of French citizenship, see Hufton (1992), Gordon (1994), Wells (1995).
6 David Held, for example, distinguishes seven clusters of rights corresponding to seven key sites of power: health, social, cultural, civil, economic, pacific and political rights. These bundles of rights are, Held contends, the key to successfully entrenching the principle of autonomy and facilitating free and equal political participation (Held 1993, pt. I; 1995).
7 Other feminists argue that citizenship is 'an articulating principle' and hence inherently contestable. See Mouffe (1993, 84).

PART I

Theoretical Debates

CHAPTER 2

Differential Citizenship

Wayne Hudson

What is citizenship? Is it more than a quasi-technical term for 'membership' or 'ability to exercise a capacity'? Contemporary theoretical debates attempt to disarticulate citizenship from the nation-state and from sovereignty. They flag problems of multiple and pluralist citizenship. This chapter intervenes in these debates by arguing that a coherent notion of citizenship is not what we need. Instead, we need to register the plurality and disorder surrounding citizenship and enlarge our understandings of citizenship to include notions not only of *differentiated*, but of *differential citizenship*.[1]

Currently citizenship is an overused word deployed as a code term for attempts to renew older social and political projects based on the desirability of social and cultural uniformity. Citizenship cannot bear this, or many of the other burdens currently placed upon it. Nor should it be assumed that citizenship is necessarily desirable or a good thing (Hindess 1993). Nonetheless, a realistic understanding of political citizenship does not preclude coming to terms with contemporary cultural, ethnic, religious and moral diversity. On the contrary, a republican approach to the array of citizenships to which Australians have access can do justice both to the need for determinate tests, especially for political citizenship, and to the need for reflexive engagements with a greater diversity of citizenships than the classical discussions of citizenship had in mind (Heater 1990, 1996).

Definition

Differential citizenship is a non-traditional approach to citizenship which implies that:

- citizenship is different on different sites and in different contexts and domains;
- different citizenships involve multiple capacities;
- exercises of civic capacity do not fall under a single citizenship; and
- citizenships cannot be totalised, especially for example, by reference to citizenships persons possess as members of a nation-state.

Everyone knows that what 'citizenship' means varies with discourse and context, but in the literature of citizenship the implications of this fact are seldom drawn. Often a citizen is taken to be a *member* of something. For example, a member of *a city* or *a community* or *a state* or *an empire* or *an association* or *a corporation*. At other times the stress falls on *exclusion* and clear boundaries. Who gives citizenship? Who judges disputed cases? Who is denied citizenship? How can citizenship be lost? At other times *the practice* of citizenship is held to be crucial. Citizenship, however, is not one thing, and monistic approaches conceal the heterogeneous sites on which Australians exercise diverse citizenship capacities. Some forms of citizenship are *specific to one site or particular membership*, for example, membership of a voluntary association, a church, a club, a lodge, a block of home units, a corporation. Others amount to *exercises of capacity*: those who do it are citizens in that domain. In other contexts citizenship implies *a positive evaluation of behaviour*. For example, good citizenship in corporate contexts involves behaving in ways which take account of the rights of other players and some consideration for the public good. In other cases again, citizenship is *an ethic by which existing arrangements can be evaluated and judged*.

It is also no longer controversial to refer to *multiple citizenships*, not only in the sense of cases where a person has dual citizenship, but in the sense that one person has many citizenships or, more subtly, is angled towards distinct citizenships, for example, national citizenship and reproductive citizenship, differently because of considerations of race, gender or, in some countries, religion. Even a commonsense approach recognises that citizenship varies in different domains. Hence scholars currently distinguish *local government, state, national, regional,* and *international citizenship,* and some now add *cosmopolitan, transnational* and *global citizenship* as well. Likewise, it is useful to distinguish between *political citizenship* and *legal citizenship*, where the latter is jurisdictionally specific, between *social* and *cultural citizenship*, where these relate to capacities and institutional sites, and between *economic, corporate* and *industrial citizenship*. This leaves, at the very least, the crucially different cases and terrains of *sexual, educational, media, military, environmental, ecological,* and *religious citizenship*, where these are all defined differently.

Further, the tests for each of these citizenships vary, or in some cases are unclear. This pluralisation of citizenship has major implications because *there are multiple conceptions, forms, and logics of citizenship*. Citizenship is different for different people in different contexts, depending on race, age, religion and gender. And some of these differences are incommensurable, just as some forms of citizenship are *intrinsically heterogeneous*.

When allowance is made for *discursive forms of citizenship*, the range of citizenships extends further because some forms of citizenship are simply *hermeneutical*, in the sense that there is no 'fact of the matter' to fall back on. They arise with forms of interpretation. Often they depend on discursive choices; for example, biographical decisions to bond with counterfactual belief systems. Consider the case of counterfactual beliefs which generate unusual forms of religious citizenship that do not depend on the existence of a state. Jehovah's Witnesses, for example, believe that the world is under theocratic or divine government. This government apparently began in 1914 when Jesus Christ threw Satan out of Heaven. Although the divine or heavenly kingdom is already in operation and 'established', this is not known to everyone, and so a visible organisation of 'kingdom preachers' has been set up on earth to alert people to the signs of the times. Eventually, God's kingdom government will take action to destroy all the governments of the world and Jesus Christ will go into action as a victorious king. A paradise on earth ruled by Christ will be set up, in which the dead will come to life and human beings fortunate enough to find themselves in it will live forever. Clearly Jehovah's Witnesses are members of more than one 'city', and can offer only qualified allegiance to the governments of the present world. To this extent, they remind us of the Augustianian problematic of the relationship between the 'earthly' and the 'heavenly' cities which was important for western Christian approaches to citizenship for 1500 years.[2]

Differential citizenship is an internally disaggregative approach to citizenship which takes account of declarations and option-taking, as well as formal legal authorisations of citizenship claims. It recognises multiple and irreducible types of citizenship negotiated by the exercises of multiple civic capacities. Clearly consensus about citizenships may not always exist. If discursive forms of citizenship are accepted by nation-state administrative or other appropriate bodies, this may be decisive, regardless of whether or not these positions can be grounded in fact or rendered consistent within the ambit of a single 'theory' of citizenship. Even the apparently innocent notion of 'good citizenship' unleashes a large number of citizenship statuses which do not depend on membership of any particular nation-state. Consider the case of training to exercise 'good citizenship' as a member of a school community. There may well be nation-state government policy documents pertaining to good citizenship, and these may influence how a school seeks to train students. Alternatively, a school may adopt its own approach, going beyond practices as yet current in the wider community. What is crucial is how the school citizen gets to know what responsible and appropriate exercise of school citizenship in specific contexts requires, not what passport they hold. Indeed, Chinese, Korean and Japanese students may all attend the school and be deemed good citizens without holding Australian passports or having any intention to settle in Australia.

Once the notion of a single uniformitarian citizenship is eroded, the existence of different logics of citizenship relative to particular sites and related changes of comportment and ethics can be taken more systematically into account in the context of the promotion and good management of civil society. In the context of growing reflexivity and social differentiation (Beck, Giddens and Lash 1994; Luhmann 1998), recognising differential citizenship implies that political citizenship should be construed as something exercised among other citizenships by individuals who have or could acquire other citizenships. Like other contemporary cultural changes, this shift does not imply a break with traditional approaches to citizenship so much as *a more tensional conception of citizenship as a set of distributed comportments rather than a single ethic.*

Multiple Citizenships

The perspective of differential citizenship also questions the basic grid upon which histories of Australian citizenship have been projected, including the attempt to construe these histories in terms of a movement from 'subject' to 'citizen', where these are taken to be opposite and exclusive terms. In fact, 'subject' was a term associated with power and agency in both Roman and German private law. To be a British 'subject' in colonial Australia was to have a high dignity, and be comparatively immune from interference in foreign parts. It did not imply servitude or submission. And British 'subjects' were always expected to be good citizens in diverse contexts (a point often forgotten in the standard histories), just as they were encouraged (if male) to be 'citizens of the world', and were taught *ad nauseam* that the just belonged to a heavenly city beyond the transience of earthly cities and states. A differential approach to citizenship qualifies the standard literature on Australian citizenship in so far as this assumes a single exclusionary citizenship and a slow teleological transition from 'subject' to 'citizen' (cf. Davidson 1997a). It reveals that the standard accounts underestimate the multiple identities and *personae* available to Australians, and the ways in which they exercised positive agency in deploying them for their own ends. All this implies that Australian civic identities deserve closer study. There is much more to Australian traditions of civic identities than the standard histories of citizenship suggest. And this, in turn, means that the spaces in which Australians would be active as 'citizens' have not yet been adequately understood.

The term 'citizen' was used in vague senses by Australians until at least the First World War.[3] Hence when Australian women, Chinese and other groups excluded from legal citizenship in the new Commonwealth insisted that they were 'citizens', they meant that they were reliable and responsible members of the community (Irving 1997). Indeed, it is impossible to understand many Australian civic identities without recognising the existence of multiple citizenships.

There were at least four quasi-political citizenships. One was Imperial or Empire citizenship. Thus Ernest Scott, Professor of History at the University of Melbourne, was still able to declare in 1911 that:

> Australians are very strong Home Rulers – that is, so far as Australia is concerned – and they are apt to look with suspicion upon any proposal which may seem to carry with it any curtailment of their power to govern themselves, or any check, however insignificant, upon the free exercise of the legislative or administrative functions of either Commonwealth or states. But this statement must not be misunderstood. It is not meant to assert that there is in this country no regard for the Empire, no Imperialism, in the true sense of the word. Australian loyalty, as already pointed out, if vague and unformed, is yet very real; we are proud of our Empire, and of our citizenship therein; of the glories, the traditions and the memories in which we, in common with all Britons, have our part.[4]

And even as late as 1926, T.R. Bavin distinguished between the different duties which came with the different citizenships Australians possessed. First, the citizenship of the city. Second, the citizenship of the state. Third, the federal citizenship of the Commonwealth of Australia. Finally, citizenship of the Empire which made the Australian 'more than a Britisher'[5] (Arnold et al. 1993, 23). The change in the sense of Britisher shows how cultural and ethnic identity could move, even when political citizenship remained the same. Differential citizenship also explains how nineteenth century Australians negotiated many exchanges in the 'civil society' of particular colonies.[6]

In the same spirit, consider the case of John Dunmore Lang, the leading Australian republican of the nineteenth century, and a notorious controversialist in matters ecclesiastical, political and civil. Lang was simultaneously a Scot, British, New South Welsh, and Australian. Though an ardent republican, he remained a British loyalist committed to the Empire as the work of providence in world history, and regularly cheered for the Queen as proof of his loyalty. The same Lang advocated Australian independence from Britain, but he was not anti-British. Nor did his republicanism imply a demotic bias. Lang's republicanism was Presbyterian and influenced by theological theories of Thomas Chalmers. It was a matter of the right to local government at *all* levels, in every state and city, not only nationally. His republicanism was also indebted to the Dutch precedent of the United Provinces, and he was cosmopolitan enough to draw on relevant resources wherever he found them.

For Lang republicanism originally existed by divine appointment, even though this republic was also a theocracy:

> it is matter of sacred history that the only form of human government that was ever divinely established upon earth was the Republican – in the wilderness of Sinai – and that God himself interposed, in the person of his own accredited minister, to protest against the unwarrantable innovation, when that form of government was at length set aside in the commonwealth of Israel, and monarchy established in its stead. Monarchy doubtless prevailed for a long period in that country, *by Divine permission*, as many things else do in this lower world, that are certainly not of Divine appointment; but Republicanism existed from the first *by Divine appointment*; and it cannot, I submit, be a very bad form of government, which can plead such an authority in its favour. (1870, 124–5)

Indeed Lang declared:

> in the original *Magna Carta* of Israel – that famous *Constitutional Act* which came down from Heaven, bearing the *Sign Manual* of the Eternal, for the establishment of a Republic, more glorious, and happier far, while it subsisted, than those of either Greece or Rome ... we find all the principles of manly freedom established and developed – universal suffrage, perfect political equality (combined with one of the most beautiful and affecting devices imaginable to preserve it) and popular election; the three grand fundamental principles of Republican government. (1870, 125–6)

Lang's project of an Australian Empire was also unintelligible without his commitment to spreading the rule of Christianity throughout the world:

> Australia is at this moment one of the most important centres of moral and Christian influence on the face of the globe. It possesses this character in a degree incomparably higher than the United States of America. The forty millions of the Mahometan and Pagan inhabitants of the Indian Archipelago, whom Christian Europe has left almost entirely uncared for these three centuries, are now within a few days' sail of our actual settlements on the Gulf of Carpentaria. New Guinea, one of the largest islands in the world, is at our door; *and the multitude of the isles* of the Western Pacific are close upon our seaboard, while China looks in the distance from the northern extremity

of the land. There is clearly, therefore, no part of the habitable globe on which it is of more importance at this moment to plant a thoroughly Christian people than the shores of Australia, and the islands of the Western Pacific. With half a million of such people – and there would be no difficulty in finding them – Australia would have a moral machinery to bring to bear upon the heathenism of the earth, unsurpassed by that of any other Christian country of equal population in the world. I confess I entertain the highest hopes of my adopted country in this important particular. (1870, 436–7)

Lang spoke of the independence of colonies as 'the law of nature and the ordinance of God' (1870, vi). He envisaged an Australia Empire which would be a 'National Government for the colonies on the Pacific Ocean'. This Empire would colonise New Guinea:

New Guinea would very soon become a province of the Australian Union, and would prove like the East and West Indies, to the adventurous youth of the southern provinces, who would there grow tropical productions by means of Aboriginal, Malayan, or Chinese labour. (1870, 429)

Lang had no sense that he was a subject but not a citizen. On the contrary, he addressed his writings to his 'fellow citizens' (1870, vi) by which he did not only mean those who were British subjects. Like other nineteenth-century colonists, Lang had a sense of a 'citizen' as one who resided in and exercised civic capacities in a certain place.

Lang's own civic capacities were obviously wider than his nationality, itself uncertain (Scot, British, Australian). And these capacities sometimes modified in crucial instances his ability to exercise his political citizenship as a British subject. Lang's activities as a minister of religion meant that he exercised civic capacities under Presbyterian ecclesiastical law, and it is important to recognise that the secularisation of politics was by no means complete in nineteenth-century Australia. On the contrary, in his ecclesiastical capacity Lang denounced specific developments in the English law of divorce as an abomination to God. As a minister of religion, he was also excluded by Imperial statute from standing as a candidate in the first elections under responsible government in New South Wales. Conversely, the Imperial state had only a very limited role in the regulation of his ministerial capacity. Indeed, Lang needed a specific non-state ecclesiastical mechanism to maintain this civic capacity in tact. Hence when he was rejected by the Presbyterian Synod of Australia and deposed from the ministry, he established his own Synod of New South Wales to legitimate his activities.

Lang's case may be thought untypical. It can also be taken to represent the confused situation before Federation, as opposed to the much clearer situation which allegedly prevailed after it. In reality, however, the complexities his case displays also have a role in twentieth-century Australia. And so far from being defects of the Australian political experience, this diversity is basic to a proper account of Australian civil society, which rests on negotiations between multiple identities and exercises of civic capacity.

Many writers assume that the freedoms of Australians derive from and are limited by the Australian state, and that the law of Australia is the law relevant to them. But this repeats the myth of a single citizenship.[7] For Catholic Australians, however, the right to church marriage has always depended on Roman church law, and often on the decisions of Roman ecclesiastical courts over which the Australian state has no control. Similarly, the fact that Australian Labor leaders sympathetic to independence from Britain were often unwavering subjects of an absolute monarch, the Roman pontiff, means that there were hidden sphere and domain distinctions behind their democratic rhetoric. No Australian Catholic leader ever suggested that Roman church law or sexual ethics should be determined by a popular vote. Likewise, the involvement of many Australian Liberal politicians in Freemasonry qualifies the extent to which they were prepared to treat other Australian citizens equally in the context of employment and social honours. In effect, in both cases a more specific civic identity qualified the way in which a wider civic identity was interpreted and deployed. And in more recent times plural civic capacities have continued to characterise Greek, Italian, Vietnamese and Chinese Australians. Complex questions have also been raised about the diverse citizenships of Islamic and Jewish Australians, both in the context of religious law and in the context of alleged allegiance to a foreign power.

Institutionally Embodied Forms

Recognising that a wide diversity of differential citizenships need to be taken into account does not mean that institutionally specific forms of citizenship are unimportant. On the contrary, institutionally embodied forms of citizenship often make a plurality of other citizenships possible, and provide the security in which they can be effectively pursued. To this extent, the formal management of differential citizenship may actually require a strong emphasis on the institutional bargain dimension of Australian political citizenship: on citizenship as a form of negotiated settlement with the national community which confers entitlements and duties (Walter 1996). Accepting that citizenship is not 'a concept' or 'one thing', and that citizenships are plural and involve different types of entities on different sites, does not exclude a strong form of political citizenship allied to specific arts of governance.

Moreover, this citizenship can address the heterogeneities opened up by notions of differential citizenship if it draws upon broadly republican approaches to governance (cf. Pettit 1998; Hudson and Carter 1993). Australian political citizenship can and should include an obligation to recognise and respect exercises of citizenship by others over a large number of different domains.

A case for strong *republican* political citizenship can be made for some but not other *personae*, without reducing it to allegedly permanent attributes of a single human nature. Strong *republican* political citizenship means that each intra-societal citizen is committed to the norms of the polity in which she or he resides, and has extensive rights and duties by virtue of that fact. It implies public concern with and for the civic formation of citizens, whether they be human persons, companies, or associations. This public concern is not simply the need to secure a healthy *res publica* in which public officials are kept honest. It is to secure the basic preconditions for free individuals to live in co-operation and concord, where those goals require *inter alia* strong national institutions to promote the public good, the maintenance of multiple and diverse public spaces, institutional support for free associations, organisations which promote social solidarity and collective will – formation among citizens with diverse thick identities, and political arrangements which regularly reproduce informed, disciplined and self-initiating citizens.

In this context, accounts of citizenship which construct citizens primarily as subjects produced by and then regulated by the apparatuses of states need to be supplemented by strong accounts of agency, so that citizenship is understood in terms of dispositional possibilities, as well as in terms of the impact of historically variable forms of political, economic, and legal regulation. Precisely because republican citizenship is about the formation of citizens, republican citizenship needs to be explicitly associated with a philosophical anthropology which takes account of both the human body and its suffering (Turner 1993) and of historically changing physical, pyschological, and civic capacities.

Strong *republican* political citizenship can be both culturally specific and universal. It is compatible with claims that governments must treat their citizens in certain ways, and must forbear from other conduct towards them. It also implies that citizens have extensive duties to one another as well as rights against the nation-state. As the notion of differential citizenship suggests, today more emphasis needs to be placed than in the past on discursive negotiation, the self-reflexivity of agents, and procedures which allow exceptions. For example, cases may well arise in which citizens of a nation-state opt to pay more taxes if they are allowed to insist that no part of their taxes should go to the support of the military. In this way, the state may come to negotiate with rather than to merely command citizens in key areas such as taxation and war. In the same way, strong *republican* political citizenship is compatible with a more decentred understanding of 'community' as 'togetherness' which does not imply homogeneity or identity.[8]

Of course, the question of when and how Australian political citizenship relates to the other forms of citizenship to which Australians have access remains a difficult one. Can the various citizenships – political, social, economic, cultural, sexual, or military, environmental and so forth – be brought together, especially since some of them are heterogeneous and site-specific? In actual cases it often turns out that political citizenship has decisive effects on other citizenships: for example, sexual citizenship, military citizenship and environmental citizenship. To this extent, there is a case for expanding political citizenship to address *how political citizens may be expected to behave across their citizenships*. As James Walter argues, a clear program of citizen rights serves as a check on both the state and the market, and is an expression of the sort of civil society we want (Walter 1996). Whether this means we need a Bill of Rights, either explicit or implied, remains a disputed question (Brennan 1998). But it is clear that we need to think the pluralities of contemporary citizenships without necessarily attempting to treat them as all equally transparent, and without necessarily attempting to totalise them in a single unified citizenship. And in this chapter I have argued that Australians need to embrace strong republican citizenship to protect and promote differential citizenship, even though this means breaking with both nostalgic forms of traditional republicanism and with forms of postmodern pluralism which underestimate the need for a powerful and ethically committed structuring state.

Notes

1 *Differentiated citizenship* is usually taken to mean that differences between types of citizens or groups of citizens need to be recognised and taken into account. On differentiated citizenship, see Young (1989). *Differential citizenship* emphasises that political citizens have access to a vast diversity of citizenships which cannot be collapsed into a single inclusive uniformitarian citizenship.
2 On Christian citizenship, see P. Riesenberg (1992). The importance of the Augustinian tradition is frequently underplayed in Anglophone writing on citizenship out of a covert Protestant bias. Orthodox Christian conceptions of the state and citizenship are also neglected.
3 See now Helen Irving's exceptional study *To Constitute a Nation: A Cultural History of Australia's Constitution* (1997), especially chapters 6 and 9. My reading of the evidence is consistent with Irving's but places more emphasis on the consequences of different exercises of civic capacity for different

forms of citizenship. For a related argument, see Hudson and Bolton (1997, ch. 11).
4 E. Scott, 'Australia and the Empire', in J. Arnold et al. (1993), *Out of Empire: The British Dominion of Australia*, p. 22.
5 T.R. Bavin, 'Empire Citizenship', in J. Arnold et al. (1993).
6 For more detailed historical material on why it is a mistake to construe Australian civic identities in terms of a single form of citizenship, see Hudson (1998).
7 Further evidence for this view is provided for Freemasonry in early New South Wales in A. Atkinson (1997). *The Europeans in Australia: A History*, vol. I. Melbourne: Oxford University Press, ch. 12.
8 For recent French attempts to rethink 'community' in pluralistic terms, see Blanchot (1988), Nancy (1991), Agamben (1993), and Lingis (1994); cf. Corlett (1989). Jean-Luc Nancy catches the exterior, even shallow, character of the model of citizenship coming from Aristotle and the relativistic politics it implies, and contrasts this with the interior, absolute virtue model of the subject coming from Plato. He argues that both need each other. See *The Inoperative Community* (1991).

Further Reading

Bohman, J. and W. Rehg (eds) (1997). *Deliberative Democracy. Essays on Reason and Politics*. Cambridge, Mass: The MIT Press.
Chesterman, J. and B. Galligan (eds) (1999). *Defining Australian Citizenship: Selected Documents*. Melbourne: Melbourne University Press.
Irving, H. (1997). *To Constitute a Nation: A Cultural History of Australia's Constitution*. Cambridge: Cambridge University Press.
Janoski, T. (1998). *Citizenship and Civil Society. A Framework of Rights and Obligations in Liberal, Traditional and Social Democratic Regimes*. Cambridge: Cambridge University Press.

CHAPTER 3

Republicanism and Citizenship

Philip Pettit

The republican tradition is the tradition of thinking in which government is regarded as a *res publica*, a public affair, and not as a province in which prince or party can legitimately pursue more sectional interests. More specifically, it is the tradition within which government is seen as a public affair, because the end or telos of government is conceived as the liberty or freedom of the individual and that liberty is itself represented as a public achievement. From the time of the earliest, self-conscious republics, liberty was taken to be more or less equivalent to citizenship: that is, to a status that presupposed the existence of a state. 'At Rome and with regard to Romans', as one writer puts it, 'full *libertas* is coterminous with *civitas*' (Wirszubski 1968, 3; see too Crawford 1993, 1).

The republican way of thinking about government dominated European thinking down to the end of the eighteenth century, when it gave way to the new way of conceiving of the role of government that came to be described, initially in tones of abuse, as liberalism. Where republicans had insisted that the freedom of citizens was a public affair – that it was a product of how government and society were organised – the new liberals tended to think of freedom as something that pre-existed government, and indeed citizenship, and that was consummated in the private, non-civic realms of family and friendship, contract and commerce. Liberals represented government as an unfortunate necessity, not as something intimately tied to the ideal of liberty, and they thought of the ideal government as a way of organising society so as to maximise people's enjoyment of pre-political liberty; the idea was to have only the minimal government required for keeping the peace.

I have been arguing in a number of publications that we should return to the republican tradition of thinking as we seek, in this time of transition, to reconceptualise the role and responsibilities of the state (Braithwaite and Pettit 1990; Pettit 1996, 1997). The republican way of thinking of freedom, and of citizenship, gives us a conception of the goal that the state ought to espouse which is at once plausible and substantial.

The republican approach ought to be particularly appealing in contemporary Australia. It offers a way of conceiving of the state we ought to support, and the citizenship we ought to nurture, that connects closely with local themes and traditions. It connects with the drift away from the British monarchy, of course, but much more importantly, it connects with broader habits of simultaneously recruiting government to large tasks and viewing government with suspicion and distrust. It also holds out a way of recasting the role of government that can celebrate the diversity of our culture and population, while being faithful to our European heritage. Something of this should appear later in my discussion.

The discussion is in three sections. First, I characterise the republican notion of freedom. Next, I show why the realisation of such freedom can be described as coterminous with the enjoyment of a suitable form of citizenship. And then, in the third section, I mention two revisionary principles of citizenship which the modern republican should borrow from opponents; one is liberal in provenance, the other is communitarian. In a short conclusion, I argue that, contrary to some assumptions, however, there is no need for modern republicanism to borrow from populist ideas of democracy in reconstructing its notion of citizenship; the tradition already supplies a perfectly adequate notion of democracy.

The Republican Notion of Freedom

The republican tradition of thinking has a long history. It is the tradition associated with Cicero at the time of the Roman republic; with Machiavelli – 'the divine Machiavel' of the *Discourses* (Machiavelli 1969) – and various other writers of the Renaissance Italian republics; with James Harrington and a host of lesser figures in and after the period of the English civil war and commonwealth; and with the many theorists of republic or commonwealth in eighteenth-century England and America and France.

These eighteenth-century theorists can be taken to include less radical figures like Montesquieu and Blackstone – the author of the famous commentary on the laws of England – as well as the antimonarchists responsible for the United States Constitution and for the various declarations emanating from revolutionary France. If such figures did not seek a political republic – if they were happy with a constitutional monarchy – they still espoused a conception of freedom that linked them with the republican tradition; they looked for what we might describe as a judicial republic. Thus for them England was 'a nation', in Montesquieu's (1989 [1748], 70) unmistakeable reference, 'where the republic hides under the form of monarchy'.

The conception of freedom that we find in this long tradition sets up freedom in contrast to slavery (Patterson 1991). Where the slave or servant lives at the mercy of their master, the freeman – and the tradition does focus on men – lives at the mercy of no one. He is able to stand on his own two feet and to look others squarely in the eye, conscious that no one can interfere with him at will or with impunity. The slave is subject to interference on an arbitrary basis. The freeman is subject to no arbitrary power. The slave is dominated or subjugated by their master; the freeman is dominated by no one. Freedom does not consist just in the absence of interference, as later liberal theorists hold; freedom consists in the absence of domination: in the absence of vulnerability to arbitrary interference.

There are two aspects of this way of thinking of freedom – this way of casting freedom as non-domination – that are particularly worth remarking. The first is that while all state activity involves interference – the interference of taxation, legal coercion and the imposition of legal sanction – this interference need not compromise people's freedom as non-domination, provided that it is not arbitrary in character. The state may do a lot of good for people's freedom as non-domination, because it can undermine the power of arbitrary interference that some people enjoy over others: it can undermine, say, the petty fiefdoms of husbands, or employers, or creditors. And in doing that good, so this first observation emphasises, the state need not itself represent a compromise of anyone's freedom, even the freedom of those whose power it curbs. Like natural obstacles, good laws will put limits on the range of choices open to people but if the limitations are not arbitrary, then they will not represent a form of state domination; they may reduce the extent over which freedom as non-domination is enjoyed but they will not reduce the intensity or quality of that freedom.

An act of interference is perpetrated on an arbitrary basis, we can say, if it is subject just to the *arbitrium*, the decision or judgment, of the agent; in particular, if it can be chosen or rejected without reference to the interests, or the opinions, of those affected. An act of state interference will be non-arbitrary to the extent that it is forced to track the perceived interests of the people affected; it does not come of a relatively unfettered power in the authorities. The act will be non-arbitrary, for example, if the political institutions allow those affected to contest it and to gain a ruling on whether it fails to track their interests

– that is, a fair one, given their own criteria. We may live at a far cry from such institutional arrangements but the possibility is there and needs to be marked.

So much for the first important aspect of the republican notion of freedom as non-domination: the fact that it represents state interference, so far as the interference is non-arbitrary, as not itself a compromise of people's freedom. One qualification is necessary, however, before going on to the second important aspect of the notion. This is that nevertheless the notion of freedom as non-domination can provide grounds for criticising high levels of state interference. A first ground, of course, is that too much state power is going to be difficult to check and contain; it will tend to become arbitrary. And a second is that if we can restrain domination as well with fewer as with more numerous laws – if citizens can be equally well established in the enjoyment of freedom as non-domination by fewer laws – then we should always prefer the fewer. This is because even if the more numerous laws do not themselves dominate people, they do unnecessarily reduce the range of activities over which people may exercise undominated choice; they reduce the extent of people's freedom as non-domination, as I put it, even if they do not reduce its intensity.

But the republican notion of freedom makes the state look capable, in principle, of being a relatively attractive presence. It also makes a variety of relationships which have characterised contemporary societies look downright unattractive. Consider the relationship whereby a husband can interfere on a more or less arbitrary basis with his wife, an employer with his or her employees, a teacher with their pupils, a union boss with ordinary members, a creditor with his or her debtors, and so on. There need be no actual interference in such a relationship but even if actual interference is lacking, someone attached to freedom as non-domination is bound to protest. For the relationship means that one person has the capacity to interfere on a more or less arbitrary basis in at least some of the other's choices and that capacity is enough in itself to reduce the other person's freedom; it is enough to put them in a position akin to that of a slave.

The emphasis of traditional republicans on the potentially benign nature of the state comes out in their enthusiasm for what they represented as the rule of law. They conceived of the rule of law as a regime under which authority is even-handedly exercised in the perceived interests of citizens and those in authority do not enjoy a special power of domination; they are themselves citizens who have to live under an impersonal law.

The complementary emphasis of republicans on the malign character of relationships of subordination comes out in their antipathy to the notion, as it was described, of the kindly master. As Algernon Sydney (1990, 441) put it, 'he is a slave who serves the best and gentlest man in the world, as well as he who serves the worst'. Or as it was put by Richard Price (1991, 77–8) in the eighteenth century: 'Individuals in private life, while held under the power of masters, cannot be denominated free, however equitably and kindly they may be treated'. There is domination, and there is unfreedom, even if no actual interference occurs.

The notion of freedom as non-domination with which republicans operated gave way in the nineteenth century to a distinctively liberal way of thinking about freedom. On this approach freedom is non-interference— freedom is being let alone – and the two features of the republican conception are stood on their head. However non-arbitrary the character of state interference, it still constitutes a violation of liberty and can only be justified so far as it prevents more interference than it represents; thus liberals start out with a suspicion of the state that is much deeper than any misgivings that republicans might have harboured. And however great the domination that a husband or employer may enjoy over wife or employees, that domination does not mean that those in the subordinate positions suffer in the freedom stakes; freedom is unaffected by power and is lost only if there is actual interference.

These two reversals meant that classical liberals tended to look for a minimal state – a state that imposed a minimum amount of legal interference – on the one hand; and on the other that they tended to be fairly complacent about the existence of relationships of power in the workplace and the household. They often argued, for example, that albeit the employer or the husband had dominating power in relation to employee or wife, they had no rational incentive to exercise that power in actual interference; thus, so they speculated, employee and wife could be expected to enjoy a high level of freedom as non-interference. Their urgings in these regards of course came to be strongly opposed by those socialists and feminists who, drawing on republican ideals and catch-cries, railed against the wage-slavery of industrial employees and the subordination of married women.

Republican Freedom and Citizenship

So much by way of explicating the republican notion of liberty. I began this essay by saying that for republicans freedom is equivalent to citizenship in a suitable polity or state. I now want to explain, in the light of my explication, just why this is so.

The explanation takes the form of a syllogism.

a. Citizenship in a given polity means full incorporation in its institutions: full susceptibility to the rights and responsibilities that those institutions impose.
b. Freedom as non-domination, so far as it is available to all the citizens of a polity, is constituted – constituted, not caused – by their incorporation in the institutions of the polity.
c. And so their citizenship is what constitutes whatever freedom as non-domination that the citizens of a polity enjoy in common.

The first premise of this argument should be accepted on all sides; it is a more or less standard explication of what citizenship means. All of the weight falls, therefore, on the second premise. I need to explain the sense in which the freedom as non-domination which citizens enjoy is constituted by their incorporation into the local political institutions.

Suppose that we have institutions in place, maybe these, maybe those, which confer a perfectly undominated status, over whatever area, on each and every citizen in the society. People all live in one another's society but no one is subject to the arbitrary interference of another; the institutions distribute power and protection in such a way that the only interference accessible is non-arbitrary: it is not interference that may be guided by unshared interests or ideas. Now, assuming that we have such perfect institutions in place, what is the relationship between them and the non-domination which they serve to establish?

Consider first of all the relationship between such institutions and the non-interference – the non-interference, not the non-domination – that people may enjoy under them. This relationship is certainly going to involve a familiar causal element: the institutions themselves interfere with people but they also have the effect of inhibiting others from interfering and so the actual level of non-interference that people enjoy is a function of this causal impact. The striking thing about the relationship of the institutions to the non-domination that they put in place, however, is that it does not have the same causal character.

The people who live under the institutions do not have to wait on the causal effect of the institutions in inhibiting potential interferers before they enjoy non-domination. To enjoy such non-domination, after all, is just to be in a position where no one can interfere arbitrarily in your affairs and you are in that position from the moment that the institutions are in place: from that moment it is true that no one can interfere in your life at will and with impunity; no one can interfere on an arbitrary basis. True, it is bound to take time and some causal interaction for your non-domination to become a matter of common awareness, and for potential offenders to be deterred. But the non-domination as such antecedes such causal sequences. It comes into existence simultaneously with the appearance of the appropriate institutions; it represents the reality of those institutions in the person of the individual. Montesquieu (1989, 187) implicitly recognises the point when he talks of liberty as it exists, now in the constitution, now in the citizen.

But though the relation between state and non-domination is not causal, neither is it mysterious. The presence of certain antibodies in your blood makes it the case that you are immune to a certain disease but it does not cause your immunity, as if the immunity were something separate on which we had to wait; the presence of those antibodies constitutes the immunity, as we say. By analogy, the presence in the polity of such and such empowering and protective arrangements makes it the case that you are more or less immune to arbitrary interference but it does not cause that immunity, that non-domination; it constitutes it. To be immune to a certain disease is to have antibodies in your blood – maybe these, maybe those – which prevent the development of the relevant virus. The presence of the antibodies represents a way of realising the immunity; it is not something that causally leads to it. To be immune to arbitrary interference, to enjoy non-domination, is to have inhibitors present in your society – maybe these, maybe those – which prevent arbitrary interference in your life and affairs. And the presence of suitable inhibitors – suitable institutions and arrangements – represents a way of realising your non-domination; it is not something that leads by a causal path to that non-domination.

The upshot is that enjoying freedom as non-domination amounts for citizens just to their being incorporated in the local, political institutions; it amounts, in a word, to their being full citizens of the local polity. Their freedom is constituted by the institutional reality of their citizenship. It is one and the same thing.

Some people may think it an ominous feature of freedom as non-domination that it is an institutional reality, in the sense explained. They may say that if freedom is conceived of as something that the state constitutes – if it is conceived as citizenship – then it is not going to represent a criterion by which the state can be judged. But that is nonsense. Freedom as non-domination is an institutional reality in the sense that it is constituted, not caused to exist, by the institutional arrangements that put it in place. But we can still compare the freedom as non-domination that different sets of institutions, different forms of citizenship, may constitute and we can still find that one set does better than the other in respect of such freedom: we can do this in just the way that we could compare the kinds and levels of immunity against a certain disease that different sorts of antibodies might conceivably provide.

Two Revisionary Principles

This essay, so far, has been an uncritical celebration of the republican notion of liberty and citizenship. Opponents of the republican approach will rush to point out that, however attractive in other ways, there are two features of how republicans thought of citizenship that are downright repellent. First, they always imagined an elitist republic in which citizenship was extended only to a minority. This may have been for reasons of feasibility, since the neo-Roman tradition that infused republicanism always asserted human equality. And second, republicans conceived of the minority who were to enjoy citizenship as a very homogeneous lot: propertied males in a monocultural society. Both of these criticisms are just, and if we are to reappropriate the republican way of thinking of freedom and citizenship, then we need to espouse principles that mark off our republicanism from that of traditional thinkers.

The first criticism can be resisted so far as we make it clear that citizenship has to be extended to at least all the responsible adult members of the society. There may be a distinction to be drawn between residents who are not properly citizens, and perhaps do not wish to become proper citizens – they may be denied the right to vote, for example – but in substantive ways all responsible adults should have access to the same freedom as non-domination. Citizenship must be a universally available status, not an elitist one. This principle might be described as a borrowing from liberalism. Liberal theorists have always argued that human beings are entitled to equal citizenship, even if they have sometimes held back in practice on the equality of women and blacks and others.

In passing we should note that it may even have been this universalist commitment which led early liberals like Bentham and his school to give up on the rich old republican conception of freedom in favour of a diluted notion of freedom as non-interference (Pettit 1997, ch. 1). Once it was admitted that in principle all human beings should have access, it must have seemed difficult to continue to espouse the notion of freedom as non-domination; after all, that notion would have required a transformation in the position of women and servants, as feminists like Mary Astell had seen (Hill 1986, 76). Thus the very influential William Paley argued against thinking that freedom required non-domination, and in favour of the conception of freedom as non-interference, on these lines:

> those definitions of liberty ought to be rejected, which, by making that essential to civil freedom which is unattainable in experience, inflame

expectations that can never be gratified, and disturb the public content with complaints, which no wisdom or benevolence of government can remove. (Paley 1825, 359)

But if we associate freedom with citizenship, and extend citizenship to all responsible adults, what happens regarding the position of children and of adults who are not deemed responsible? They cannot be given a large range of choice, due to their immaturity or incapacity. But the denial of choice does not mean the presence of domination: after all, a rule of law denies all citizens a certain measure of choice and yet it does not dominate them. The crucial requirement is that when children and non-responsible adults are denied certain choices – when they are subjected to a certain control – the pattern of denial and control is effectively dictated by their interests, as impartially conceived, and not by anyone else's. While not being given full freedom, the individuals involved need not be rendered unfree; while not being given full citizenship, they need not be treated as if they lacked all status and standing

The second failing in the traditional republican conception of citizenship is that it projects a homogeneous image of citizens: in effect, an image of citizens as monocultural, propertied males. As we need to borrow a liberal, universalist principle to reform the traditional republican approach, so this shows that we need to borrow a reforming principle from another important camp in contemporary theory: the group of thinkers who are loosely described as communitarian. As liberals stress the need to include everyone equally in a polity, so communitarians stress the need to respect the affiliation of different individuals with different cultural and ethnic and gender identities. The principle that we need to borrow from communitarians is one which makes clear that common citizenship is consistent with such differences of identity; it need not be assimilationist in character (Young 1989, 1990).

The principle required is not a hard one to defend. Consider how even liberal theorists are prepared to grant that the shared rights of people in a society may require very different expenditures to cater for different sections of the population. The right to vote is easily and cheaply accommodated in an urban environment, for example, but it may be difficult and expensive to extend it to remote rural residents. The right to a basic education may be readily met in the case of the normal, talented child but may require special, expensive schooling for someone who is handicapped.

These examples show that one and the same right may ground different claims, depending on the different circumstances of the individuals involved; and this, by lights that most of us share. Thus we need have no hesitation about admitting that one and the same right to citizenship – one and the same right to freedom as non-domination – may ground different claims, depending on the different affiliations and identities of people in the society. What is needed to ensure non-domination, effective full citizenship, for a woman may differ in various ways from what is needed for a man. Or what is needed in the case of someone who belongs to the mainstream culture may differ from what is needed for someone who belongs to an ethnic minority or an Indigenous population.

I cannot explore the significance of this principle further in the present context. But I would like to emphasise that it is not just a supplementary principle, designed to make up for an inherent weakness in the republican approach. The very best prospect for those who have been traditionally marginalised may be offered by the discovery of a common ground with others – the ground of a shared, republican citizenship – on which they can make claims for different treatment. Make special claims on the basis of a special status and you are likely only to generate resentment and resistance. Make special claims on the basis of a shared status and your chances of success increase.

Conclusion

Is there need for a third revisionary principle, as well as the two principles associated respectively with liberalism and communitarianism? Some may say that as the republican tradition – like every tradition up to the later eighteenth century – was elitist and monoculturalist, so too it was less than fully committed to democracy: that is, to the effective sovereignty of the people, even of the minority of people who constituted the citizenry. They will say that as modern republicanism has to learn from liberalism and communitarianism, so too it has to take a lesson from populist notions of democracy.

This idea I strongly resist. When republicanism insists that a republican rule of law – a regime designed to promote people's freedom as non-domination – need not itself dominate people, one central assumption is that the rule of law will be democratic in a certain way. It will be democratic in the sense that people have access to government of a kind that should help ensure that government actions in their regard will track their perceived interests, or at least those of their perceived interests that are compatible with living under a shared arrangement of government: in other words, those of their perceived interests that are politically avowable in their dealings with others.

Republicans did not conceive of the access required for democracy in purely electoral terms, though they certainly favoured the election of officials – or at least their selection by lot – over any form of hereditary or colonial rule. They thought of the access required as being mediated equally through the courts and, more generally, through arrangements that would enable people individually or in groups to challenge and force a review of what government was doing or proposing to do. This conception of democracy as involving a power of contestation, as well as a power of election, is already evident in the veto that the Roman constitution gave to the tribunes of the plebs. But it recurs in other forms throughout the later tradition, culminating in the notion of having judicial and other arrangements for the review of government action.

Traditional republicanism needs to become inclusive and nuanced in its conception of the citizenry: it needs to take on board the two principles mentioned earlier. But it does not have to recast the older understanding of democracy. On the contrary, it can draw on that understanding to articulate a notion of democracy in which the important thing is not the triumph of the collective, popular will – that could be the worst form of domination from the viewpoint of a minority – but rather the responsiveness of government to people's perceived and avowable interests. In this as in so many other respects I find the tradition congenial and inspiring.

Further Reading

Australia's Republican Question (1993). *Australian Journal of Political Science* 28, Special Issue.

Hudson, W. and D. Carter (eds) (1993). *The Republicanism Debate.* Sydney: New South Wales University Press.

McKenna, M. (1996). *The Captive Republic: A History of Republicanism in Australia 1788–1996.* Cambridge: Cambridge University Press.

Pettit, P. (1996). 'Our Republican Heritage.' *Eureka Street,* 6(6), 41–5.

Pettit, P. (1998). 'Reworking Sandel's Republicanism.' *Journal of Philosophy,* 95, 73–96.

Sellers, M.N.S. (1995). *American Republicanism: Roman Ideology in the US Constitution.* New York: New York University Press.

Skinner, Q. (1997). *Liberty Before Liberalism.* Cambridge: Cambridge University Press.

CHAPTER 4

Postmodernism and Citizenship

Peter Beilharz

What is a citizen? or, who is a citizen? and, where are we now? These are the kinds of questions that come up when we conjugate categories such as the 'postmodern' with others such as 'citizenship'. I shall argue in this chapter that changes associated with postmodernism and, increasingly, with globalisation, make it less clear who counts as a citizen. The sense of fixity or stability which surrounds the image of the good citizen, paradigmatically, say, in the figure of Kant, citizen of Königsberg, seems increasingly distant from the world we inhabit. Is all then lost? Only apparently, as a case can also be made for the tentative emergence of something like postmodern forms of citizenship, associated now, as they were in a way earlier with Kant, more with city or cities, locale or localities, region or regional identities. Further, the idea that citizenship is exclusive is hardly new. Citizenship claims have always been caught up with claims to exclusion or inclusion, whether to do with the nation-state or, before it, the city-state, whether to do with geographical boundaries or with property ownership. The institutions of citizenship have always had their flaws. The value of citizenship, like that of democracy and equality, is nevertheless worth retaining, and arguing for.

Myths of Foundation

Modern political culture is based on two normative myths of foundation. Western cultures use a dual frame of reference in claims to citizenship. The first is provided by the image of Athens. The second is constructed around the images of the French Revolution thrown up two thousand years later. Both of these imaginary sources of meaning confer insight, as well as obscuring it. Thinking about the image of Athens reminds us that claims to citizenship precede the invention of the nation-state. Claims to citizenship of a city, a locality, today a metropolis may actually be more pertinent again than are claims to national belonging, national identity, 'being' Australian, barbecues, beach, bush.

Who in any case is an Australian? Elsewhere, visiting North America or the Continent, we discover that we become Australians, rather than inhabitants of Nathan or Northcote. Being antipodean, belonging to the realm of the great southern land, this elsewhere means being Australian. Being Victorian, or from New South Wales, this kind of appellation makes no sense, except perhaps in parts of Britain where the resonances are local. The extent to which modern citizenship has been caught up with nations and nation-building has always been, to some extent, exaggerated and phoney. The citizens of Athens belonged to Athens. Did the citizens of the French Revolution belong to 'France'? No. They lived in a city called Paris. Think back not to Kant but to Aristotle. *Zoon politikon*, the political animal, the citizen is a city-dweller. The life of the polis, political life, is the life of the city. What we call the French Revolution made the French; the 'French' did not make the French Revolution. They were too busy trying to scrape together a living to care about the week's escapades in Paris. They discovered they were French after they were told so, just as Bavarians became Germans, and the Welsh or Scottish discovered they were British.

So what makes us Australian, any more than a Sardinian is an Italian? It's a question of what we are told, if we are careless enough to ask the question 'who am I?' in the presence of the authorities. The sources of identity otherwise will be less national than local. Your friends, relatives, colleagues, people who make up our lives here and elsewhere will likely tell you different. For the sources of what we called 'modern' citizenship have also been strikingly 'traditional', governed by place or people of origin.

Naming, as the saying goes, makes up two-thirds, maybe half, of human activity. We are symbolically active animals. We call ourselves citizens, others not; we name ourselves, construct ourselves in particular ways, within the matrix of visual and bodily constraints which make us sexed, variously pigmented, placed linguistically or phonetically, able or disabled. The less powerful are named by those with more power and authority. We call ourselves postmodern to set ourselves apart from modern, by which we often (ironically) mean *not* modern but traditional. Why then should we describe ourselves as *citizens*?

Evidently the core philosophical value which underpins the pursuit of citizenship is *autonomy*. But to claim autonomy is already to beg various other questions, for the related value of 'independence' only makes sense with reference to the facts of dependence. We are all always dependent, just as we are always irredeemably social. Individual identity can never be constructed outside the context of the social. Yet postmodern identity, it could be argued, is also quite readily subsumed to commodification, to the passive life of the consumer. Postmodern identity, on this case, may well be possible, but not necessarily as civic identity. Postmodern identity is private, rather than public. Well, yes and no. Postmoderns also live in public, in public spaces, at sidewalk cafés if not in the agora. And they argue, and sometimes disagree, about how we might live. The culture of the French Revolution also had its coffee houses, newspapers and its presentation of self, its favoured patterns of dress and forms of address. Have we really changed so much since then?

Athens, in any case, is by other criteria so distant, so remote, as to make us wonder what the connection might be between us and them, except in the myths of foundation. To speak about a new world civilisation like Australia since invasion is to connect up less to those images of Athens, relatively simple societally, relatively small, and more to evoke images like those of the French Revolution, which sociologists claim inaugurated the modern project itself. And they are right, in one sense at least. For modernity has been deeply implicated in the ambiguous project of nation-building, to the extent that the path in particular of the twentieth century has both been blighted by the negative effects of nationalism and has seen the nation-state serve as the institutional focus of major projects of class compromise and social reform. The Keynesian welfare state only makes sense with reference to the consolidation of national projects of reform, and it is that setting which generated Marshall's famous claims for citizenship (Marshall 1950).

Modern to postmodern

What might it mean, to be the citizen of a nation rather than of a city? Into the twentieth century the eighteenth-century implications become more clear. To be a citizen male is to bear arms, to fight for king and country, to return to a system of repatriation which runs in effect as a separate and invisible sphere of the welfare state (Skocpol 1992). To be a citizen female is to reproduce this system, to provide a different system of welfare or reproduction, literally and metaphorically (Beilharz, Considine and Watts 1992; Lake et al. 1994). For those men who fought, the identity acquired was compulsory, ANZAC, independent Australian Briton. The implication of ethnic homogeneity is plain. No krauts, no dagoes, no Chinese, women and girl children to the rear, boys into training. Multiculturalism plainly upsets this, and the logic of assimilation which followed from Gallipoli into the 1960s. 'New Australians' were obliged to drop one singular identity and replace it with another, as though the path of the twentieth century had not already made it abundantly clear that displacement and migration would become normal rather than exceptional, not least of all in new worlds like Australia where, as the cliché has it, we are all immigrants anyway, all bearers of multiple passports.

This is where modernity (or the postmodern) catches tradition up. For the logic of modernist claims to citizenship has identified 'culture', or language or genetic stock with citizenship and identity. 'Citizens' have counted as 'people', Nazis or Aryans as citizens. Less infamously, this is also part of the story which follows from the great French Revolution, where not only peasants and provincials find themselves 'French' but so too do the visitors, the Arabs, Africans and Greeks, those who discover that the civilising purpose of the French state is to assimilate rather than to accommodate difference. But if citizens are different, and often hyphenated, Italo-Australian, German-Australian, then abstract claims to universal identity or belonging become tyrannical rather than emancipatory (Kymlicka and Norman 1994).

The idea and practice of modern citizenship, then, is deeply contradictory and ambivalent. Citizenship has often been used politically or systemically to integrate or modulate rather than to diversify. This fact helps to establish exactly how contradictory modernism is, for it is simultaneously conservative and radicalising, simultaneously given to homogenisation and to difference. The modern state becomes subsumed to highly traditionalistic yet practically innovative claims of nation-building and race-building. The erosion of these kinds of claims to citizenship is a positive step forward, for they are less claims, rights to voice, than genetic entitlements.

What, then, might be meant by the idea of postmodern citizenship? Inasmuch as modernity or modernism at least has been identified with nation-building as an authoritarian project, the prospect of postmodern citizenship sounds like something of a relief if not a promise. Those who remain more committed to the modernist project will be unconvinced. They will argue that there can be no citizens without a nation, therefore no claims to citizenship which are not simultaneously claims to national belonging or else they will insist, as modernists are wont to do, that talk of the postmodern is a sign of decadence or frivolity, not to be taken really seriously, a mere fad that (like the Rolling Stones) will pass.

In all disputes like these, there is both a great deal at risk and a great propensity for mutual caricature. The point, however, in this context is that for better and for worse, the identification of politics and citizenship with the nation-state which sets the twentieth century apart is slowly coming unstuck. Obviously nation-states are here to stay; we cannot imagine a global order in their absence. A globalised world is still a world of nation-states and regions. But at the same time, regional and local loyalties are reviving, and national governments are less inclined than at any previous time since the previous century to view national problems – health, housing, poverty – as nationally solvable (Beilharz 1994a, b). The national claims of social democracy or the Keynesian welfare state presumed a will to power, a will to reform. Especially after the Second World War, it was presumed that all members of the population could become citizens. That consensus, which held together liberalism over the twentieth century, is now over. We no longer commonly presume that there is such a thing as education for democracy, that health-care systems should enable, that civics should be part of socialisation (Civics Experts Group 1994). We no longer share the strategic optimism of, say, Marshall, that one process of reform might combine with or encourage another, that democratic horizons might institutionally expand rather than expire (Marshall 1950).

The name 'postmodernity' can also be taken to refer to this, not that we progress into a superior condition after modernity, but rather that we no longer find modern dreams entrancing. Modernists are social engineers; postmodernists believe less in progress than in the minimisation of cruelty (Rorty 1989). In other words, 'what we easily call the "postmodern" is not an epoch which follows the modern at all; it carries over with all the same problems of the human condition, but no longer views them as fixable.' Postmoderns then confront all the same problems as moderns did, but without the residual optimism which humanists possessed, that the mess humans generate might at least be shifted.

Citizenship as City-dwelling

The name 'globalisation' can also be invoked to explain this process. Sociologists, again, will routinely instruct us that modernity, the period inaugurated by French and Industrial Revolutions, opens up dramatic changes by way of social and geographical mobility. Nowhere is this more apparent than in arguments about the new class, those highly mobile, culturally elastic middle-class folks who have no deep loyalty to place, taste or tradition. Indeed, the logic of arguments such as those of Robert Reich is that middle-class workers, technocrats and intellectuals are *not* citizens, rather are guilty of a kind of national treason, failing to serve country or nation rather than themselves, wherever money, influence and work take them (Reich 1992). Certainly there is something in this case, if only in the reference to speed, complexity and mobility as constitutive of the fabric of modern life. Traditional views of citizenship, Athenian or Parisian, presume sufficient leisure via property to allow democracy to happen. These days no one has any time for democracy at all. The intensification of life, the pluralisation of roles and obligations make it difficult to imagine the older models of citizenship or civic life as working at all. Today's cities are indeed run by the bourgeois, the financier, the technocrat, but not by the citizen, not by the people. Does a word like 'globalisation' then offer to explain this better than another, like postmodernism? Does it make sense to talk of a global citizen?

The short answer to the last question is no. Reich and other writers on globalisation have made this point well enough: citizenship needs some kind of sense of belonging or participation, which is not compatible with a kind of empty cosmopolitanism. To be everywhere, after all, in a certain sense is to be nowhere at all. On the other hand, however, to be at all modern (or postmodern) is by definition to possess multiple forms of identity. Think of all those that you have – make up a list. Parent, or carer, lover, father/son, mother/daughter, teacher/worker/writer/consumer, occasional citizen or demonstrator, domestic labourer, bearer of the traditions you inherit and the forms of association you elect into ... we are all of us all of these, and more, and this is exactly why the modernist form of citizenship has collapsed, for we will no longer be defined 'essentially', as Australian, equals British/worker at home or factory, nationalist, bearers of the national ethos/bushmen or women/ANZACS or lifesavers.

Globalisation itself is nothing new – a century ago Marxists and liberals called it imperialism. In shorthand, you can read it as Americanism. In the Pacific, and in Canberra a synonym is Asianisation. This is regionalism, not in the strictly local, but transnational sense. Can we be citizens of Asia? Not really, not any more than Indonesians or Malays. The message, again, is an old one: it concerns the internationalisation of economic relations, which undermines political claims to national sovereignty. The complication for Australians today is that increasing Americanism in economic life also involves Americanising the superstructure, social policy or state form. The will to include citizens of a homogenised kind, which was a key to the Keynesian welfare state, is now increasingly replaced by the will to encourage difference through markets. Globalisation, presented to us as economic necessity, is in fact a political choice in favour of deregulation. Its effects are extraordinarily uneven, and unpredictable. Globalisation will not advantage those whose hold on citizenship has been tenuous, dependent on jobs in manufacturing or other hitherto protected sectors. Its encumbent policy packages, like those indicating privatisation, will not obviously advantage others whose claims to citizenship are potential more than actual.

Deregulation, in a setting like contemporary Australia, involves a redistribution of risk, life chances and property rights across transnational rather than national frames. On this basis, those who already have some possession of autonomy may well acquire more, elsewhere. Those others, who are denied what they had or could have claimed, will be unable to take their capacities elsewhere, as the new class might. But this is to refer less to the contemporary paradox of citizenship than to the eternal bind, that the conduct of citizenship depends in the first place on the power prescribed by property ownership.

What is new about the present crisis of citizenship is rather to do with the capacity and complexity of social forms. Not only postmoderns, but moderns such as Marx and Weber and Simmel and Lukács, pointed already to the new forms of enchantment generated by modernity. Modernity is, after all, that newly created social form which more than any preceding it takes on a life of its own. Modernity is the regime of the sorcerer's apprentice. It is that which, with the fetishism of commodities, is wilfully created by us as social actors, and which becomes so much more opaque, beyond understanding control or even steering. It is the simulacra which is so overpowering that we no longer know what is real and what not, what is changeable and what is beyond us. Arguments concerning citizenship rest upon various senses of will, decision, reason and control. If these then all fail us, if the space for modern politics – that Prometheanism which earlier thought it could do all – simply evaporates.

Alongside the simulacra, the surreal, however, there is still us, struggling with everyday life in our various identities, carers, workers, producers, consumers, friends, and citizens. The irony of this story, then, may well be that after this massive forced march through modernism and nation-building, our forms of citizenship now begin again to resemble the earlier politics of citizenship as city-dwelling. By modernist standards, postmodern citizenship will not make sense. But it is arguably those very modernist standards which no longer give sufficient meaning to us today. Chances are, our loyalties henceforth will be to places rather than place, to tradition and to the sources of identity we choose. Chances are, this may be a prospect with less apparent danger, and more possible prospect, than modern citizenship has so far managed to achieve. The lives of moderns may be fugitive and ephemeral, but the cities in which they are lived out are also enduring. The cities and suburbs we inhabit in Australia are not yet so massive or opaque as to be impossible. Citizens may yet still live within them; perhaps they already do. Perhaps we may end then as, in our mythology, we started, as citizens of cities.

Further Reading

Beilharz, P. (1994). *Postmodern Socialism-Romanticism, City, State.* Melbourne: Melbourne University Press.

Bridges, T. (1994). *The Culture of Citizenship: Inventing Post-modern Civic Culture.* Albany State: State University of New York Press.

CHAPTER 5

Democracy and Citizenship

Alastair Davidson

On 8 May 1997, the Hon. Dr David Kemp MP, Minister for Schools, Vocational Education and Training, launched the Discovering Democracy program. This would provide young Australians with the core of their civics and citizenship training during their pre-tertiary education (DEETYA 1997). His speech contains the Australian state's view of what democracy is and should be. Since the program was designed by a group revamped from the ALP's earlier Civics Experts Group which had designed the new civics education for Australians, it is not unfair to see it as the shared political consensus about democracy and citizenship of both major political positions.

Dr Kemp's speech states that democracy is something that has evolved throughout Australian history. While there may be a few areas needing updating, our political practices, procedures and institutions amount to a democratic regime of which Australians should be proud, and which they should be prepared to defend. What we should study to understand democracy is Australian political history.

What this paper maintains is:

1. that a partial history is told;
2. that the real story is quite different;
3. more importantly, that no understanding of democracy can be reached by simply recounting a history of what Australians have called 'democracy';
4. that that account has to be measured against what state-of-the-art political theory states democracy to be – practice must be measured against what ought to be;
5. that when that is done, what exists in Australia does not meet adequate standards for democracy in (a) a modern nation-state; (b) a modern nation-state facing a globalising world;

6. and, consequently, Australian citizens are not empowered to cope with the challenges which face them in the public realm as we enter the twenty-first century.

Democracy and History

The claim of Discovering Democracy is that Australia is one of the 'world's pioneering democracies' with 'deep roots in the history of Britain and Europe'. It is through understanding its history and institutions that students will grasp what democracy is. There has been a long debate through Australian history which has led to acceptance that everyone is equal, even the dispossessed Aborigines. The history is sketched thus:

> Today's students are heirs to one of the most remarkable democratic initiatives of the nineteenth century. Just after 1850 [note the date – a third of white history on this continent is omitted] hundreds of thousands of people began to pour into this country in the great gold rushes. Among them were many who were frustrated at the slow development of democracy in Britain and who were determined to establish a fully democratic society in their new land. They joined with and gave momentum to those already pushing towards representative institutions of government.
>
> Australia provided these people with unique opportunities to translate their reforming spirit and egalitarian principles into the democratic framework we enjoy today. Realising that democracy required educated citizens and a moral and ethical society they not only looked for gold, but also built schools, churches and universities.
>
> An impressive record in democratic and social progress began. Australia was one of the first countries in the world to abolish the property requirement for voting in a popular assembly, to give all men and later all women the vote, to pay salaries to members of Parliament (so that those without independent incomes could seek office), to provide public education and old age pensions, to introduce the 8-hour day, and to establish the secret ballot – known throughout the world as the Australian ballot – so that everyone could cast their vote free from intimidation. By the second half of the last century, Australia had some of the most radically democratic political institutions in the world.
>
> In this century 100,000 Australians sacrificed their lives to defend their democratic way of life against militarism and totalitarianism – and to help other nations defend their democracy. (DEETYA 1997, 2)

In his speech Dr Kemp projected this rosy and self-congratulatory story nearly into the next century, saying:

> The remarkable civic stability and cohesion of our society demonstrates convincingly that, as proposed, debated and amended during the 1890's and finally established in 1900, the Constitution, which had been approved by the Australian people through direct democratic processes, including approval by

the people at referendum, has provided a secure basis for our system of democratic government which has endured for nearly 100 years.

And, he went on, this meant that students should study our institutions. Using judicious quotations from Bernard O'Dowd (!) and others, he insisted in particular that our history showed a continuous if peaceful national drive towards democracy and 'an equality [which] challenges every entrenched position of privilege and status'. Not only was the drive towards egalitarianism present even in the convict period, but it made Australia the first to grant women the vote and Vida Goldstein (after whom his electorate is named) the first woman candidate for election to Parliament in the British Empire. It also led to equality for the Aboriginal people and equality in the application of laws to all people.

While we might object to the details – and in particular to the omission of terrible genocide against the Aborigines which lasted into the 1970s (see the UN Convention on the Prevention of Genocide, Art. 2e) – overall this history is unexceptionable. But it is partial, and by a sleight of hand identifies the undoubted Australian social egalitarianism with the procedures and institutions required to guarantee power from below (Kelsen 1945).

Australia has had from 1842 until this day terrible malapportionment in its electorates. In some places one person's vote was worth 11 times another's even in the 1980s. This was recognised as a fatal flaw needing rectification in the report of the Constitutional Reform Commission of 1988. Even today there is no right in Australia to a vote of equal value.[1] Where that right does not exist there can be no democratic power from below in any definition of democracy known to political theory. How, to quote Rousseau back at Dr Kemp, can we be free if we do not live under laws of our own making? How can we make such laws if some people are more equal than others at the ballot box? Moreover, the responsible government principle that guarantees the accountability of any government to the democratically elected house has been repeatedly denied, most dramatically in the Whitlam dismissal of 1975, but in fact throughout all Australian history since 1850 (Davidson 1991). Finally, unless it is impossible for a head of state who is not democratically elected to act independently of the advice of a government enjoying majority support in the lower house, there is no control from below. Yet gubernatorial overriding of Parliament is also a repeated feature of our history.

That negative history is omitted, and so a critical point of view designed to improve the situation is not fostered. This could no doubt be rectified if a more critical history were also told: a history of exclusion emphasising the undoubtedly totalitarian state system that existed until 1850, which even Liberals like F.A. Bland made the cornerstone of their theory in the 1940s and 1950s.

Nevertheless, the problem would remain that democracy cannot be properly understood if a study of history is used to exclude a study of its normative and political nature. Democracy can only be understood as a standard and goal, one that can never be reduced to any particular practice because contexts are always changing. What democracy is can only be found in political theory. A focus on history – in this case the struggle of the Australian people for a just society – fosters what has aptly been described as the 'heritage' notion of citizenship (Duschesne 1997). In this, ethics and morality are defined in relation to our debt to our forebears and acknowledgment of their achievements, even if their goal was not attained. There is undoubtedly some merit in this. An account of the current system in England could not be easily understood if we did not go back to the Reform Acts of 1832, 1867 and 1884, all of which marked moves toward democracy. On the other hand the limits of that telos could not be grasped without understanding the demands of the Chartists and, more particularly, how their desire for a written constitution and a bill of rights was based on an abstract model of what ought to be. This model implied, moreover, a criticism of the limits of all the past history. But once the notion of a debt is set up it becomes emotionally difficult to criticise the past. Respect for the men and women who died 'defending our democracy against totalitarianism' discourages criticism of their conception of democracy along the lines that it was, for instance, exclusionary and racist.

So a critical perspective is minimised by the notion of debt. This is why even a progressive history of the struggle against tyranny as recounted in the Australian legend is liable to block understanding of democracy and citizenship. It cannot be emphasised enough that the attachment to the common law and the Westminster system, so lauded in Discovering Democracy and in Australian political discourse, can only prevent understanding of both categories. While there is no space in so short an essay to go into this issue, a short digression about what is excluded is in order.

Democracy as a Normative Ideal

Dr Kemp cites Rousseau's dictum that men are born free but they are everywhere in chains, and then draws a rapid parallel with the condition of convicts here. No doubt there is an element of truth in the implication that there was a yearning to be free of the chains placed on them in the old world. But Rousseau meant more than that. And so did the 1791, 1793 French revolutionary constitutions from which we get the modern notion of a democratic citizen. The rejection of the chains of the old world meant a desire to turn against the fathers, the experts, the legacy of the past. This rejection informs the notion of the abstract equal individual with universal rights expressed in the French constitutions. These documents also assume an anti-historical, consensual notion of the good. (Incidentally, the French revolution and the entire 'European' tradition of democracy and human rights was usually bitterly attacked in Australia, whose institutions are in no way based on a European as distinct from an Anglo-Saxon tradition.)

More, a critique of the French revolution would emphasise how it moved away from or ignored its own premises to confuse the sovereign people (who could come from anywhere) with the nation. The vaunted open republic – which Discovering Democracy suggests is the ideal in Australian history – was immediately damaged by this confusion of democracy with a people as a closed community or nation. Democracy and human rights became what they were defined to be by the French revolutionary people at their origins, and thus a historical cultural artefact which was non-negotiable by new arrivals. No clearer example could be given of the danger of historicising even the most progressive concepts. Once they become the patrimony of any nation they become modes of exclusion. Discovering Democracy also slides from the principle of democracy into the idea that it is our national creation, to be defended against attack and criticism by the blood of warrior citizens. Indeed, how could any historical approach do otherwise?

The effect is to tend to exclude any consideration of what democracy and citizenship in theory means today. We cannot, therefore, measure our practice against those ideas to see how far we have to go. Such theoretical notions are numerous and necessarily in a construct which asks first why people wish to have control over the public realm; then what they think the latter context is; and finally what the appropriate procedures are to ensure the control from below in a context which is ever changing both quantitatively and qualitatively. It is appropriate to state here that most commentators agree that there has been a major qualitative change in the last few years as we move from economies governed by nation-states to economies governed by a 'global' market. This marks a transition in democratic thought in which both the nation-state and the global are contexts, instead of the latter being bracketed out as earlier by more or less effective national borders.

I can take only two political-theoretical-normative ideas about what democracy might be in this new context. One is highly political/practical and has been endorsed by all the world's regions except the Asian. The second is highly theoretical. Both are forward looking and normative as they see democracy not primarily as something which is inherited but as something which is built and rebuilt.

The first is the statement of democracy embodied in the Strasbourg Consensus of 1983. Its inspirers were the members of the Council of Europe, the place *par excellence* where nation-state and regional/global contexts overlap in decision-making (Strasbourg Consensus). This lists the requirements for a pluralist, parliamentary democracy in the following fashion:

> Human freedom and human dignity, freedom of speech, freedom of thought and freedom of conscience, the right to criticise and the right to freedom of movement [all of which] are indispensable foundations of human coexistence
>
> Their protection and enhancement are central to all action by the state. This is served by:
> - the citizens' right to choose and change government in elections conducted under universal suffrage and by secret ballot
> - the right and duty of those representatives to regulate life in society by means of laws and to control the executive.
>
> A democracy is an open society in which all state power is derived from the people. It implies:
> - the right to participation and consultation in political decision-making at local, national and regional level
> - free access to information and free choice between different sources of information
> - the freedom of the press and media
> - the freedom to form political parties and to stand for office
> - freedom of association, including the right to form trade unions
> - the right to participate in the determination of working conditions
> - freedom from slavery and the exploitation of human labour.
>
> Democracy guarantees human dignity. This implies:
> - the right to life, liberty and respect for the human person
> - freedom of speech, thought and conscience
> - freedom of religious observance
> - freedom of movement of persons, goods and information
> - the right to school and post-school education preparing the individual for life in a democratic society.
>
> Equality before the law regardless of sex, race, creed or birth, requires:
> - an independent judiciary
> - the possibility of subjecting all decisions of the executive to judicial scrutiny
> - the subordination of the police and the armed forces to the elected government
> - the right to privacy and protection of personal freedoms.

This is clearly a document of procedures designed to secure power from below in a stable existing democratic regime. As such, it accords with the theme of Discovering Democracy. Yet, if such a document were set up as a measure for existing Australian practice, it would become crystal clear how far short our procedures and institutions fall. Even where it could be claimed that, say, the equality before the law section resembles what we have in Australia, the Australian legal decisions are restrictive in the extreme of the rights listed when compared with those of the European courts. We have only to advert to the attempt to destroy the Maritime Union of Australia, or the attempted reversal of the Wik decision, to show the gap between the promise and performance of the Australian state.

Yet the gaps with respect to such practical political documents are much less than those with respect to advanced democratic theory. Slightly defensively, Discovering Democracy points out that democracy was not established here with a revolt of the people against the tyrant. It was emulatory and (though this is not stated) introduced from above. We have no glorious revolution, nothing that corresponds with 1776 or 1789. Nor do we have the clarion clear statement that a people tired of being nothing intended to become everything against its rulers, for evermore jealously calling them to account when and how it wished.

No one would wish to assert the need for repetitions of those revolutions. The reality is, moreover, that the complexity of modern states and government makes regular hands-on participation so difficult that most of the time the populace will agree to what Rousseau deemed slavery between elections, leaving the day-to-day handling of the public to politicians and administrators. But in the face of this, something is needed to remind the latter that the people remain sovereign. Again a brief digression is in order: until very recently the notion of the popular sovereign was under suspicion because of the fear of a majority tyranny. The separation of powers was lauded at the expense of direct democratic participation (Bobbio 1976, 1984; Gauchet 1989; Pettit 1997). The wheel has turned as it becomes clear that the managerialist response to globalising society means democracy is disappearing in practice, while being criticised in theory (Zolo 1992; Kaplan, A. 1997).

One author (Brossat 1996) argues interestingly that in the managerial society the moment of democracy comes when the people go en masse to demonstrate in the streets. This happens when they feel that enough is enough, and signal that feeling (and their power) to the rulers by their anarchic, spontaneous protest. They show that the power of the ruler rests in the last instance on the popular sovereign. So, far from democracy being everyday participation, it is reduced to a moment of assertion, the assertion that human beings are not nature to be manipulated but anti-nature, against all order of things. In assessing, say, the late 1990s' mass demonstration of over 100 000 people in favour of the MUA, such a view is highly relevant. It reminds us that the rule of law, and the agreed subjection to those rules so often harped upon by decision-makers, rests in the end on the political conviction that the populace decides what right is and what rights are. This was obvious at the time of the French Revolution, but has become obscured by debates about the functioning rather than the foundations of democracy.

While it could be argued that these examples are partial, and that there are many other versions of what it is to be democratic in the literature, they at least remind us that any model for the future requires a critical assessment of what now exists. Discovering Democracy definitely does not emphasise an analysis of democracy and citizenship as something forged or created collectively within particular spaces.

Democratic Citizens in a Global Context

It is the analysis of what our context will be which is most lacking in the Discovering Democracy speech (compare Davidson 1997a). The nation-state is assumed as the almost exclusive context, with the rest of the world seen as Other. No doubt the nation-state will remain the primary context for deciding what procedures are appropriate, but we are moving towards superimposed global spaces of economic and social life that are already making borders porous and impossible to control. No individual can be empowered any more if that individual is empowered only within a national or local space. This reality is glaringly obvious from the development of enormous foreign labour forces in even the most ethnically homogeneous states of the world. Their displacement to (Nair 1997) and temporary residence in places where they are not citizens has disempowered them. Before the new nationalist reaction manifested itself throughout the world, there was a relaxation of barriers to naturalisation; acceptance of multiple nationality; a vast human rights regime established by the UN and other bodies for all human beings; and in the European space, the ending of the requirement that only nationals can have political rights in a particular country. Elsewhere I have referred to this as the emergence of the citizen who does not belong (nationally), and argued that this is progressive, especially when compared to the sort of communitarianism which runs from Etzioni and Walzer to Le Pen and Pauline Hanson.

Dr Kemp's neglect of the salient human feature of globalisation, of the arrival of whole populations of completely foreign workers, many of whom do not intend to stay or belong, and who through rapidity of communications no longer are obliged to, who do not assimilate in the old sense, even over two generations (e.g. Eade 1997: 159), is mind-boggling in a multi-ethnic Australia. While immigration has forced multiculturalism on this country, newcomers have nevertheless had to accept as non-negotiable Australia's legal and political institutions.

These are, of course, often presented as the fruit of 600 years of superior British wisdom about appropriate political arrangements. But the silencing of the voices of a quarter of the Australian population about such matters can scarcely meet any criterion of democracy, let alone the rights listed in the Strasbourg Consensus (Davidson 1997b).

The result is that we fail to hear voices which would remind the Australian state and old nationalist Australians that the loyalties and identities of these new arrivals are multiple and lead back to other parts of the region and world. This failure to see the impact on national citizenship leads to a failure to study what it means for Australia to be part of a regional economy. If it continues, this will lead to even greater difficulties. People should reflect on what procedures will be needed to empower citizens in such a future overarching polity and where the problems will lie. The main guide to those lies in the positive experience of the European Union.

The Europeans have long recognised that empowering the citizen in a regional world requires a welfare state, or some means of providing for the economic, social, educational and health minima to allow a citizen the necessary autonomy to be active politically. This means bringing the state back in and ending a unilateral understanding of the citizen as 'agin the government'. But the endeavour to achieve justice for all through affirmative action to empower disadvantaged minorities, groups and regions has meant new procedures and institutions as well.

First, there is the development of local government (often coinciding with ethnic divisions within existing nation-states) as the main site of everyday citizen decisions. The locals spend their money according to their hierarchy of needs and cultural particularities. The nation-state level certainly remains but its capacities are much reduced as it is obliged to observe rules which come from the third semi-federal level of government. This regulates what is again a multicultural space facing common problems, mostly in the economy and finance but also covering migration, criminality, pollution and health. None of these problems stop at national borders or are controllable within them.

The basic innovation is more democracy in more places. But racism and other problems are not eliminated simply by returning local government to ethnic or religious minorities. To protect individuals within systems recognising the right to cultural difference, vast and ever-extending human rights regimes have been introduced. To make them work, it is essential to allow outside interference in local affairs where human rights are concerned. No nation or minority can ever simply argue that they can do what they like in their own space. Practically, minorities are increasingly using avenues of appeal which leapfrog the next higher instance to reach a legislature or tribunal which by definition always consists of a majority of 'foreigners' vis-à-vis any particular nation-state. In Europe it is accepted that democracy needs human rights to work, just as the converse is true.

The major procedural problem comes at the highest level of government. Here a parliament would have to be so big – even if its jurisdiction were limited – that it would be unwieldy without some sort of division of labour within. Debate continues on what a regional parliament that is truly democratic – inspired by the principle of one person, one vote, one value – might look like. In the meantime, interesting discussions and experiments in electronic democracy are under way. These could eliminate the problem of representation in many areas by introducing a direct democracy of citizens based on issues rather than identity of values (Davidson 1996).

Conclusion

In sum, the new civics program devotes little attention to what will be the major citizen concern of the twenty-first century in our region and, indeed, in the vast spaces of Australia itself. The introduction of electronic democracy might quickly obviate the claimed need for malapportionment based on problems of distance and thinness of population. Such malapportionment is never consistent with democratic principle.

The European experience is not advanced here as a panacea for an Australia facing globalisation. Europe is a region which rests on a common Judaeo-Christian heritage and on commitment to democracy and human rights as principles. In the Asian free economic region, there are few such commonalties. This is obvious if we compare, say, Australia and New Zealand with the People's Republic of China or with South Korea. Not even the mediation of Japan and the Philippines could bridge a gap where many local traditions are diametrically opposed to the civic virtues listed in Discovering Democracy. If democracy and citizenship are really limited to the notions discussed in Discovering Democracy, then the abyss seems unbridgeable. But if the notions elaborated in the European Union are used as a guide to what it is to be empowered as a citizen in a global world, then it is much narrower.

What is clearly no longer viable in a world where former enemies are now neighbours is the notion of the citizen as primarily a warrior fierce in defence of democracy and human rights. Such a person is a nationalist who 'bristles' and for whom tolerance, mildness, forgiveness and love of the Other are the last consideration. His/her values are self-referential. They can lead to the attitude expressed by Pauline Hanson when she said that if to be patriotic is to be a racist then she is a racist. No conviviality allowing the evolution of understanding, and ultimately shared values, is encouraged in such a world. The next generation of citizens should be taught to live with others, not against the Other. Civic education for the democratic citizen of today – faced by multiple and irreducible difference and no shared collective conscience – should include those virtues. It does elsewhere. Why not here?

Note

1   *McGinty v Western Australia* (1996). 70 ALR 200.

Further Reading

Davidson, A. (1997). *From Subject to Citizen: Australian Citizenship in the Twentieth Century.* Cambridge: Cambridge University Press.
Zolo, D. (1997). *Cosmopolis: Prospects for World Government.* Cambridge: Polity.

CHAPTER 6

Feminism and Citizenship

Eva Cox

The concept of citizenship in the modern democratic state usually presumes that the public sphere is based on rule-driven rationality and universality of rights. Relationships within the spheres of public life are defined by laws and rules of governance. This type of citizenship presents many problems for women, as it allocates to the private sphere many of the functions and roles ascribed to women. Free males in the Greek polis were the only citizens, and echoes of that divide were reinforced when industrialisation processes moved production from the home. Men were defined by the public, political and reasonable while the private, nurturing and emotional was left to women. Even when women were allowed to vote, they were presumed to acquire male rights and duties.

Today, unpaid work in the home, the processes of care and nurture and reproduction are relegated to the relatively unseen and presumably unregulated areas of private life. Passionate and particularistic relationships are not seen as appropriate for public scrutiny. While this may have had some resonance in times when the state had a more limited role, the divide fits badly with the gradual transfer of services from homes into the community or market. Household services have followed household production into the paid sector. The movement of married women into paid work over the past three decades has also blurred the separation of home and work, and new technology has decentralised work, so more are now working from home again.

Responding to such changes, feminists over the past three decades have moved many areas of presumed privacy onto the public agenda, including domestic violence, incest, rape and other aspects of relationships formerly often de facto ignored by the legal systems. Claims that women's rights must be seen as human rights, and that rape in war is a war crime, have made it clear that women have lifted many of the presumed blinds which screened the private from public view. However, these gains have often required that the problems be defined in terms acceptable to the dominant views of what constitute public issues, in order to invoke the claims of women as citizens. To use an instance from my own experience, childcare had to be defined as an economic experience, not a nurturing one, to ensure its expansion.

If citizenship for women seems currently possible only when women can translate their causes into neoliberal, masculinist terms, the concept may be too limited to continue to be useful for feminist analysis. Yet economic and political changes have undoubtedly created renewed interest in concepts such as citizenship and civil society. The possibilities of using citizen rights and charters as counters to economic rationalism, and civil society as part of the counter to state power, form part of recent debates on the shifting roles of state, society and markets.

Overlapping these changes in the last two decades has been the rise of various feminisms and the increased involvement of women in public life and governance. This chapter will examine both citizenship and civil society from a feminist standpoint, to see whether it is possible to rework these concepts to reflect changing perceptions of gender and difference. The recent introduction of the concept of social capital in relationship to civil society offers some interesting possibilities for reworking differences and divides.

Not a New Problem

Constructing citizenship in the Australian context can be traced back 100 years, to the very practical debates on defining citizenship for a new nation. Helen Irving (1997) in her history of federation, describes the problems our founding fathers faced in defining citizenship in the late nineteenth century (158ff). Even though 'citizen' was a term more common in republican systems, it was already in wider use in political discussions relating to participation in civic or other public debates and actions. Indeed women's groups used their involvement as citizens as part of their claims for the vote. Irving writes that 'women argued for the vote, not in order to become citizens but because they already were citizens'. By this they meant, as they pointed out, they were already making a civic contribution by 'taking an equal part in the religious and moral development of the people, and doing more than half of the educational, charitable and philanthropic work of society as presently constituted' (A Petition from the Womanhood Suffrage League of NSW, to the Convention in Adelaide, 1897, in Irving 1997, 158).

Women claimed it was both their private and public involvement that formed the basis of their claim to citizenship, which then led to their claiming the right to vote. Women gained the vote in South Australia in 1894, one of the earliest grants recognising that many women were new women, modern women moving out from the home and hearth. Women in their political role were seen as civilising influences both on male behaviour and on their political agendas. Women becoming 'people' required that they be capable of the restraint that it was assumed men acquired through their participation in public life (Irving 1997, 181), in other words, that they be reasonable and fit into a masculinist Anglo-white definition of the model citizen.

The state in the Australian context is particularly important because it has been the solver of problems, the provider of resources, and a legislator with a brief to create the egalitarian ideal. The 'workingman's paradise' (Castles 1985) had constructed centralised wage fixing with a basic men's wage as early as 1907, regulated working conditions, public housing, pensions and so on. It is not surprising that the Australian women's movement generally shared the expectation that the state would be the vehicle of reforms required by women also.

Second wave feminism appeared in Australia in the 1960s and 1970s and coincided with the end of the postwar industrial boom and of postwar conservative political rule. The 1970s were the high point of publicly influential feminism. The advent of the reformist Whitlam government in 1972 offered unparalleled opportunity to use the state for intervention on behalf of former outgroups. Even the strong Marxist elements in many early women's liberation groups slowly accepted that the state and its resources were important for funding refuges and women's health services.[1]

So a strange compact was shaped between women and the state which produced many gains in areas such as equal opportunities, equal pay, childcare, and domestic violence. The Australian experience gave us the term 'femocrat' and some very innovative and successful ways of using politics and bureaucracy to manage the processes of collaboration or, as some would see it, co-option (Eisenstein 1996, passim). However, by the late 1970s, changes in the international economy and rising neo-liberalism were influencing women's relationship to the state. Women's groups were also becoming more diverse and specialised and often involved in substantial funded services, not just advocacy. Many questioned difference, power and whose interests were being served. The debates on the power relationships within feminisms were also emerging by the early 1980s. Women in the bureaucracy set up specialist units initially to advise governments on women's needs because there were few women in politics or in senior ranks of the public service. At the time many feminists welcomed the special status of these units (Sawer 1990). Though women's groups still complain about their more recent abolition and downgrading, these units in fact often became co-opted and isolated 'women's issues' from the 'mainstream', allowing the public policy agendas to be divided on gender lines.

Recent governments, both Labor and conservative, were trying to follow neoliberal precepts and attempting to reduce the role of the state, just as demands for new care services and social programs were increasing. The ageing of populations, the movement of women into paid work, the increase of excluded and distressed victims of changing demands for labour meant that education, community care and health services were inadequate.

Governments started cutting programs and demanding that individuals be self-reliant. Public funding became a competitive arena where groups sought to press their claims by being the most piteous or politically acceptable. Many so-called women's issues, such as domestic violence, were reworked into pathologies with women as victims to be serviced. The women's movement arrived at the state gravy train just as changes in international finance capital and the end of an expectation of growth were setting the scene for the ideological decline of the role of governments.

Governments have involved themselves in further care via a range of public policy initiatives such as childcare and care for people with disabilities. At the same time, however, the reductionist state redefined care services as marketable commodities, setting up 'standards' and possible subsidies, acknowledging the move of care into public spheres. Pushes by feminist groups for counting unpaid work in households made this visibly the largest industry in Australia, if tallied by commodified financial accounting (ABS 1994). This assessment of the market value of unpaid household services using economic models leaves little space for discussion of other aspects of care. Relationships and emotion are generally excluded, as are the differences between paid jobs, voluntarism, conscription and obligation, or even how to measure the quality of the services provided.

Recognition of unpaid work has always been problematic in a political and economic environment where the costs of replacing unpaid care is seen as prohibitive and the shift, whether market or state sponsored, undesirable. The policy responses have been and are again based on constant re-invention of the family to provide non-market care. This demonstrates the discomfort of transferring the caring role into public view. Forms of institutional or paid care are presumed to be less satisfactory than private unpaid care. Some small financial concessions through social security or tax systems have been made to maintain a false private, public divide and to encourage people to stay full-time in unpaid work in family services. This policy approach ignores the fact that most people, or at least most women, combine paid and unpaid work.

Feminist Critiques of Citizenship

The above examples illustrate some of the problems involved in conceptualising citizenship as elastic enough to cover the roles and relationships that have in fact been excluded. Moreover, some writers argue that some features built into concepts of citizenship are irreconcilable with many feminisms (e.g. Gilligan 1982). The basic divide that most feminists identify is that between universality and justice based on rationality, and an ethic of care based on particularistic and affective relationships. If citizenship is defined in terms of the first, the second area associated with traditional women's roles and, in some cases, a different moral perception is incompatible. Iris Marion Young in 1987 and Carole Pateman in 1988 employed some of the earlier critiques of the capacity of liberal theories of the state to be used as part of the emancipatory processes of women as citizens. Both claimed that present theories of the democratic state failed women either because of the unequal structure of the social contract (Pateman), or the constructions of liberty and fraternity (Young) and the conceptual division of reason from affect and desire. Young sees male ideas of citizenship as based on legalistic concepts designed to set up a universal that is not able to deal with difference or with non-masculine constructs of the public sphere.

Young argues that we should be able to use the concept of 'the personal is political' to create a public sphere from which nothing is excluded except self-determined privacy (1987, 59). She offers the image of 'a heterogeneous public with aesthetic and affective, as well as discursive, dimensions'. Young argues that the current distinctions between public and private express a will for homogeneity, so the private is allocated those areas which do not fit, for example, nature, emotion, irrationality. Universality is not inclusive but exclusive, because it forces out those areas of daily life which involve feelings. She claims that emancipatory processes require a redefinition of the public to extend its scope so as to include the affective and particular.

Peta Bowden in her book *Caring* (1997, 6) calls on Gilligan's work that looks at the voicing of care versus justice. Care perspectives, she claims, cannot be separated from their contexts of responsiveness to others. Responsibility in relationships 'resists abstract formulations of moral problems' In a justice model, 'emphasis is placed on rights, duties and general obligations and moral reasoning is marked by schematic understandings of moral problems which allow previously ordered rules and principles to be applied to particular moral cases'. On citizenship, Bowden declares:

> Indeed the formal associations of citizenship are frequently used to distinguish precisely those aspects of relations between persons which is constitutively limited or in which partiality of personally engaged attentiveness signals undue bias and favoritism. Citizen relations are more likely to denote interpersonal connections that eschew the values of intimacy and personally engaged care. (1997, 141)

The partiality of thick and intimate relationships, or known connections, do not fit with objective application of rules.

Citizenship practices, she claims, express the most generalised forms of interpersonal interaction where personal attributes give way to predictability, stability and control of the outcomes of activities. Citizenship replaces care with justice, commitment with duty and goods with rights and rules. These definitions suggest that we can be separately public citizens and private beings, rather than recognising that we are most likely to be both at the same time. We may act differently in certain settings but all our actions are based on prior relationships, expectations and feelings.

Social Capital and Citizenship

I now want to explore ways in which models of social capital may make links between these two apparently incompatible parameters. Social capital is accumulated through experiences of relationships and expectations, and offers ways of reconceptualising citizenship in a more holistic framework. Social capital is expressed as levels of trust that maintain norms and values essential for functional citizenship and civil societies (Cox 1995). Norms of civic life should allow us to function as social beings, and to civilly manage differences and debates.

Unlike citizenship, where the focus is on the individual, social capital binds the diverse elements of civil society through collective social and political processes. In some definitions civil society is described as the 'space' between the state and family, that is, the community or third sector of organised groups. Again, I would dispute the drawing of such lines as offering both gendered and inadequate descriptions of the complex interactions of individuals within households through community to politics. I am using civil society here to include both the family and the state in many of their functions.[2] However, many roles such as educator, service provider, funder of cultural and other services and standard setter, cross from state to family. The state is part of the expression of the will of the people and performs functions, in Australia at least, which are similar to those performed by community groups and families. The difference is that it does so with some legitimacy because of its mandate of popular sovereignty.

I want specifically to include many functions of the family because its exclusion is one of the primary problems of gendered divides. The role of raising and protecting the future generations is already and increasingly a partnership between community, state and families. Since the public instruction acts last century, the state has asserted its responsibilities and the right to have a say in the rearing of the young. Unpaid family services also replace lost state and expensive market services.

Since services, demands and resources flow between the various sectors, the above definition recognises that the sectors are permeable and that the lines will be redefined and contestable. Rational theorists do not recognise that rules only work when people feel they are fair and trust their provenance. Trusting the system is a prerequisite to compliance; trusting other people is also necessary if daily interactions are not to be overlaid with costly processes of enforcement.

Social capital is therefore accumulated through the same processes which make us good citizens and our societies more civil. We bring diverse views and needs to our interactions, and social capital provides the trust necessary to resolve differences. Seyla Benhabib (1992, 8–9) describes some forms of problem-solving as moral conversations. This, I am suggesting, fits with core aspects of social capital. The concept of using conversations, not to find consensus but to see others' standpoints and come to agreements, fits with processes of developing trust and working collectively for the common good. Drawing on the work of Hannah Arendt, Benhabib claims participants in society are the concrete Other rather than the universal Other. The universal Other is the compleat citizen – the rational, rule-driven individual who exists only in theory; the concrete Other is us, mixing our cultural, social and other experiences. The reality is that we are all feeling, connected beings who mediate rationality with expectations and levels of trust.

Annette Baier (1994) suggested that 'appropriate' trust can mediate between reason and feeling since

> to trust is neither quite to believe something about the trusted nor necessarily feel some emotion towards them – but to have a belief informs an action influencing attitude. In my terms trust allows us to combine the possibly particular with the general, to test over time, the components as possibly being fair and sustainable. (1994, 10)

Her view suggests that the connections between justice and care are actually quite tight in practice, and can be linked theoretically. The social capital model extends these links.

The 'care' element relates to the development of trust, and this tends to be part of ethical familiarity; the justice elements are involved in setting boundaries and expectations. These set rules of engagement and rights that do not have to be invoked unless breached. The key difference is that trust is linked with, but not synonymous with, the processes of justice because it requires fairness of process to maintain its levels. Sustainable trust is only produced in situations with egalitarian, participative processes that are not subject to gross inequalities or exploitation. So rationality and rules provide the framework which is invoked when care becomes exploitative or too partial to be fair.

This is suggested also by Bowden (1997, 143) who notes that the caring aspects of socialisation are obviously important in developing the sense of both moral virtue and justice that the citizen is presumed to require: 'The virtues of citizen relationships in terms of adhering to norms, co-operation, and trust are closely derived and related to the private sphere' (1997, 143).

Particularistic relationships are not necessarily fair, nor is there necessarily equality of power in decisions, nor do they necessarily operate equitably. If care relationships fail this test, some rule-driven frameworks are needed to cover the informal sphere and offer some criteria by which inequities can be challenged. The liberal conception of citizenship rights is useful, for example, in empowering the consumer. Rules and entitlement become the means by which the non-trust relationships can be made to work. Rights, obligations and entitlements are put in place to ensure that collective or individual claims can be made to gain equity and to offer predictability and accountability. They are essential for interactions where there is no opportunity for building the long-term interpersonal relationships that engender trust and fit into civic mores of egalitarian societies.

Rights discourse has a long and distinguished history of putting the issues of inequalities on the agenda. The construction of the rights debate is limited by the need to develop categories to compare, to work within, to rationalise and simplify. The reductionism essential in rights discourse tends to be addressed by defining more and more categories of claimants. It is possible to look at the different groups of claimants as Bowden does by saying recognition, respect and listening can be added, allowing for some subtleties of difference within the claimants' system.

Conclusion

Rules of public behaviour may seem irrelevant to the sphere of private care but they are pervasive in practice. The maintenance of groups and the development of links are intrinsic to caring work. The liberal state, confronting complex and embedded relationships, has problems in framing bureaucratic and legislative bases which do not militate against the responsiveness and flexibility of ethical care. The affective aspect of nurture, the feeling of being the special focus of individual concern, may conflict with norm-driven mandated programs in institutional format but are essential to meeting diverse needs.

Social capital is a useful framework for examining citizenship and the rights debate. High social capital gives communities, societies and nations the capacity to deal with conflicting demands from diverse groups and to solve them within a framework of acceptable process. It is based on processes which encourage the constituent groups to trust the goodwill of others rather than the game theories of liberal rationalism.

The construction of processes of relatedness, of expectations of goodwill and optimism about the possible relationships, mean that connections between people become part of the pattern of citizenship. It is valid to see the claimant position as an antidote to the loss of trust that occurs in social systems where there is no possibility of face-to-face development of relationships of trust.

The care debate is somewhat stuck in its idealisation of close personal relationships characterised by intimacy and attachment. The levels of exploitation and power maldistribution already identified by feminisms in intimate relationships need a wider scrutiny. Similarly, constructing citizenship without care is no longer an option. Feminist citizenship and civil society need to start from the premise that nothing is too priviate to be scrutinised for fairness and nothing is so public that particular and diverse needs are not to be noted and respected. An ethics of care and a framework of justice and fairness must both be accommodated as parts of the constant processes of civil societies.

I want to conclude by noting that feminist citizenship is not about feminising justice, or changing or masculinising care. It is about recognising that current definitions are too limited to be functional descriptions of good societies. In practice these have always made judicious amalgams of care and justice models. The problem is to recognise the components and validate the interrelationships as well as the outputs.

Notes

1 I was present at the many arguments in 1975, when money was offered to celebrate the UN International Women's Year, and at the bitter debates there and later in Victoria about accepting government funds for refuges, etc.
2 I would exclude the public order aspects of the state, and its defence functions, as being uncivil, in a current and older sense.

Further Reading

Cox, E. (1995). *A Truly Civil Society*. Sydney: ABC.
Lister, R. (1990). *The Exclusive Society: Citizenship and the Poor*. London: Calvert's Press.
Putnam, R.P. (1993). *Making Democracy Work: Civic Traditions in Modern Italy*. Princeton: Princeton University Press.

CHAPTER 7

Limits to Citizenship

Barry Hindess

Discussions of citizenship commonly treat it as largely concerned with the relations between an individual and the state of which s/he is a member, but citizenship also has an important international dimension. At this level citizenship is an index of membership of one or other national community. It refers to a membership status which may be recorded in a passport and other documents. Governments use such documents to inform their own officials, and officials of other governments, that a person is a member of their society, and they use related documents (such as visas) to regulate the movement of non-citizens.

This international dimension of citizenship, in which it serves as part of an international regime of population management, is of considerable political importance in the contemporary world. However, when governments and other organisations seek to promote citizenship, or to appeal to the rights and the duties which it entails, they clearly invoke more complex understandings of what it is to be a citizen. Such understandings vary but, at least in the democratic societies of the late twentieth-century west, they usually share an image of the citizen which is derived somewhat loosely from the city states of western antiquity. The citizen, Aristotle (1962) tells us, is 'he who has the power to take part in the deliberative or judicial administration of any state', while a state 'is a body of citizens sufficing for the purposes of life' (*Politics* 111, 1275b, 19–22). Here citizens are seen, not just as belonging to the population of a state, but as occupying an important status within that population (they take part in government) and as belonging to a political community or state of a very particular kind (one that is governed by citizens). Citizens are autonomous persons, at least in the sense that they are not dependent on others (on a parent, an owner or master, or a husband) for their status as members of the state. The state to which they belong as citizens is a community of fate rather than of choice, and its members are normally themselves the children of citizens. It is usually thought to be a moral community whose members share a common culture which serves both to regulate their interaction and to distinguish them from members of other such communities.

Finally, citizenship in the modern west differs from that of its classical predecessors in two fundamental respects. In Greece and in Rome for most of its history citizenship was the privilege of a small minority. Now, most adults are likely to be citizens of the state in which they live, although there are also very significant numbers of resident foreigners. Also, modern states are generally regarded as being too large to be governed by the collective activity of citizens themselves. Citizens in the twentieth-century west play a part in government, but for the most part indirectly. Citizens do not govern themselves, but governments are expected to be accountable to them, primarily through some kind of electoral process. This, of course, requires that the work of government can be rendered visible to the citizens at large.

It is these more complex 'internal' understandings of the citizen in relation to the state of which s/he is a member that particularly concern me in this paper. I focus on what the language of citizenship suggests about the character of the state or political community to which the citizen belongs before turning in my final paragraphs to the issue of accountability. We can begin by observing that nobody seriously regards Australia, or any other contemporary state, as a self-governing community of citizens in quite the sense of the above description. Indeed, discrepancies between the image of such a community and mundane reality are commonly acknowledged. Short of the most drastic ethnic cleansing, for example, the cultural and ethnic pluralism of national populations is clearly here to stay. As a result, governmental multiculturalism is a feature of most societies in the world today – not just of those, like Australia, Canada and the USA, who tend to present themselves as nations of immigrants. Even in Europe and Japan, where the image of a national political community whose members share both a common culture and a common descent frequently surfaces in the rhetoric of a national and racial chauvinism, that image has never been entirely realistic.[1] Or again, it would be foolish to pretend that substantial differences of income and wealth, or the fact that a small minority are able to possess a second or a third home, or substantial holdings in a chain of newspapers, a television channel or a football league, do nothing to undermine the equality of status which all Australians share by virtue of their common citizenship. While Australian governments and most Australian parliamentarians routinely claim to act in the interests of all Australian citizens, it is abundantly clear that some of those citizens are far more equal than the rest.

Other examples could easily be found, but these two will serve to make my point – which is not so much that the image of Australia (or any other country) as a community of citizens is unrealistic in many important respects (Hindess 1993) but rather that it is generally recognised as such. The significance of the language of citizenship in Australia and other western societies, then, is neither that it provides a realistic account of conditions in these societies, nor that it seriously misleads their inhabitants about those conditions. What the language of citizenship does provide is a framework for political discussion which is widely regarded as legitimate: that is, it provides the terms in which governments can appeal for support and be criticised by their opponents, demands for special treatment (of Indigenous peoples, advantaged and disadvantaged minorities) can be advanced or disputed, and so on. To say that the language of citizenship is legitimate here is simply to say that political demands framed in its terminology will not be regarded in these societies – as they might still be in some parts of the world – as either treasonable or revolutionary, although they will often be seen as impracticable, misguided or unreasonable.

The language of citizenship is only one among several influential ways of conceptualising relationships between a state and members of the population under its control. The latter might also be seen, for example, as consumers or taxpayers, as belonging to a distinctive ethnic, national or religious community, or as subordinate subjects of a superordinate sovereign. While these alternatives continue to be influential, the language of citizenship has been regarded as legitimate in most western societies at least since the end of the second world war, and in several of them for considerably longer. It has also become a more prominent part of the public rhetoric of western societies in the last two decades. Governments, parties and other organisations are busily promoting their preferred understanding of citizenship. Thus, the figure of the citizen regularly appears in defences of the welfare state and right-wing responses to the dependency culture which state welfare is said to produce, demands for citizenship education, proposals for a citizens' charter, campaigns to restrict immigration, proposals to develop new, multicultural and post-nationalist forms of citizenship, and so on.

How is this recent upsurge of interest in citizenship to be understood? The fact that it has been taken up in support of diverse and often conflicting political objectives indicates that we are far from witnessing a concerted push to realise the citizenship ideal, for example, by making governments more properly accountable or citizens more nearly equal.

On the contrary, I suggest that the widespread invocation of citizenship in contemporary Western societies reflects a kind of nostalgia for a recent past in which, so it is now believed, certain ways of thinking about the government of populations – precisely in terms of the imagery of self-governing communities of citizens – had more purchase than they do today.

Nostalgia, like the hard-headed realism which pretends to be its contrary, is a play of comforting illusions and, while it knowingly misrepresents the past, it also provides powerful distraction for the present. My point, then, is not so much that conditions in contemporary western societies have changed (although, of course, they have), but rather that perceptions of those conditions have changed in such a way as to make the comforting discourse of citizenship appear less relevant to the work of government than it may recently have been – thereby prompting the reaction that citizenship (the thing itself) needs to be reinforced, or even reconstructed, if it is to meet the challenges of the twenty-first century.[2]

Conditions are thought to have changed in many ways, as the massive and heterogeneous literature on postmodernism demonstrates all too clearly. The changes which are particularly relevant to the nostalgic invocation of citizenship are those relating to the perception of Australia and other western societies as political communities able to control their own affairs, and as communities governed by their citizens. What is at issue in the first is reflected in Dahl's notion of final control of the agenda of government, by which he means that the community can decide what areas of the life of the community should be brought under the control of its government and what can reasonably be left either to regulate themselves or to be governed by other agencies (Dahl 1989).

This idea of final control of the agenda of government has usually been tempered by perceptions of both the normative and the practical limits to government. Many commentators have suggested that the latter have become more consequential in recent years as the internationalisation of trade and finance, and the widespread deregulation of financial markets, have undermined the effectiveness of established regimes of national economic management. There is, of course, a substantial element of nostalgia in such a suggestion.[3] However, what should be noted here is that the widespread loss of faith in the effectiveness of macroeconomic management at a national level can be seen as part of a more general shift in perceptions of the ability of governments to manage affairs within their own societies, and one which is by no means confined to the economic sphere. The movement of people, narcotics, cultural artefacts and distinctive lifestyles across national boundaries has also served to undermine the perception of the national community as a cultural unity.

These changing perceptions of economic management have developed hand in hand with changing perceptions of the economy itself. Western social thought has tended to understand the economy as a self-regulating network of interdependent activities endowed with a natural propensity to expand. The economy has been regarded somewhat ambiguously, sometimes as operating within the boundaries of a national territory, and sometimes as extending far beyond them. While features of the economy have been seen as setting objective limits to the capacities of national governments, the implications of those limits for governmental reflection on economic matters are radically different in the two cases.[4] In the first case, the economy has been presented both as a largely self-regulating system and as a *national* economy, whose boundaries more or less coincide with those of the relevant national territory. This perception suggests that a national government should treat its economy with respect, and that if it does so, then increasing prosperity can be expected to follow. Should increasing prosperity not follow, or not follow quickly enough, this will be seen as a result of extra-economic obstacles – local customs and traditions, government sponsored monopolies and 'political' interferences of various kinds – which it is the responsibility of government to clear away. In this respect, the idea that the economy works best in the absence of political interference nevertheless provides governments with considerable scope for justifying their own interventions. This perception of the national economy as essentially benign (if only it can be made to work properly) is the key to the rosy view of national economic management which sustained social democratic parties, and many of their political opponents on the right, throughout much of the twentieth century.

In the second case, the national economy is no longer seen as a self-regulating system, but rather as a fragment within a substantially larger self-regulating whole – and one which no merely national government could possibly be in a position to control. Thus Robert Reich (US Secretary for Labor in the Clinton administration) laments that soon there will be no 'national economies, at least as we have come to understand that concept. All that will remain within national borders are the people who comprise the nation' (1992, 3). On this view the responsibility of government for economic management is less a matter of clearing away the obstacles to the proper functioning of the national economy considered as a system, and more that of ensuring that domestic economic activity is able to respond effectively to conditions determined elsewhere. It is in such ambivalent terms that the internationalisation of economic activity has traditionally been seen, both as offering great opportunities to established national communities, and, if they fail to respond effectively, as threatening their national integrity and way of life.[5]

While the development of economic rationalism in Australia and related developments in other OECD countries have clearly been influenced by the rise of neoliberalism, they also reflect an important shift away from the perception of the national economy as a relatively self-contained functional unity – especially in countries like Australia and New Zealand, which are particularly dependent on international trade. The declining salience of this view of the national economy affects the image of a self-governing community of citizens in two ways. First and most obviously, it suggests that national governments cannot exercise the control over their economic affairs which the idea of self-government has traditionally required. Rather, it seems that the task of government is now to respond rapidly and effectively to the domestic impact of powerful outside forces which it has no hope of being able to control. On this view of their responsibilities, governments, like military leaders, may well be held accountable for their policies at some point, but it would be unrealistic to suggest that the actual conduct of operations be subject to democratic control by the troops.

Second, the older conception of the national economy as a self-contained system sustained an important view of how governments could be held accountable for national economic management. Aggregate measures of unemployment, growth, inflation, and so on could all be seen as serving to inform both policy-makers and citizens. On the one hand, governments could be seen as responsible for controlling the relevant economic aggregates and, on the other hand, the behaviour of those same aggregates rendered the actions of government in the sphere of economic management visible to their citizens.

This point brings us directly to the perception of Australia and other western societies as communities governed by their citizens – or rather, by those citizens working indirectly through representative institutions. The idea is that citizens elect representatives who constitute a government which issues laws and other instructions and establishes the means to enforce them. The presumption of their (imaginary) prior agreement implies that, if these laws and instructions are issued in the proper fashion, then the great majority of citizens will go along with them – although this aspect of government may be backed up by other devices for dealing with any recalcitrant minority. On this view, the work of government will be accountable to its citizens primarily though the electoral process. This is a version of what Foucault calls the 'city–citizen game': a representation of governmental power which, while it is by no means entirely fanciful, nevertheless covers only a small part of the government of contemporary national populations.

Foucault also insists on the importance in western societies of the 'shepherd–flock game', a representation of relations between sovereign and subjects in which the former appears as a superior being who nevertheless looks after the interests of the latter – often in ways which they fail to appreciate (1981, 223–54). While, in contemporary western societies, the image of superior sovereign and subordinate subjects has been partially displaced by versions of the city–citizen game, the idea that the ruler knows best still retains a powerful hold on the thinking of governments.

I noted earlier that relations between governments and members of the population which they control might also be understood in terms of the image of the person as client or consumer. Indeed, there are many contexts in which the quality of interactions with government agencies is more nearly captured by such an image than it is by the image of the person as citizen. In practice, of course, nobody believes that the 'city–citizen game' provides a realistic portrayal of any existing society. The fact that it does not is nevertheless worth emphasising, if only because the image of community of citizens frequently leads academic political analysis, and non-academic political debate, to focus primarily on the law-making aspects of government, thereby relegating to a position of secondary importance much of the mundane work of government – and therefore many of the interactions between government and its citizens.

If the image of a community of citizens promotes an influential, but remarkably limited, view of relations between government and people, there are also problems with the notion of accountability which that image suggests. In effect, the idea that government is accountable to the people primarily through public debate and the electoral process requires that the people are able to evaluate what the government is doing in their name. It requires, in other words, that the work of government be rendered visible to the citizens at large in the form of an overall picture – for example, through aggregate measures and expert assessments of performance in the relevant policy areas, the provision of departmental reports and specialised inquiries, and perhaps a few case studies to illustrate general policy issues. Such devices are not necessarily problematic in themselves, but they invariably leave much of the work of government in obscurity. Composite measures tell us little about the impact of government policies on the individuals most directly affected – for example, the clients of social welfare and other government agencies, or the victims of planning decisions. Furthermore, such overall pictures – of national economic accounts, unemployment, the environmental impact of a new runway, a freeway or an industrial development – are highly susceptible to manipulation by governments and by powerful private interests. As a result, those who are in a position to see part of what is obscured by such pictures and to mount a protest can be dismissed all too easily, both as merely promoting their own sectional interests and as failing to appreciate the whole picture (which is really clear only to the minister concerned). There is a nicely ambivalent relationship between the view of modern representative government promoted on the one hand by the language of citizenship and representation and, on the other, by the language of sovereign and subjects in which, as noted earlier, the sovereign appears as a superior kind of being – and elected governments commonly appeal to both of them. Thus, a governmental commitment to the promotion of citizenship can easily co-exist with the belief that government knows better than any insufficiently powerful group of citizens who suffer the consequences of its actions.

Finally, there is a certain complicity between the view that government is accountable through the electoral process and the relatively benign image of the national economy as a largely self-contained system of interaction. In both cases, government is seen as acting primarily by means of regulation which is centralised and visible – although in practice it is widely recognised that there are significant activities of government which this view leaves in obscurity. Thus, even if it were possible to set the problem of governmental arrogance and duplicity to one side, the changing perception of economic management noted above means that we should expect the publicly visible – and in that sense publicly accountable – aspects of the work of government to become even less significant overall.

To conclude, I have focused on two limitations of the contemporary language of citizenship. This language is limited because it invokes an ability on the part of the state, as a body of citizens, to manage its affairs which is now widely (and in many respects correctly) regarded as seriously misleading. As a result, it promotes an anachronistic vision of the capacities and responsibilities of national governments. The language of citizenship is also misleading because it provides a remarkably limited account of relations between governments and members of the population living under their control. However to say that the language of citizenship is misleading in important respects is not to say that it should be abandoned. Insofar as it helps us to maintain a measure of free and relatively informed political debate, and to campaign against the arbitrary impositions of governments and their mistreatment of weak minority groups, then the language of citizenship is well worth preserving, in spite of its substantial limitations. But, in the world of the late twentieth century, the image of a state that is governed by its citizens cannot be regarded as a viable political ideal.

Notes

1. On the contrary, the experience of cultural diversity has been the normal human condition throughout recorded history. See McNeill (1986).
2. This is a major theme of David Held's recent work. See Held (1995, ch. 4 and 5).
3. Hindess (1994). For a careful survey of literature on the impact of globalisation see Hirst and Thompson (1996).
4. The arguments of this and the next few paragraphs are developed more fully in my 'Neo-liberalism and the National Economy,' in Dean and Hindess (1998).
5. The threat looms large in Pusey (1991). See also the symposium on Pusey's book in *Australian and New Zealand Journal of Sociology*, 29(3), 1993.

Further Reading

Dean, M. and B. Hindess (eds) (1998). *Governing Australia*. Cambridge, Cambridge University Press.

Held, D. (1995). *Democracy and the Global Order. From the Modern State to Cosmopolitan Governance*. Cambridge: Polity.

Hindess, B. (1996). *Discourses of Power: From Hobbes To Foucault*. Oxford: Blackwell.

Hirst, P. and G. Thompson (1996). *Question: The Myths of the International Economy and the Possibilities of Governance*. Cambridge: Polity.

PART II

Different Citizenships

CHAPTER 8

Political Citizenship

Mike Salvaris

Citizenship is an idea with many meanings and dimensions. It is often defined barely, as a formal status, 'the legal bond between the individual and the State', and related rights and responsibilities (Australia, Parliament 1994, 11), but it also contains or has acquired in centuries of development, social and ethical dimensions, based in belonging, solidarity and nationalism (thus the exclusion of 'non-citizens'), and more recently, in universal values of dignity and human rights (Barbalet 1988; Heater 1990; Turner 1993, 78).

Foremost and unavoidably, however, and certainly in its historic origins, citizenship is a political condition, realised in political activities and institutions. It is, first, about membership in a political community. Its rights and duties must ultimately be guaranteed by political systems. Aristotle assumed active political participation in government by ordinary citizens to be a public good, although whether this is possible or desirable in complex modern states is contested (Dahl and Tufte 1973). But since the eighteenth century, citizenship has been fundamentally linked to the political principles of democracy, equality and self-government, and thus most fully realisable in a civic democratic republic. The citizen is the basic political unit of democracy, as the subject is in a monarchy (Davidson 1997a).

In the late twentieth century society, citizenship has also become 'a strategically important idea' in both practical and theoretical politics (Kymlicka and Norman 1994). Practically, it is believed necessary to reassert the 'fundamental political legitimacy' of citizenship to counteract 'the worldwide trend towards monetarism and ... markets' and the rapidly growing power of global corporations, which gravely threaten citizenship and democracy (Roche 1992; Saul 1997) and make potential

'Quislings' of national politicians captured by their interests (former Australian Chief Justice Brennan 1998). For many political theorists, the concept of citizenship has become re-charged in the 1990s, not just because of the new political contexts, but as a 'natural evolution in political discourse which seems to integrate the demands of justice and community membership – the central concepts of political philosophy in the 1970s and 1980s' (Kymlicka and Norman 1994, 352).

Nearly half a century ago, T.H. Marshall wrote of citizenship as a kind of benchmark for political progress: 'societies in which citizenship is a developing institution', he said, 'create an image of an ideal of citizenship against which achievements can be measured and towards which aspirations can be directed' (Marshall 1950, 29). But the suggestion of inevitable and uniform progress is misleading. The ideal of citizenship is under constant challenge in all political communities and in various guises, and so too inevitably are the concrete political forms (rights, institutions, etc.) developed in its name. Thus while 'the justice of a nation's basic structures' is important, the strength and vitality of the civic culture that sustains them may be more important in the long run: 'without active, knowledgeable citizens, the forms of democratic representation remain empty; without vigilant, informed citizens there is no check on potential tyranny' (Civics Expert Group (CEG) 1994, 16).

If, therefore, we seek to define the criteria for strong and healthy political citizenship, we should look for strong institutional forms and practices in laws, and especially the Constitution, in public policies and administrative practice defining clear and concrete standards, and hand in hand with these, an active, well-informed and self-confident citizenry, in whom the ethics and values of the public interest are well embedded. How does Australian citizenship measure up to these standards? How can it be strengthened? And what might be the impact of the transition to a republican constitution?

In Australia today citizenship is a 'somewhat clouded concept' (Stephen 1993). It is neither well understood nor firmly defended by the citizens themselves, often misleadingly and manipulatively portrayed in the media and public culture, minimally defined in political and administrative structures as a basis for coherent rights or policy. And in recent decades, even its primary and historical rationale as a paradigm, and an ethical basis, for defining relations between government and the individual has been challenged.

For most Australians, the concept itself is not an emotive one: it describes a dry and formal legal category, redolent of earnest but long forgotten 'civics' classes.

If you asked the person in the street what citizenship meant to them, you would probably get an answer along the lines of the right to vote or be elected to Parliament, the right to a fair trial or to carry an Australian passport. (Australian Catholic Social Welfare Commission (ACSWC) 1993, 5)

As a nation, Australians claim an instinctive affinity for some of the core values which sustain strong citizenship (egalitarianism, a fair go, mateship, social solidarity, etc.). History shows these values were often misapplied to promote social and racial exclusion rather than its opposite (i.e., in the 'White Australia Policy', the exclusion of Indigenous people, and the gender bias of the 'workers' welfare state'). But Australia can still fairly claim to have pioneered some of the political forms of modern citizenship, even to have been a kind of 'social laboratory' a century ago (Thompson 1994; Castles 1985; Beilharz et al. 1992, 18).

How real are these values in the 1990s? On the face of it, Australian society appears a reasonably fair and tolerant one, 'fortunate in its enjoyment of the amenities of citizenship' (CEG 1994). Progress in multiculturalism, equal opportunity, and Indigenous reconciliation over three decades seemed to confirm this. But since the early 1980s, a closer look shows a much less fair and inclusive society. Among modern democracies, Australia is unusually reticent in spelling out the form and substance of its citizenship. In law and policy, it is difficult to find unequivocal statements about the underlying values of citizenship, much less a clear definition of the actual rights, duties, institutions and policy standards that give it flesh and bone. As a monarchical democracy, we have been reluctant to enshrine what others took as the core principle of democracy: the political sovereignty of the citizen as the supreme source of authority. Yet other 'core national values' find no meaningful entrenchment either, even if they are now finding symbolic expression in 'non-binding' constitutional preambles.

Concepts of the 'fair go' are not put down anywhere in writing. Because Australians were subjects under a constitutional monarchy, rights were not articulated in the Constitution and the various citizenship acts say nothing of rights and duties and give no clue to the definition of civic virtue (Ideas for Australia 1994).

The current Australian Constitution has almost nothing to say about citizenship: what it means, what are the citizens' basic rights and duties. This is intentional: a century ago, the 'founding fathers' were not designing a citizens' charter, but a treaty between governments, state and putative federal. They focused efficiently on their core tasks: dividing powers between signatories, and setting up the basic structures of a new government. In many ways the Constitution was a compromise settlement to overcome the concerns of reluctant state politicians on bread-and-butter issues like free trade. Interestingly, there was a brief flirtation with the idea of defining 'a broader and more dignified' form of 'national citizenship', but that idea foundered on the twin rocks of state conservatism and imperial deference, 'citizen' was thought an inappropriate term for 'subjects' of the Empire (Quick and Garran 1976 [1901], 957).

Australia has a citizenship act, proclaimed in 1948 and currently being redrafted (it had been described as 'a masterpiece of legislative incoherence' by Stephen (1993)); but it will essentially continue to focus on the formal processes for admission to citizenship rather than the substantive content. What many Australians think of as 'basic rights' of citizenship are in fact quite insecure, lacking clear definition and adequate guarantees of delivery. Civil, political and legal rights lean too heavily on the frail shoulders of judges and a system of 'common law' that is neither comprehensive nor especially sympathetic to poor and excluded citizens. Social and economic 'rights' (public education and health, the 'right to housing', the 'right to a job') could best be described as discretionary benefits or aspirational policy goals. In both classes of rights (civil/political and social), Australia has signed international conventions comprehensively promising such rights to its citizens, but, by and large, governments have failed to incorporate these rights where it matters most: in domestic law. Finally, as recent Australian history shows, both classes of 'rights', no matter how long or painfully acquired, can be quite easily legislated away by simple parliamentary majority.

Australian citizenship could thus be fairly described as structurally weak, both in its political forms and in its popular support. 'The anaemic profile of the citizen in political discourse' can be explained in part 'by its shallow historical roots' (Beilharz et al. 1992). These roots grew mostly from British soil; in many ways, the story of our citizenship has been one of 'gradual extrication from law and custom made in London. Citizenship devolved on to Australians. It has not been established as a birthright – and in consequence there are few guarantees' (Jayasuriya 1994, 93). The historical legacy included a British monarchical (and imperial) model of government rather than a European republican or revolutionary tradition; reliance on British common law rather than wider universal principles of human rights or citizenship as the basis for rights; a national Constitution that is (as we have seen) essentially silent on citizenship; and a tendency in public policy to follow narrow and increasingly passive models of citizenship rather than seeing it as an actively developing and democratic political category. This tendency first constructed the 'worker citizen', and then in the postwar era, the 'welfare citizen', a product of the gradual 'slides' in the British and Australian debates 'from a political to a sociological definition of citizenship' and the growth of the welfare state (Davidson 1995, 30–1; Habermas 1992, 11). The most recent stage in this evolution, discussed below, is the 'consumer citizen', the citizen of the markets. This transition has been compounded by the 'narrow understanding' and lack of public debate on the practical and symbolic meaning of citizenship in Australia. This has simultaneously led to weaker 'functional forms' of citizenship and limited the ability of many citizens to participate actively in the life of the community (Cappo 1993).

In the decades since the Second World War, these structural weaknesses in Australian citizenship were masked by a process of bipartisan consent. In the first half of the period, agreement between labour and conservative parties on at least the 'core values' of Australian citizenship and the maintenance of a minimal welfare state was sustained by steady growth in the economy and government spending, and boosted from time to time by some unarguably significant policy changes promoting social and political participation: most notably, with the 1970s Whitlam government programs such as Medicare, free tertiary education and the Australian Assistance plan – a period described as 'the strongest moment of citizenship claims in modern Australian history' (Beilharz et al. 1992, 48).

Then, since the 1980s, an increasing concern with citizenship as culture, national identity and lifestyle has tended to distract attention from its essential weakness as democratic political practice. The new discourse often relies on the 'cynical and self-interested deployment' of a certain kind of bombastic masculinism, and makes endless calls to 'celebrate' being Australian, especially on ritual occasions like Anzac Day and Australia Day. The discourse obscures the material relations within which we all live and seriously depletes our ability to understand our true commonalities and to imagine a better and more democratic society. 'Australians', says Graeme Turner, 'have become used to hearing the nation talked about as if it were a brand name, rather than a social community, whose interest politics should protect' (Turner 1994, 156–7). Since the early 1980s, the steady advance of economic rationalism in government and public life has brought profound changes in both the form and conditions of Australian citizenship, and more fundamentally, in its ethical and political rationale.[1]

Most obviously, economic rationalism has shown itself in the rapid and wide-ranging transformation of the public programs and institutions that sustain citizenship, and create the possibilities for equality and equity, for participation, community and social inclusion. Programs cut, abolished or diluted include: key social services including public education, public health and dental services, social security; the equity of the tax system; work rights, unemployment programs and wage protection; legal aid and human rights enforcement; childcare, public housing, public transport and public broadcasting. Many of the institutions and services which have stood for decades as the visible symbols of the public sphere, of the community and the common property of citizens, have disappeared: sold, commercialised, or shut down, often leaving communities significantly poorer.

The catalogue of public assets and services 'privatised' in a mere 15 years tells the story of an extraordinary national movement from public interest to private profit at all levels of community life, from huge public corporations to the humblest municipal service: telecommunications, gas, electricity, water supply, buildings, lands, forests, national parks and state reserves, banks and insurance offices, airlines and railways, airports and sea-ports, roads and freeways, hospitals, ambulance services, nursing homes, aged care services, government audit, judicial functions and court reporting, police records, prisons and youth detention centres, childcare centres, town halls, schools and universities, cemeteries, swimming pools, garbage collection, parking enforcement, health and building inspection, camping grounds, meals on wheels.

During the period of these changes, Australia has steadily become a more unequal and more stressed society, with sharp differences in income and wealth (including close to the most unequal distribution of earned income in the OECD, widening gaps between executive salaries and wages, the top 10% of wealth-holders having 55%, and the top half 98.4%, of total wealth); high and growing levels of poverty, especially among women and children (24.2% of all dependent children in poverty in 1995–96 compared to 20.7% in 1985–86); high and sustained levels of unemployment, especially long-term (now about a third of all unemployment) and the young; huge losses in the number of full-time jobs, estimated at 3.3 million in the past 12 years; internationally low levels of spending on social services; an extraordinary growth in the imprisonment rate (57% from 1987 to 1997, now one of the highest international rates); high and growing rates of youth (male) suicide, homelessness and drug overdoses; internationally high rates of homicide; high differentiation in socioeconomic outcomes for Indigenous Australians in almost all measures of equality and social well-being from health, welfare and education to income, employment and justice; a very high proportion of children educated at private rather than public schools; increasing centralisation of media power. International comparisons of Australia to countries with similar income and political systems show a poor to mediocre performance on many measures of social well-being and equity. Since 1992, Australia has fallen from 7th to

15th on the UN's Human Development Index (which measures income, health and education levels), the third largest relative decline for the top 20 countries); our human rights ranking is 15th in the 20 main OECD countries. On a weighted comparison of international best practice across 29 key indicators of economic, democratic, social and environmental well-being, Australia ranks 15th out of the top 23 (largely OECD, industrial) countries.[2]

At the heart of the ethical issues, citizenship raises the relationship between the moral idea of the citizen and the amoral nature of social exchange in the marketplace (Turner 1993). The citizen, fundamentally, has 'a status independent of economic standing' (Plant 1991). The rapid and mostly unchallenged elevation of economic rationalism as a central principle of public policy (despite its problematic claims even to economic truth), and the growing reliance on the market to solve political and social problems, which has characterised many liberal democracies in the past decades, have become 'a savage attack on the principles of citizenship' (Turner 1993). This is because it attacks not just the visible forms of citizenship (rights, public policies, etc.), but the fundamental ethic on which it depends. 'The promotion of the concept that the untrammelled, self-sufficient competitive individual will maximise human welfare damages deeply the possibility of ever creating a truly cohesive society in which everyone can participate' (Ormerod 1994, 211). Without individuals and organisations prepared to participate and take responsibility, without a concept of the public interest, without the values of tolerance and compassion, and some sense of solidarity and belonging, citizenship would be impossible and democracies become difficult to govern, even unstable (Kymlicka and Norman 1994). In the course of these profound changes in Australian society and public life, it now appears that it is the basic paradigm of government and citizenship, the nature and rationale of their relationship to each other, that is changing.

Where do we go from here? How will we retrieve the situation? How can we make a more coherent and stronger form of political citizenship in Australia? Is the republic and constitution debate salvageable, or will the defeat of the most recent proposal merely confirm people's disillusionment and alienation from the political process and postpone the possibilities of popular interest and pressure for republic citizenship democratic reform for a decade or more? Certainly we need to have *a new debate about citizenship.* At beginning of the 1990s, looking back over the turbulence, change, etc., and forward to a new century, many commentators called for a renewal of Australian citizenship, a new social compact, and many saw the republic and constitution reform as the ideal vehicle to bring about this change, and the new century and millennium as the spur and the incentive, and indeed they were excited about what seemed to be an extraordinary historical opportunity. What is needed is a rekindling of the basic ethic and legitimacy of citizenship with a focus on concrete benchmarks and standards and measuring well-being, incorporating those standards into government and constitutions. New processes are also needed to bring citizenship and democracy to people, including new incentives to elevate and reward citizenship (Saul 1997). Citizenship in local government particularly needs to be strengthened. But the issues are much broader. The underlying issue for a renewal of Australian citizenship is the question of *what kind of society we want Australia to be.*

Australians can reassert the 'the lost legitimacy of citizenship' (Saul 1997), but they will need to focus on the hard content of citizenship in terms of rights, duties, institutions, programs and policies which support a 'truly civil society', and which have been so sweepingly and apparently so effortlessly weakened by the advent of economic rationalism. This will not be easy. Indeed, there is a grave danger that the ideal of active Australian political citizenship will be lost forever. If this is not to happen, then Australians will need to understand their present relative powerlessness as citizens with no access to a process of citizen-initiated constitutional reform, as persons subject to largely undemocratic practices and institutionalisations of government. Today Australian governments acknowledge no basic stewardship. Instead, policy is devised to achieve largely short-term ends. If Australian political citizenship is to become a reality, we will need to change this through specific and institutionally particular reforms, including the use of indices for the achievement or non-achievement of citizenship.[3] In this context, the coming of the republic is not enough. Australians will remain subjects under the control of governments until such time as a much better democratic practice of political citizenship is established at the heart of our national political life.

Notes

1 A good definition of economic rationalism by Michael Pusey can be found in Shafritz (2000). Three useful Australian studies of the impact of economic rationalism on citizenship and public policy are: Rees, Rodley and Stilwell (1993); Stretton and Orchard (1994); Rees and Rodley (1995).
2 Chief sources of Australia national data are found in: Stilwell (1993); Australia, Parliament 1995: 49–52, citing various sources; Hogan and Dempsey (1995); *Sydney Morning Herald* 20 Oct. 1997 (full-time job losses, citing Australian Bureau of Statistics figures); Australian Bureau of Statistics (1997, 1998); Fincher and Nieuwenhuysen (1998); Eckersley (1998, 1999).

International comparative data is from: Humana (1992); UNDP (1990, 1998); Institute of Social Research, Swinburne University of Technology (1999).
3 A 1996 report by the Senate (Legal and Constitutional References Committee) recommended 'as a high priority' for government the establishment of a 'system of national citizenship indicators and benchmarks' to measure and set national standards for legal, economic, social and cultural well-being, and with special reference to social and political participation and human rights (Australia, Parliament, 1996). The Senate committee also commended the work of a national research project (the National Citizenship Project) that has been underway since 1994. This project is a university–community collaborative project (Swinburne University of Technology, Deakin University, University of New South Wales, Victorian Council of Social Service) and is developing a system of citizenship indices similar to that envisaged in the Senate report. The benchmarks and indicators are derived from three principal sources: a review of 'international best practice' (most notably, UN human rights standards and comparable national systems); citizenship theory and applied policy; and a national survey of public attitudes to, and priorities for, national well-being standards (Burke 1997).

Further Reading

Australia, Parliament, Senate Legal and Constitutional References Committee (1995). *Discussion Paper on a System of National Citizenship Indicators*. Canberra: Senate.
Salvaris, M. (1998). 'Citizenship and Progress.' In R. Eckersley (ed.), *Measuring Progress: Is Life Getting Better?* Melbourne: CSIRO Publishing.
Saul, J.R. (1997). *The Unconscious Civilisation*. Ringwood, Vic.: Penguin Books.
Walter, J. (1996). *Tunnel Vision: The Failure of Political Imagination*. St Leonards, NSW: Allen & Unwin.

CHAPTER 9

Indigenous Citizenship

Tim Rowse

On 'Australia Day' (26 January) 1938, Indigenous people staged a 'Day of Mourning' in the midst of the colonists' Sesquicentenary of British invasion. A meeting of one hundred in Sydney resolved their protest against:

> the callous treatment of our people by the whiteman during the past 150 years, and we appeal to the Australian nation of today to make new laws for the education and care of Aborigines, and we ask for a new policy which will raise our people to full citizen status and equality within the community. (quoted in Horner and Langton 1987, 29)

The assertion that Indigenous people are being denied their rights as citizens has been, since the 1930s, one of the potent idioms of Indigenous political mobilisation.

In this essay I want to outline a perspective on Indigenous citizenship that emphasises *citizenship as capacity* rather than *citizenship as right*. As Valverde has recently reminded us, some seminal formulations of liberal notions of governance have insisted that individual liberty is founded on an individual's capacity to govern him or herself. She quotes John Stuart Mill's introduction to *On Liberty*: 'It is, perhaps, hardly necessary to say that this doctrine is meant to apply only to human beings in the maturity of their faculties' (cited in Valverde 1996, 360). The meaning of the phrase 'their faculties' and the criteria of their 'maturity' are both open to conflicting views. Indeed, I suggest that the politics of Indigenous citizenship is a struggle not only over notions of right but also about ways of being present and effective, that is, about capacities for Indigenous participation. I will argue that Indigenous Australians have challenged governments to reinvent their citizenship as a set of communal, not merely individual, capacities and rights.

I am aware of a serious limitation in my perspective: I have not tried to address the transformations in non-Indigenous citizenship that should complement the enhancement of the civic capacities of Indigenous people. My essay is thus marked by the same colonial asymmetry that has always required 'them' to be more like 'us', without ever rendering problematic the constitution of 'us', not only as citizens but as colonists.

Uplift

The phrasing of the 'Day of Mourning' resolution can be read as alluding to the problem of the 'faculties' of Indigenous Australians. That is, the resolution sought 'education and care' and it allowed a reader to imagine what kinds of 'education and care' would 'raise' Aboriginal people 'to full citizen status'. A clue to the ways in which 'education and care' would change Indigenous Australians can be found in the assumption, among some activists, that not all Indigenous people in Australia were ready, in January 1938, to exercise citizenship. One of those present, William Cooper, had written in 1936 that 'the dark man must be taught to be self-reliant and industrious and to win his rights by sheer worthiness' (Markus 1988, 39).

As Heather Goodall has pointed out (Goodall 1993, 1996), some Koori activists of the 1930s judged that it was not necessarily wise to proclaim unqualified pride in their Indigenous heritage. Goodall shows that in the ideologies of Koori and Murri protest at this time the value of heritage came to be qualified by respect for modernity. For example, from 1925, the Australian Aboriginal Progressive Association (AAPA) made claims to land security and to freedom from state (New South Wales) interference with family life. The AAPA's rhetoric included confident assertions of Indigenous heritage and identity. However colonial oppression, taking many forms, persisted, and was intensified as the Depression diminished the demand for Indigenous labour. The search for a language in which to assert Indigenous interests took Indigenous leaders into associations with defenders of the other Australians who suffered in that crisis. Some of the activists who became prominent in the 1930s enjoyed strong support from the trade unions and the Communist Party of Australia. Goodall points out that the radical labour movement criticisms of NSW government practices were grounded in liberal democratic principles of equality of opportunity, appealing to an ideology of modernity. The effects of this political culture on William Ferguson and Cecil Patten can be seen in their pamphlet *Aborigines Claim Citizen Rights!*, in which they assured the public that: 'We have no desire to go back to primitive conditions of the Stone Age. We ask you to teach our people to live in the Modern Age, as modern citizens' (cited in Goodall 1993, 91).

Two points follow from Goodall's historical investigations. First, it is misleading to take any one statement by Indigenous leaders as definitive of their political consciousness. The terms of Indigenous self-representation were (and remain) discursively promiscuous, rather than internally consistent and rigorous. Geoff Stokes may have overstated the contrast between the 'citizenship' rhetoric of the 1930s and the 'identity' rhetoric of the 1970s and 1980s (Stokes 1997; and see McGregor 1993), but his thesis of changing rhetorics is undeniable. Second, *one* of the ways in which Indigenous protest has sought to be persuasive has been to insist that Aboriginal people are capable of acquiring the *capacities* to be politically and legally equal as citizens. On my reading, this theme is stronger in the 1930s. Nowadays it is implicit in the Indigenous enthusiasm for organisational development, albeit in the 'Aboriginal way'.

Partly as a result of the protests between the two world wars, the suggestion that Indigenous Australians could 'improve' and thus qualify for citizenship attracted support among those Australians who wished to reform welfare policies. By contrast, the argument that the Indigenous heritage already qualified them for the rights they asserted – notably their rights to land and to freedom from interference with family life – fared badly in Australian politics from the 1930s to the 1960s, the era of 'assimilation'. The 'assimilation' policy that arose as a selective response to the protests of the 1930s sought to end discrimination against Indigenous Australians but failed to concede an Indigenous right to land. 'Assimilation' also gave new legitimacy to the established practice of removing children from their families in order to 'improve' their prospects.

The most articulate and thoughtful advocate of assimilation in any Australian government, Paul Hasluck (later Sir Paul), Minister for Territories in the Menzies government 1951–63, once argued that Indigenous Australians had never *not* been citizens. Rather, he insisted, they were citizens to whom special laws – some enabling, many restricting – had been applied. It was the duty of governments to review continuously the extent of these laws' application. As Indigenous people acquired the capacities to live in the manner of other Australians, they should be exempted from the special laws. In 1953, 'at the stroke of a pen', Hasluck exempted those known as 'half-castes' from the Northern Territory *Aboriginals Ordinance*. He was responding to a campaign by Northern Territory people of mixed descent who protested at being lumped in with 'full bloods'. By 1965 the Commonwealth government had removed most remaining regulations from those Aboriginal people whom the government had continued (from 1953 to 1964) to class as 'wards'. Other states paralleled this progressive dismantling of the laws restricting Indigenous peoples' movement, their associations, their earning capacity and their consumer choices. By the 1970s, Queensland's remaining restrictive legislation stood out as unconscionable state 'paternalism' (Chesterman and Galligan 1997, ch. 2).

Hasluck did not see these reforms as the granting of 'citizenship' to Aboriginal people. Reformers, he argued, should cease to demand that Indigenous Australians be 'given' citizenship. Rather, his critics should say: 'The Aboriginal has citizenship as a right; remove the State laws which restrict him in the exercise of his rights' (Hasluck 1965, 446). Hasluck's point may seem no more than sophistry to those who chafed under his Administration's (and the states') restrictions on their liberty, but his plea is defensible on two grounds. Legally, Hasluck could have cited the *Nationality and Citizenship Act* of 1948, by which all persons born in Australia were deemed citizens of Australia. Politically, Hasluck's view is embedded within a conception of state responsibility which is familiar and widely accepted in Australia: the state has a duty to regulate the conduct and circumscribe the rights of certain citizens if they lack the capacities essential to conducting themselves as citizens. Hasluck compared some Indigenous Australians to other categories of 'incapacitated' citizen: the mentally afflicted, children and youths under 21. It is an essential feature of Hasluck's liberalism that he did not see Indigenous Australians as disabled by virtue of their race or their genes; rather, their 'incapacities' were cultural and historical and therefore open to correction by education. In his view, some acquired more quickly than others the capacities to conduct their lives without special regulations.

This way of thinking about 'assimilation' and citizenship was enlightened 'common sense' in Australian politics until well into the 1960s. Nonetheless, there were sharp controversies about the implementation of policy – about the pace at which the state could and should lift from the shoulders of Indigenous Australians the yoke of its tutelary controls, about the number of people who should still be covered by such laws, and about how to treat those portions of land known as 'reserves'. My point is that Hasluck could have cited, as an Indigenous mandate for this schema of emancipation, *some* of the language used by Kooris in the 1930s. That is, when health, education and other welfare programs had the effect of enhancing Indigenous peoples' capacity for citizenship, and when that achieved capacity was recognised by the state's amendment of a person's legal status, was not the state obliging the 'Day of Mourning' resolution's call for 'education and care' so as to 'raise our people to full citizen status'?

To give 'assimilation' such a political lineage is to risk scandalising much contemporary opinion. There is now a widespread if contested sense of national disgrace about some of the programs of assimilation, especially the gross interference in Indigenous family life and the attrition of the Indigenous land base in the longer colonised regions of Australia. Indigenous people have much to be angry about: the raising of their children by (often well-intentioned, but often racist) non-Indigenous parents, against the wishes of the child's family of origin; the materially neglectful, but confidently authoritative, regimes of some missions and settlements; the forcible disbanding of 'mission' communities as reserves was revoked; the marginal jobs attracting low wages; the exclusion of Indigenous peoples from the services and amenities of country towns; 'welfare' authorities' control of Indigenous peoples' money and other property; the devaluation of Indigenous traditions other than those which could be sentimentally or aesthetic-ally indulged. Entrenched within state administrations, the white supremacist, authoritarian and neglectful habits of 'welfare' persisted in much of Australia, despite Hasluck's mild and civilised exhortations from Canberra.

However, I suggest that we do not let our contemporary horror at the specific *mechanisms* of tutelage overwhelm our understanding of the historical development of Indigenous citizenship.

'Escaping Notice'

The assimilation era helped to produce a skilful and articulate Indigenous critique of this oppression. Hasluck was ambivalent about the tendency of assimilation policy to bring forth an articulate Indigenous constituency. In 1965 he referred to the necessary capacity of citizens to challenge government actions by legal or political processes. Some Indigenous people lacked 'familiarity with legal processes', he regretted. Nor did they enjoy 'such ready access to the courts as do other citizens'. Accordingly, Indigenous people were simply unable to deal with the powers sometimes exercised arbitrarily by police and employers. Nor were Indigenous people politically effective: 'Their political protest may either not be made because of their ignorance, or fail because it may appear not so much a protest against officialdom as one against their neighbours' (Hasluck 1965, 440). However, if Hasluck wanted Indigenous Australians to be legally and politically effective in their citizenship, he did not want them to be effective as *Indigenous people*. He opposed the idea of a distinct Indigenous citizenship. Hasluck condemned what he saw as the divisive championing of Indigenous Australians' rights. In 1959, he complained of the ostentation of much of the debate about welfare policies: it militated against the gradual elimination of Aboriginality itself. He warned against the kind of concern which has the effect of 'heightening race consciousness on both sides'. Any

> heightening of race consciousness becomes an obstacle to the process of assimilation ... we do not want to become more and more conscious of their differences from us but of their likenesses to us. ... When we see them taking themselves naturally and escaping notice for heaven's sake keep their privacy sacred. (Hasluck 1959)

The political virtue of Indigenous invisibility is also a theme in Hasluck's final effort to justify 'assimilation', his book *Shades of Darkness* (Hasluck 1988).

By then Hasluck had witnessed the realisation of his fears: the Indigenous assertion of an unextinguished identity and the recognition by some governments of distinct Indigenous rights. As a tertiary-qualified central Australian Aboriginal leader once warned a (Liberal) shadow minister for Aboriginal Affairs: 'You know what assimilation produced, don't you? Cunts like me!'

His words were only partly true. The assimilation program gave him the opportunity to leave his family and country and to acquire formal training. However, it was only in the post-assimilation era that he could deploy these individual capacities as the director of a major Indigenous organisation. Such organisations are the product of Indigenous challenge to governments to rethink their approach. In the 1960s, critics began to argue that Hasluck's persistent efforts to govern Aboriginal people as individuals and as discrete households overlooked the *communal* dynamics of Indigenous life. They urged governments to harness, rather than undermine, these communal capacities.

Assimilation policy aspired to enable individuals by destroying the communities in which they were unhelpfully embedded. The closure of reserves and the constitution of the isolated (or integrated) Indigenous household among non-Indigenous households was an assault on Indigenous traditions of communality. In at least one passage of Koori remembrance, this was the assault of 'citizenship' itself. For Bill Lovelock, the reserves had been Indigenous property since the reign of Victoria:

> you know, granted, gazetted and all this kind of thing and this is why the reserves were just reserves. You could go there and they could camp, they could build a humpy, they could knock it down, and let the next bloke build another one if he wanted. They could shift to another one, see, and this is what upset them when the '67 referendum come in and all this passed by because of the uranium and all that up in – Comalco up there in the north

and all these rich deposits on these Aboriginal reserves were taken away, the power away. Like the constitution was altered through the referendum, the 1967 one. Any how, since then the Aboriginals sort of split up – our relations, there was no more mixing and stay for a couple of months, six months – they can't do that. (quoted in Cohen and Somerville 1990, 76)

The alteration of the Constitution in the 1967 referendum is often recalled by Kooris younger than Lovelock as the event by which Indigenous people 'got citizenship'. Lovelock's memories draw on a different oral tradition. His version of that change is a tale of decline: the moment of 'citizenship' is when reserves were closed and Indigenous community, persistent throughout the 'welfare' days, was eclipsed. A lot could be lost if Indigenous people left (or were pushed out of) their communities and began 'escaping notice'.

Towards Indigenous Collectivism

The possibility that Indigenous peoples' 'emancipation' as individuals could exact such a heavy price was not lost on Charles Rowley, the director of the Social Science Research Council's 1960s research project on the history and current circumstances of Indigenous Australians. Rowley argued that they should be allowed to retain their communal traditions. His argument owed nothing to cultural nostalgia. Rather he was drawing the lessons of the failures of the policy of assimilation:

> The aim of 'assimilation' has been to winkle out the deviant individual from the group, to persuade him to cut the ties which bind him and his family to it, and to set him up as a householder in the street of the country town. But policies which aim to change social habit by educating individuals, while ignoring the social context which has made him what he is, can have only limited success. A program involving social change must deal with the social group. (Rowley 1971, 417)

The form in which the social group would be politically and perhaps economically viable was the company, he suggested.

Rowley's point was taken up by the Council for Aboriginal Affairs and eventually bore fruit as the Fraser government passed the *Aboriginal Councils and Associations Act* in 1976. Governments now deal with an Indigenous constituency consisting mostly of statutorily defined and locally based councils and associations. Incorporation is arguably the most significant act of Indigenous political enfranchisement ever accomplished by Australian governments, because it creates the political technology through which to give practical expression to the idea that Indigenous people have a distinct set of rights – most importantly, rights to land and to self-government. The emergence of these Indigenous capacities for collective political action is therefore a central topic in any consideration of the contemporary conditions of Indigenous citizenship.

Native Title and Indigenous Citizenship

Since the early 1970s, Australian governments have made an effort to define nationhood in 'multicultural' terms. 'Aboriginality' has been selectively 'solicited', rather than extinguished. Consummating this challenge to mono-culturalism, the High Court's judgments in 1992 ('Mabo') and 1996 ('Wik') have gone far beyond any official exhortations of multicultural tolerance by declaring that in Australian common law the Indigenous customary law remains a potent, living legal tradition. Over a very large proportion of the Australian land mass, 'native title' may provably remain to some degree.

One apparent casualty of these decisions has been an Indigenous view that emerged in the late 1970s and gained many adherents in the 1980s that Indigenous Australians should not see themselves as citizens of Australia. To be a citizen of Australia, it was argued, conceded British sovereignty and so betrayed the principle of unextinguished Indigenous sovereignty. Critics lamented that this principle was politically unproductive (Reynolds 1987, 175–8). Their alternative strategy – to frame Aboriginal land claims within the traditions of the colonists' law – has borne fruit in the High Court. Indigenous lawyer Noel Pearson has argued that the High Court's decision vindicated the strategy of working within the evolving legal apparatus of the colonial state (Pearson, N. 1993). By postulating 'native title' (even while conceding that it is easily extinguished by the Crown) the High Court accommodated what was crucially different about Indigenous Australians – their status as original owners of the continent – while reasserting that Indigenous and non-Indigenous Australians are commonly citizens.

The various 'land rights' laws (Northern Territory 1977, South Australia 1966, 1981, 1984, New South Wales 1983, Victoria 1984, Queensland 1990) *created* a communal property right by legislation. The 'Mabo' decision *recognised* an Indigenous tradition of law, and ruled that Australia's common law must respect that tradition. At a time when the push for 'land rights' appeared to have stalled politically, the High Court's decision challenged Australians to give effect to Indigenous law in new policies, laws and institutions.

This brings us back to our focus on the need to produce *capacities* for effective citizenship. So far I have argued that Australian governments have responded with two contrasting policy emphases to the Indigenous demand that they be accorded citizenship. The first policy emphasis –

assimilation – placed a high value on the individual and discouraged his/her attachment to the lands and the families on which persistent Indigenous identities were based. The second policy emphasis – land rights with self-determination – recognises continuing communal attachment to land, the value of Aboriginal family life and the necessity for incorporated forms of Indigenous communality. Although it is common to think of 'self-determination' policy as succeeding and replacing 'assimilation', I suggest that in the 1990s government practices towards Indigenous Australians and Indigenous actions towards government have included both individual-oriented and communally oriented programs and laws. The politics of Indigenous citizenship is a persisting interplay and, at times, contest between these two modalities of government and law.

This can be demonstrated by the dilemmas which 'Mabo' – the litigation and its political sequels – raised for both governments and Indigenous people. Nonie Sharp (Sharp 1996) has drawn attention to the difficulties which the Murray Island plaintiffs encountered in explaining Meriam customary law to the Supreme Court of Queensland and then to the High Court of Australia. She argues that the courts found it difficult to grasp the ways that land belonged to 'families' or lineages. The 'lineage or family group' could be presented in such a way as to emphasise either communality or individuality – the key individual being the recognised head of the family. The Mabo case was referred by the High Court to the Queensland Supreme Court so that certain matters of fact, including the facts of Meriam tradition, could be authoritatively determined. Arguing before Justice Moynihan in the Queensland Supreme Court, Ron Castan QC put forward:

> claims to specified allotments of land, not to a system of clan or collective ownership as argued in some African cases, or in the Yolngu case heard by Justice Blackburn. They were classified in Australian law as individual or private rights. (Sharp 1996, 108)

However, these individual rights were presented by Castan as being embedded in a 'collective overall context'. Sharp comments that: 'As it transpired, the selection of the court category of "individual" rather than "communal" rights to land may have helped Justice Moynihan to find ownership rights among the Meriam' (Sharp 1996, 109). Sharp says that although Meriam title is neither communal nor individual but familial, entitlement may be colloquially stated in an idiom of individual rights. Such colloquial accounts, she says, always entail the responsibilities of a crucial 'nameholder' to his/her kin. The introduction of laws of property inheritance seems to have provided further opportunity for ownership to be stated by contemporary Meriam in individual terms.

After Moynihan's determination of the 'facts' of Meriam custom, the Mabo case resumed in the High Court. But the 'individual/communal' issue was not yet resolved. The High Court became perplexed by the evidence that was being presented for David Passi's and James Rice's ownership of land portions on Murray Island. Had Justice Moynihan found individual rights or some kind of 'group holding arrangement'? the High Court asked. Eddie Mabo's claims having been exposed as too weak, counsel for the plaintiffs regarded the individual rights of Passi and Rice to be their strongest case for establishing that the Crown's ownership of Australia was burdened by Indigenous customary law. But the High Court judges saw little evidence of a proprietorial link between any one individual and any one Murray Island plot. Accordingly, on the last day of the High Court's hearing, counsel for the plaintiffs amended their claim, radically but effectively, to one of group ownership (F. Brennan 1994, 34–6).

The Keating government aspired to legislate in the spirit of the High Court's views on Indigenous rights. As well as passing the *Native Title Act*, they proposed the ATSIC Amendment (Indigenous Land Corporation and Land Fund) Bill to create a fund to buy land for those whose 'native title', in Australian law, has been extinguished forever. In the Senate debate over this Bill, in October/November 1994, the appropriate forms of Indigenous property entitlement were in dispute. The Bill stipulated a specifically 'Indigenous' *communal* form of title. Coalition and Green Senators found this restrictive: beneficiaries of the fund, they said, should be able to choose their forms of land title, including individual ownership. They accused the government of trying to deny land fund beneficiaries the full range of forms of ownership enjoyed by non-Indigenous Australians.

These objections questioned one of the philosophical bases of 'land rights' policies enacted by both Labor and non-Labor governments since the 1960s. Indigenous 'group life' has been affirmed in land rights legislation. Legislated land rights since 1966 (when South Australia led the way with its *Aboriginals Land Trust Act*) have refused to vest title in individual Aboriginal people. Land-owning entities have been created by legislation conferring title which is 'communal' and 'inalienable'. Justice Woodward, recommending the 'lands trust' as title-holding entity for Northern Territory Aboriginal people, said that he believed that it would be 'in harmony with traditional Aboriginal social organization' (Woodward 1974, 13). Twenty years later, leading the government's defence of communal title, Senator Evans summarised three reasons for the act to *prescribe* corporate ownership: it would widen the number of beneficiaries; it would maintain a traditional style of ownership; and it would give a statutory basis for the accountability of beneficiaries. Of the three reasons, it was the second which he chose to emphasise:

> It is, of course, the case that Aboriginal people traditionally invariably held a communal form of title – moreover, an inalienable communal form of title. They are totally familiar with operating on a corporate basis. It is totally consistent with Aboriginal custom and tradition so far as land ownership is concerned. (Senate Hansard 1994, 2492–3)

Senator Kernot concurred: 'The basis of their society is really communal; it is collective and not individual' (Senate Hansard 1994, 2494).

Conclusion

The Indigenous constituency has become governable as an ensemble of corporations, councils, land trusts, 'representative bodies' (in the terminology of the *Native Title Act*), and other associations. Indigenous collectivism, in this sense, has become part of the technology of government and the practical terrain of Indigenous leadership. In health policies, social security policies, in the provision of essential services to remote communities and in the inscription of Indigenous land rights into the Australian system of land tenure, incorporated Indigenous groups play roles which are essential to program design and delivery.

As 'native title' comes to be incorporated into the Australian land tenure system, it is likely that governments, of whatever ideology, will find it practical further to encourage Indigenous capacities for collective action. For example, it is in the Howard government's interests (and in the interests of natural resource companies) that 'native title' claims are orchestrated by representative regional associations, rather than presented as a series of cases or as cases in which there is more than one claimant.[1] Once a land portion is acknowledged to belong to Indigenous people, governments and other interests will find it convenient to discuss development proposals with a single regional body (staffed with appropriate professionals) rather than with a myriad of individuals and families. The administration of Australia's post-'Mabo' system of land tenure will otherwise be chaotic.

My emphasis on the creative role of governmental and legal processes is intended to suggest that governments create the terms in which rights are effected. However confidently Woodward, Evans and Kernot may have aligned the corporate model with 'Aboriginal custom and tradition', contemporary Indigenous organisations have not arisen easily and spontaneously from Indigenous social forms. Some of the capacities for corporate action, such as norms of bureaucratic impersonality and unprecedented procedures of representation and accountability, are patiently being developed by Indigenous people. In this sense, many Indigenous Australians are committed to reinventing their citizenship. And this commitment will lead to further innovations. Recent studies of Indigenous organisations already show the difficulties these organisations have because they are simultaneously accountable to a grassroots constituency and to the governments and corporations with which they transact (Smith 1995; Martin and Finlayson 1996; Sullivan 1996; Fingleton 1996).

Can the same be said of non-Indigenous citizens? Hardly. The onus of 'reinvention' has been placed on the colonised. It could be argued that if the efforts made by Indigenous people are to be rewarded with social justice, there must be parallel reinventions of the ways in which non-Indigenous Australians conceive and enact their citizenship. Yet there is little pressure on the colonists to do so. Rather, reforming policy intellectuals have combined with an emergent Indigenous leadership to constitute a new social policy paradigm: incorporated collectivism or communalism. Starting in the 1960s, the notion of distinct Indigenous rights won powerful advocates within the political elite and secured a position within public opinion (Goot and Rowse 1991). But were those rights to be effected in an individualist or in a communal mode? The terms in which the High Court recognised Meriam title and the subsequent debate over the Indigenous Land Fund Bill demonstrated the strength and persistence of the collectivist or communal model of Indigenous empowerment. The state may solicit individualism in other spheres. For example, the 1989 *ATSIC Act* constituted the Indigenous electorate as an ensemble of individual voters, against advice that organisations and communities should be the electors of regional councillors. In land rights, the courts and the legislature have been resolutely 'communal' in their modes of recognition and empowerment. I do not suggest that there is something wrong with this. That is for Indigenous Australians to debate. My point is simply that it is never enough to speak of Indigenous citizenship 'rights', for such rights are conferred, recognised and exercised as determinate citizenship 'capacities'. And so Indigenous Australians continue to build these capacities – from cultural materials they inherit from their Indigenous culture and from the lessons that they draw from their colonised circumstances.

Notes

1 Part of the Howard government's 'ten point plan' in amending the *Native Title Act* was to facilitate the formation of such local coalitions of interested Indigenous parties. This point owes much to the experience of the Indigenous leaders in cobbling such coalitions together.

Further Reading

Goodall, H. (1996). *Invasion to Embassy: Land in Aboriginal Politics in New South Wales, 1770–1972.* Sydney: Allen & Unwin.

Martin, D.F. and J.D. Finlayson (1996). 'Linking Accountability and Self-Determination in Aboriginal Organisations.' CAEPR Discussion Paper no. 116. Canberra: Australian National University.

Reynolds, H. (1996). *Aboriginal Sovereignty: Three Nations, One Australia?* Sydney: Allen & Unwin.

Smith, D.E. (1995). 'Representative Politics and the New Wave of Native Title Organisations.' In J. Finlayson and D.E. Smith (eds), *Native Title: Emerging Issues for Research, Policy and Practice.* CAEPR Research Monograph no. 10. Canberra: Australian National University, 59–74.

CHAPTER 10

Multicultural Citizenship

Mary Kalantzis

This chapter tackles the question of the relation of the citizen to the state in the Australian context from two perspectives: from a theoretical point of view and from the point of view of Australia's practical experience of managing diversity. My argument is that, at a time when cultural and national differences are increasingly becoming a life and death issue, Australia has been moving towards a new civic pluralism, and has the potential to lead the world with its practical example.

Being on the verge of something however, produces anxiety. The more strongly the possibility of civic pluralism presents itself, the more loudly will its opponents claim – 'diversity and social cohesion don't go together'; 'multiculturalism is divisive'; 'we're giving away too much of our local identity in the rush to globalise'. For a few years now, under a coalition government in reaction mode, we have heard the jarring clatter of cultural confrontations between unions and industry, between monarchists and republicans, between indigenous people and pastoralists, and, most perniciously, between so-called 'special interest groups' and a blatantly manufactured ideal of the 'Australian battler'. The coalition government has dumped multiculturalism and allowed racial divisions to ripen in a country which is, quite clearly, far from feeling 'relaxed and comfortable' about its future.

I could focus on these negative developments here, but I won't. In this chapter I will argue that negotiating diversity is now the only way to produce social cohesion, that pluralistic citizenship is the most effective way of holding things together, and that an outward looking, internationalist approach to the world is the best way to maintain the national interest. To achieve these ends, however, Australian multiculturalism needs to develop into a fuller civic pluralism, one which offers the possibility of a genuinely post-nationalist sense of common purpose. To this end I will be arguing the necessity of a robust politics of culture, a politics that is able to negotiate local and global differences. In this way I am voicing a strategic optimism based on long-term possibility rather than on a sanguine assessment of the current state of the nation. By moving in the direction of civic pluralism, we will be making a new social contract, one which addresses some of the fundamental global issues of our time.

The Global Challenge

Two changes have occurred in the last decade which make diversity a far more critical matter than ever before in world politics. The first is the end of the cold war. A politics of ethnic or indigenous assertion and of lobby groups has taken the space held until recently by socioeconomic class-based arguments about the distribution of resources. Disputes over resources are now phrased in the language of cultural symbolism. Representation of identity and its symbols, cultural differences themselves, are now critical (Kalantzis 1995). The second change is rapid globalisation. The local becomes global as immigration transforms once-homogeneous local communities into global communities. The universal processes of globalisation perform a function opposite to the one anticipated: instead of imposing homogeneity, they accentuate diversity, deploy diversity as a means of product differentiation and use local diversity as the basis for making global connections. No country is immune to the effects of internationally global/mobile capital, markets and trade, communications and labour. In this context, nations all over the world are struggling with identity, national constitutions and social rights, sometimes in hideously painful ways.

Over the past two decades, and connected to these developments, the century-long trend towards an expanding, interventionist, welfare state has been reversed, and the domain of citizenship has diminished. In this context we need a reconstructive alternative. Instead of the old idea of a core culture and national standards, the civic needs to become a space where people have the chance to expand their cultural and linguistic repertoires so that they can access a broader range of cultural and institutional resources.

In order to achieve civic pluralism, states must become strong enough to act as effective arbiters of difference. The state remains a distributive mechanism to ensure equitable access to resources and participation, but now it must also be a broker of symbolic and cultural differences as claims become increasingly expressed through discourses of identity and recognition. Today we live in an environment where subcultural differences of identity and affiliation are becoming more and more significant. Gender, ethnicity, religion, generation and sexual orientation are just a few of the words used to denote these differences. The challenge for a civic pluralism is to make available public space in which different lifeworlds can flourish, to create places where local and specific meanings can be made. The paradox of the increasing divergence of lifeworlds and the growing importance of differences is the blurring of boundaries. The more autonomous lifeworlds become, the more movement may arise: people entering and leaving, whole lifeworlds going through major transitions, more open and productive negotiation of internal differences, freer external linkages and alliances. With lifeworlds becoming more divergent and their boundaries more blurred, the central fact of community life becomes the multiplicity of meanings and their continual intersection. This multiplicity is not itself new, but today it is increasing in intensity, importance and social significance.

Historically, approaches to diversity have varied enormously. Four very different alternatives present themselves as major historical and theoretical options. The first is represented by the relatively open borders of states existing before modern nationalism. The next two variants are both nationalisms, though of different sorts – a nationalism of exclusion (the second variant) and a nationalism of assimilation (the third variant). Both are powerful, yet each is significantly different in its historical practices and theoretical import. I will argue, however, for the global necessity of a fourth, post-nationalist variant that I call civic pluralism. To understand the possibility of this in multicultural Australia, we must first confront and comprehend our history.

A Developing Nationalism

A 'nation' is the organisation of human groups into large culturally homogeneous units whose geographical extent is coterminous with the borders of the state. Nationalism is the ideology of homogeneous kin. Both nations and nationalism are very new inventions. There were no nations and no nationalisms in early modern Europe. There was no nation and no nationalism of any significance in Australia until the end of the nineteenth century, and only a very qualified version of either even then.

With Federation in 1901, Australia came closer to modern nationalism. Protectionist trade policy replaced the free-trade principles of the British Empire, open immigration was replaced by the exclusionary White Australia Policy, and Australia's Indigenous peoples, formerly British citizens, were isolated to reserves under a policy of protection and denied citizenship rights. The new spirit of nationalism was founded on a white, Anglo-colonial sense of kin and community whose boundaries were drawn by the rigorous exclusion of 'others'. This was the basis of the White Australia Policy.

Speaking in defence of the Immigration Restriction Legislation in the Commonwealth Parliament, Australia's first prime minister, Edmund Barton, said:

> The doctrine of the equality of man was never intended to apply to the equality of the Englishman and the Chinaman. There is a deep-set difference, and we see no prospect and no promise of its ever being effaced. Nothing in this world can put these two races upon an equality. Nothing we can do by cultivation, by refinement, or by anything else will make some races equal to others. (Australia, House of Representatives (H of R) 1901, 26 September, 5233)

Juxtaposing allegedly immutable differences, it was argued, would produce only social conflict (Australia, H of R 1901, 7 August, 3503).

The idea of irreconcilable difference and the threat it posed to social order also applied to Australia's Indigenous peoples. Aboriginal people were subjected to a regime of protection, isolated on reserves as a 'dying race', and branded as incapable of joining the modern, 'civilised world'. These same ideas, the basis of some of the ugliest of twentieth-century racisms, produced the nationalism of exclusion.

The nationalism of assimilation, or national unification that replaced exclusionism after World War II, was substantially different. It retained the rhetorical proposition that nations must be homogeneous, but added the premise that 'people who are different can be like us'. Differences become tolerable because cultures can change. Immigrants, indigenous peoples and regional ethnolinguistic minorities are not inherently inferior. They can and should become 'civilised', 'just like us'. Perhaps the most important instrument used in the assimilation process was institutionalised schooling – teaching standardised written forms of vernacular languages; teaching the singular and non-negotiable narrative of national military and economic heroism; singing anthems and saluting flags (Commonwealth Immigration Advisory Council 1949). Social cohesion was premised on actively creating the ideal of cultural homogeneity.

During the postwar decades, the bounds of immigrant assimilability were progressively extended from northern and Eastern Europe, to Southern Europe, to the Middle East and finally to Asia and the rest of the world. More and more people, it seemed, were capable of becoming 'like us' – including Australia's Indigenous peoples. In a landmark speech in 1951, Paul Hasluck told the Australian Parliament that:

the coloured people who live in Australia should not be regarded as a class but as a part of the general community whenever and as soon as their advancement in civilisation permits them to take their place on satisfactory terms as members of that community. (Australia, H of R 1951, 18 October, 874).

This principle of nationalism allowed for open borders – often remarkably open in fact – but on the proviso that cultural homogeneity remain the crucial medium term objective. In the United States in the first half of the twentieth century, the 'melting pot' metaphor was used to describe the anticipated outcome of assimilation (Takaki 1993; Castles, Cope, Kalantzis and Morrissey 1992).

Since 1946–47, when Australia embarked in earnest on a mass immigration program, our society has become a kind of social laboratory, a place in fact where a major experiment has been successfully conducted. The experiment began with the idea of a nationalism of assimilation rather than exclusion, and it aimed at the creation of a new society built against the grain of its pre-1945 history. It would become a society well beyond the imaginations of those who devised assimilation policy in the first place. Despite the assurances of assimilationists, the long-term effect of the policy was to produce a society so diverse that racism and nationalism, unless defused, would come to present a profound danger to the social fabric. The diversity eventually became such that social cohesion could only be created through policies and practices that pointed in the direction of civic pluralism.

Multicultural Citizenship

Although assimilation policy was renamed 'integration' in the 1970s, the long-term goal of cultural homogeneity remained the same. This could only be achieved, however, by means of specialist 'migrant welfare' measures. Al Grassby, minister for Immigration in the Labor government from 1972–74, extended the welfare-reformist vision still further by saying (1973) that:

> It is in the long-term interest of all Australians – and not only the many who suffer in varying degrees from discrimination – that we eradicate those things which divide us as people and strengthen and build upon those things which unite us.

Grassby spoke about 'the family of the nation'. Citizenship was very important to this vision. 'There can be, in future, no first and second-class citizens,' he said. And this is not merely a question of helping them to share what we already have, but of encouraging them to add to it, helping them to enrich our national life and to contribute towards the creation of a new and distinctive Australia. (Grassby 1973)

Grassby's language was not yet that of cultural diversity; he very rarely used the term 'multicultural'. The fundamental welfare orientation of Labor was toward 'disadvantage' and lines of socioeconomic division. Indeed, 'migrants' (a word that would lose favour in the era of multicultural policy) were to be understood as a subset of the general class of the socioeconomically disadvantaged. The problems of migrants were considered, at root, to be general matters of social welfare and social justice. It was left to Liberal Prime Minister Fraser, along with coalition ministers MacKellar and Macphee, to frame the Australian state's relationship to the diversity of its citizenry in quite different terms, when 'multiculturalism' became official policy.

'We cannot', Malcolm Fraser said, 'demand of people that they renounce the heritage they value, and yet expect them to feel welcome as full members of our society' (Fraser 1981). Multiculturalist policy 'sees diversity as a quality to be actively embraced, a source of social wealth and dynamism' (Fraser 1981). The landmark in this process was the Galbally Report of 1978, in which multiculturalism was identified as 'a key concept in formulating government policies', confirming that Australia was 'at a critical stage in the development as a multicultural nation' (Fraser 1981). The report's core idea was 'that migrants have the right to maintain their cultural and racial identity and that it is clearly in the best interests of our nation that they should be encouraged and assisted to do so if they wish' (Galbally 1978, para. 9.6).

Galbally's multiculturalism, in sharp contrast to Grassby's 'family of the nation', was a clear, determined and extremely cost-effective element in the neo-conservative pruning and reconstruction of the welfare state. It involved shifting migrant services from the general area of social welfare to 'ethnic specific' services. This in part involved constructing 'ethnic' communities as self-help welfare agencies, and giving them a bare minimum of financial support. Ethnic groups in the new multiculturalism were implicitly viewed not as class-divided, but as homogeneous. 'Leaders' of ethnic groups could thus be viewed as 'representative', and, at the same time, potentially troublesome pressure groups could be incorporated into the state and given some responsibility for their own 'community's' welfare provision.

There were changes to the *Australian Citizenship Act* as a result of this policy shift. As the Minister for Immigration, Mr Macphee, said, 'the act of becoming a citizen is – symbolically and actually – a process of bringing one's own gift of language, culture and traditions to enrich the already diverse fabric of Australian society' (Macphee 1982). At the same time, significant parallel changes were occurring in Aboriginal policy, encapsulated in the notion of 'self-management' developed during the Fraser years and in the 1967 referendum which established that Aborigines had the right to be counted in the census.

Hawke's Labor government left these Galbally multicultural programs intact for three years, merely adding new reformist programs with traditional Labor underpinnings. The Jupp Report of 1986 (Jupp 1986) represented a rhetorical return to laborism, very much in the spirit of Grassby's welfare reformism. The term 'multiculturalism' was used very infrequently. The report's catch-cry was 'equitable participation', far removed from the Galbally model of cultural variety. 'Mainstreaming' was introduced as a new policy concept, with 'ethnic specific' services cut in the hope that mainstream institutions would assume a multicultural stance. The reactions of ethnic groups, however, forced Labor to modify its position. In Labor's 1989 *National Agenda for a Multicultural Australia*, multiculturalism was viewed both as a social description and also as a prescription in the form of 'a policy for managing the consequences of cultural diversity in the interests of the individual and society as a whole'. The *Agenda* had three dimensions. The first, cultural identity, was a resurrection of the Galbally principles. The second, social justice, was a reformulation of Labor's traditional concern with social equity. The last, economic efficiency, was perhaps the most important, suggesting as it did that multiculturalism made good economic sense (Office of Multicultural Affairs 1989). Specialist bodies were set up to provide specific purpose services in the spirit of Galbally, as well as to influence the provision of mainstream services to genuinely meet the needs of a diverse society – education, health, justice, welfare and so on. Meanwhile, expressing a similar balance of cultural issues, justice issues and issues of socioeconomic rights, Aboriginal policy moved towards 'self-determination'.

In this way a principle of nationhood was progressively developed, moving in the broad direction of civic pluralism. By the mid-1990s, following the High Court's recognition of native title in the 'Mabo' case, Prime Minister Keating was brokering the establishment of a new relationship to Australia's indigenous peoples based on a developing awareness of Aboriginal culture and history. 'The Mabo judgment,' he said, 'constituted recognition of an historic truth .... The cultural shift is occurring' (Keating 1993a). Multiculturalism, with its values of 'tolerance and openness', was an intrinsic part of this vision:

> It ... will guarantee an Australia which is not only culturally rich but socially cohesive and harmonious. Just as importantly, it will mean an Australia which counts among its primary values the capacity to find practical ways to mediate differences – not just ethnic or cultural differences but the differences between men and women, between urban and rural Australians, between Aboriginal and non-Aboriginal Australians. ... The catchword is not uniformity, but difference. It is not conformity, but creativity. It is not exclusive, but inclusive. Not closed to the world, but open to it. (Keating 1994)

The breadth and depth of the issues of political philosophy raised here are as great as those raised by Barton in 1901, but they are based now on an entirely different principle of nationhood and citizenship.

Towards Civic Pluralism

In the last fifty years, the Australian population has grown from 7 to 17 million, and about half of this growth is the result of immigration. Only Israel has had higher levels of immigration over the same period. The issue of managing cultural diversity has now reached a turning point. This should take us in the direction of the new social contract that I have called 'civic pluralism'. We currently find ourselves in the midst of many difficult debates: about dual citizenship; about the republic and constitutional reform; about what it is we will be celebrating with the centenary of Federation in 2001; about APEC and the globalisation of the Australian economy; about productive diversity as policy and practice; and about reconciliation with Indigenous peoples. Other important debates – about local government autonomy; about gender equity in the domestic and public realms; and about ecologically sustainable development, for example – also have to address issues of diversity, immigration and indigenous rights. In the principles of civic pluralism, I argue, lie the best possibility for resolving all these debates.

However, at this crucial point, the forces of reaction are stridently demanding an end to multiculturalism and Indigenous reconciliation, and a return to a mythical past in which the issues of nationality and citizenship appeared quite clear-cut. It is true that even in its most recent and most advanced form, multicultural policy had serious limitations. On the one hand, the Galbally-style focus on ethnic diversity painted groups (including Indigenous ones) into corners which were at once exotic and assumed to be internally homogeneous. On the other hand, access, equity and mainstreaming have meant in practice anything from ignoring the issue of diversity to the old-style assimilationism in a new guise now of access to the rights and resources of the dominant group. In neither case has diversity been a mainstream issue.

With civic pluralism, however, two things happen. First, diversity becomes a genuinely mainstream issue. Second, a new collaborative politics emerges in which managing diversity is a key principle of nationalism that crosses the different realms of indigenous differences, immigrant differences, gender differences, and so on. This is the new politics that should now be developing out of the policies of recent decades. Its outcome could be a new mechanism for the distribution of resources and participation, in other words, a new form of citizenship.

The issue of cultural difference is clearly a mainstream one; it is not about minorities, nor is it a matter of charity. Its significance was captured in the Australian Labor government's notion of 'productive diversity' (Office of Multicultural Affairs 1993; Cope, Kalantzis and Solomon 1994) based on the idea that cultural and linguistic diversity is a productive resource, of immediate value locally and also to Australia's ability to link into global networks. The imperative to deal with diversity arises from social, electoral and economic factors. It is clear that no government can represent the interests of all Australians unless it pays critical attention to issues of diverse lifeworlds. It must devote a part of its energies to imagining ways of ensuring cohesive sociality and the equitable distribution of resources and services in the context of diversity.

Australia's achievement thus far has been the product of a series of historical contingencies. The diversity of Australia's citizenry has given multicultural and indigenous self-determination policies particularly pragmatic bases. And our vulnerability as an export-oriented economy means that Australia has taken a leading role in regional economic integration and the World Trade Organization process to encourage free trade. For these reasons negotiating diversity has to become a foundational principle of economic and public life. Pragmatically, Australia cannot do business efficiently, service the population effectively in areas such as health and the arts, or plan education and training, without addressing diversity. Nor can we operate regionally or globally without addressing diversity or rethinking our form of citizenship.

For the last 50 years, the Australian experience has been a proactive one, anticipating change, responding constructively to change, and leading change. Another shift is now due, and the choices are clear: either to move backwards toward a nostalgic view of history, or to move forward toward the social contract I have called civic pluralism.

This particular challenge is not unique to Australia but, with its weak sense of nationalism and its history of commitment to government policies of cultural and linguistic diversity, Australia has a chance of producing the nation of the future: a nation with a post-nationalist sense of common purpose, a nation without nationalism. Australia is a nation where it is already almost possible to conceptualise the public realm as one that facilitates and negotiates diversity in such a way that groups can self-determine in significant ways at the local and personal level. Of course, we will have to reconceptualise the functions of the state and the relationship of groups and individuals to resources that the state regulates. We will also have to rethink the nature of the national identity that the state promotes through educational institutions, arts policies, media policies and the other critical symbolic interventions. Fundamentally, we have to continue looking forwards, to opt for radicalism not conservatism; and to resist the pressure to move backwards to the perceived yet illusory 'safety' of a semi-mythical past.

Participation to date has been predicated upon a set of cultural characteristics possessed by a group that tends to get tagged by the problematic terms 'Anglo-Australian', 'Anglo-Celtic Australian' or 'mainstream Australian'. Although such naming masks real internal differences, it alludes to certain ways of speaking, thinking, working and being in the world which are explicitly and implicitly valued and rewarded. Those who are, to varying degrees, outside the norm – that is, people marked because they are of Indigenous backgrounds, are non-white, are non-English speaking, or are of agrarian or of non-Christian backgrounds – have been expected to imitate the language, behaviour and ways of being of the dominant group in order to have access to symbolic representation, political participation, work and social services. Certainly this was true under assimilation and integration policies but, to a great extent, under many multicultural policies, particularly those falling under the rubric 'access and equity' which focused on enabling migrants to catch up – hence the translation services, English language teaching, and so on.

The realm of symbolic representation has remained fixed in a mirror-like relationship to the dominant group. Those not born into the dominant group have had to imitate the norms of the dominant group in order to assume the stance of belonging and hence to make an effective claim to a fair distribution of resources. Multiculturalism has meant a progressive and necessary enlargement of the national realm of symbolic representation to encompass the true variety of Australian citizens and to make of their differences a national virtue and national strength. The symbolic realm, however, is the hardest to shift. People tend to recognise that all should have a right to vote, and should have a share of jobs and social services, but there is great anxiety when it seems the Australian identity itself is challenged. Hence the current resurgence of nationalisms of both assimilation and exclusion. Hence the emotional appeal to preserve the 'rights' of an ideologically constructed

'Aussie battler'. Those custodians of the symbolic nationhood – the media, the arts and the education sector, particularly the higher education tertiary sector – have been slowest and most defensive when faced with the need to modify norms, canons or representational imagery. This is now a critical challenge. For too long those interested in change have drawn a dichotomy between the economic/political and the symbolic – it is time to bring them together.

Conclusion

The symbols of belonging, the symbols of nationhood, should represent the significant differences that exist in the body politic. This implies two new forms of relationship – direct access to the realm of nationhood without prejudice to differences; and constant negotiation between groups at a local and community level. Multiculturalism, despite its slow and evolutionary beginnings, has already opened up a much larger discussion and set of aspirations. These have coincided, not accidentally, with the policies of self-determination for Indigenous peoples. Australia's tardiness, as a colonising country, in addressing the social contract with Indigenous people has meant that this discussion has arrived alongside the discourse of democratic pluralism. This is a moment in which more and more groups are demanding the right to self-determine their lifestyles – gay communities, various youth 'scenes', religious communities, and so on. There is a growing trend for groups to want to differentiate themselves, to mark themselves off quite deliberately as different by their language, dress style and behaviour. Increasingly, it becomes the role of the public realm to facilitate these different lifeworlds and to prepare people for the difficult dialogues and the complex negotiations that diversity produces.

This development challenges the state to redistribute its resources in ways that facilitate civic pluralism. It challenges the dominant group to learn the ways of so-called minorities rather than imposing an imperative to be like the dominant group. We all will need to be multilingual and multicultural citizens. The new citizen of this new state will be a person with multiple citizenship and multiple identities. People will require a repertoire of skills to deal with a wider range of expectations and aspirations as part of a new norm. These are the skills of negotiating diversity, locally and globally, where the local is global.

In Australia, this imperative could be aided by the possibilities opened up by the accident of the date 2001. The celebration of the centenary of Federation is one opportunity among many for a new, reflective discourse (Centenary of Federation Committee 1994). In future discussions about the republic, modification of the Constitution itself, in order to represent more closely the nation that Australia has become, should be raised (Kalantzis and Cope 1993). Australia needs to state clearly in its symbols of government and rule of law that it is a nation which does not expect conformity to some dominant group's cultural and linguistic norm.

The state in the future will have a dual task: to develop community while securing diversity, and to create pathways for all while respecting differences. To do this the nation state will have to remake itself. It will have to develop a new 'mainstream' in which diversity is a core feature. To achieve this it will have to strip 'ethnicity' from the public realm, but nurture it and mediate it at the local level.

Only within such a social context will other matters of social reorganisation make sense. People will not give up the symbolic–affective realm for material gains alone. Assimilation policies can no longer be enforced. Nor will the spread of the commodity and western capitalism produce the homogeneity that was once assumed – either positively as development or negatively as imperialism. There is an imperative to produce a vision of the state for our new times. We cannot retreat into group differences and pretend that the so called 'master narrative' is not happening; we cannot look back longingly to an illusory 'golden age'. Our reality is the basis for civic pluralism. It is the beginning of the making of a new social contract. It is the basis for the making of a post-nationalist community with a new sense of citizenship.

Further Reading

Castles, S., B. Cope, M. Kalantzis and M. Morrissey (1992). *Mistaken Identity: Multiculturalism and the Demise of Nationalism in Australia*, 3rd edn. Sydney: Pluto Press.

Cope, B. and M. Kalantzis (1995). 'Making Diversity Work: The Changing Cultures of Australian Workplaces.' In D. Headon, J. Hooton and D. Horne (eds), *The Abundant Culture*. Sydney: Allen & Unwin, 163–83.

Cope, B. and M. Kalantzis (1996). *Productive Diversity: A New, Australian Approach to Work and Management*. Sydney: Pluto Press.

Kalantzis, M. (1995). 'Centres and Peripheries.' *RePublica*, Issue 3. Sydney: Harper Collins, 205–19.

CHAPTER 11

Legal Citizenship

Margaret Thornton

Interrogating Citizenship

By and large, western law has had remarkably little to say about citizenship, other than in regard to whether an individual is 'in' or 'not in' a particular national political community. The primary role of law has been to police the metaphysical boundaries in order to maintain the exclusivity of in-groups within the international community. Hence, it has been deemed more important to regulate immigration, visas and passports than the relationship between citizen and state. A superficial reading of key Australian legal texts could induce one to believe that the substantive meaning of citizenship was of little consequence. However, this appearance is deceptive, and I suggest that law is intimately engaged in a subtle constitution and reconstitution of the substance of citizenship *within* the state.

Citizenship lacks a clear legal denotation and, like many terms favoured by legal discourse, it poses as a universal of the kind that is familiar within the public realm, the realm of generality. An examination of legal texts suggests that the universality and ostensible neutrality of citizenship have served a significant ideological purpose in cloaking the play of partiality and power beneath the surface. Nevertheless, while the judicial interpretation of constitutional and legislative texts can reaffirm the power of 'benchmark men', that is, those who are Anglo-Australian, heterosexual, able-bodied and middle class, it can also provide scope for reinvention in a changed political climate.

This chapter shows how the legal meaning of citizenship is constituted and how it is always open to contest. The formalistic approach to citizenship, as contained in the Constitution and legislation, is first outlined in its historical context. Second, a High Court case is considered in order to illustrate how variable meanings can emanate from judicial interpretation. Third, it is argued that it is necessary to go behind legal texts, to consider practices such as the initiation of civil litigation, in order to comprehend the meaning of active citizenship.

Texts

The Constitution

The Australian Constitution alludes to 'citizens' only incidentally, although there are scattered references to 'subjects', 'residents', 'people' and 'persons'. The framers of the Constitution rejected a focus on citizenship because of what were perceived to be its unsettling republican origins; subjecthood was deemed more appropriate within a monarchy (Quick and Garran 1976, 957; Wishart 1986). In any case, people are important in the Constitution only in so far as they make up states, for the Constitution is primarily concerned with the allocation of powers between the Commonwealth and the states, the mode of governance of the Commonwealth, and the separation of legislative, executive and judicial powers. Although strongly influenced by the American Constitution, the Australian Constitution contains no express advertence to individual rights, such as freedom of speech or equality before the law.[1] In this respect, the Constitution was influenced by the absence of a written constitution in Britain. Westminster governance, British subjecthood and the rule of law were considered adequate protection by the benchmark men of Federation, who may well have had an interest in retaining discriminatory legislation. After all, neither women nor Aboriginal persons possessed the status of full legal persons at the time of the Constitutional Conventions, even if enfranchised, and discriminatory legislation involving 'aliens', such as the Chinese, was a feature of the times, and was to crystallise in the infamous White Australia Policy.[2]

The single reference to citizenship in the Constitution is that contained in s. 44(i), which refers to 'a citizen of a foreign power', the suggestion being that only nations other than Australia have citizens. In one sense, the allusion is unsurprising, since the creation of the Australian nation did not formally confer Australian citizenship on eligible Australians, who retained the status of British subjects until the end of the Second World War. The Australian Constitution itself, after all, is an Act of the British Parliament.[3] Section 44(i) has received remarkably little judicial scrutiny.

The High Court is empowered by Chapter III of the Constitution to adjudicate in all disputes having constitutional significance. As judges must interpret the words of legal texts, the High Court is thereby able to invest the Constitution with meaning. A formalistic approach to constitutional interpretation was long sustained by virtue of the High Court's favoured adjudicative mode of 'strict legalism', most notably associated with former Chief Justice, Sir Owen Dixon (Dixon 1965, 158). This meant that the interpretive focus was confined to the express words of the Constitution itself and to previous judicial decisions; political, social and historical matters were deemed irrelevant. The self-referential methods of legal positivism were thought to be conducive to neutral adjudication. The effect, if not the intent, has been to privilege benchmark men and the status quo. Despite the striking shifts in constitutional adjudication that have occurred since the 1980s, a deference to form has by no means been jettisoned, a proposition I shall illustrate by reference to the 1992 case of *Sykes v Cleary*.[4] This decision constrains the substantive meaning of citizenship and legitimates the residual Anglocentricity of the Australian Constitution.

The citizenship issue in *Sykes* was whether two of the candidates in a House of Representatives by-election should have been disqualified by virtue of Constitution s. 44(i) if either was a person who: 'Is under any acknowledgement of allegiance, obedience, or adherence to a foreign power, or is a subject or a citizen or entitled to the rights or privileges of a subject or a citizen of a foreign power.' Both Mr Delacretaz and Mr Kardamitsis were naturalised Australian citizens who were found not to have taken 'reasonable steps' to have divested themselves of their Swiss and Greek citizenship respectively, despite long periods of residence in Australia (per Mason CJ, Brennan, Dawson, Toohey and McHugh JJ; Deane and Gaudron JJ dissenting). Mr Delacretaz had lived in Australia for 40 years and had been naturalised for 30. At the time, he had renounced all allegiance to any sovereign state and sworn an oath of allegiance to the Queen. He had also sworn to 'observe the laws of Australia and fulfil [his] duties as an Australian Citizen' (588). However, he had not applied to the Swiss government to terminate his Swiss citizenship. Mr Kardamitsis had lived in Australia for more than 20 years and had been naturalised for 17. He was married to a naturalised Australian citizen and had three children who were Australian citizens. Mr Kardamitsis had sworn a similar oath of allegiance to that of Mr Delacretaz and had surrendered his Greek passport. Mr Kardamitsis had also taken oaths of allegiance as a requirement for serving on his local council and becoming a justice of the peace. He was unaware that there was a procedure by which he could have his nationality discharged by applying to the appropriate Greek minister. Both men held an Australian passport, the familiar indicium of Australian citizenship within the international community.

Constitution s. 44(i) was ostensibly designed to circumvent treasonable behaviour on the part of members of the Australian Parliament (Irving 1993 9), but no such evidence was adduced in regard to either Mr Kardamitsis or Mr Delacretaz. *Sykes v Cleary* highlights the distorting effect of focusing on legal form with scant regard for substance. The majority in *Sykes* held that the wording of Constitution s. 44(i) ('... citizen of a foreign power') precluded them from adopting the substantive test, the relevant test at international law.[5] Greater weight was accorded the formal words of the Constitution than the actual situation of the two men. The evidence before the court suggested that both men had done all that could *reasonably* have been expected to extinguish their original citizenship, which included a formal renunciation of prior allegiances and a long period of residence in Australia. The majority found that this was not enough. As Gaudron J (dissenting) pointed out, Parliament could not have intended that the oath and affirmation involving the formal renunciation, should be 'entirely devoid of legal effect' (614). Turning the test around, she suggested that it did not seem reasonable to expect Mr Delacretaz 'to seek release when it necessarily involved acknowledgement of citizenship that has already been formally renounced' (617). Why was it not possible for a person to be a Swiss or Greek citizen by birth and an Australian citizen by naturalisation?

While the *Australian Citizenship Act* suggests that a grant of citizenship places a person in the same position as one who was born in Australia, a majority of the High Court did not agree. In *Sykes v Cleary*, the majority judges did no more than cursorily advert to the respondents' naturalisation under the *Citizenship Act*. There was no consideration of the *character* of Australian citizenship and no acknowledgement by the court that it was creating both a bifurcation and a hierarchisation of the concept.

According to Aristotle (Warrington 1959, 1275a) and subsequent political theorists (Arendt 1958; Zwiebach 1975; Heater 1990, 201), the 'good citizen' is one who serves [his] community by actively participating in the life of the polis, that is, by holding office; a mere passive belonging does not suffice. Despite having gone through a ceremony of conferral of citizenship and receipt of a certificate attesting to the grant, Messrs Delacretaz and Kardamitsis were adjudged not fit to hold office and represent their fellow citizens in federal Parliament. Their ineligibility to stand for Parliament denied them the full capacity to be good citizens. Despite Australia's official commitment to multiculturalism, dual citizenship had the effect of downgrading them from citizens to denizens. *Sykes v Cleary* suggests that there is a residual resistance to diversity in the construction of Australian citizenship.

As Australia has at least three million dual citizens (Joint Standing Committee 1994, 177), the issue is an important one; it means that naturalisation alone is insufficient to allow one to be a 'good citizen' by standing for election to Parliament. The concept of dual citizenship is now recognised at international law. Furthermore, the events of the twentieth century have led to an increasing liberalisation within the citizenship laws of other immigrant societies, such as Canada and the United States, as well as the United Kingdom (Joint Standing Committee 1994, 182–7). The anachronistic and discriminatory character of single citizenship in Australian law is underscored by the fact that the domestic laws of some countries (such as the former Soviet Union) do not permit nationals to relinquish their citizenship.

Although the text of the Constitution has little to say about citizenship, it can be seen that judicial interpretation plays a vital role in giving meaning to the sparse words of s. 44(i). While *Sykes v Cleary* would appear to be anachronistic in multicultural Australia, the decision does not preclude the issue being revisited by the High Court.[6] Through the dynamism of judicial interpretation, a century-old constitution is capable of shaping contemporary notions of citizenship and accommodating new ways of thinking, a process that may be less fraught than altering the Constitution itself. Nevertheless, while the universal language of the Constitution provides scope for the invention of new meanings for citizenship by creative judges, *Sykes v Cleary* reveals that the outcomes will not necessarily be progressive.

The Citizenship Act

The Commonwealth is empowered to enact specific legislation regulating citizenship by virtue of several sections of the Constitution, namely, s. 51(xix): 'Naturalization and Aliens'; s. 51(xxvii): 'Immigration and Emigration', on which the *Migration Act 1958* (Commonwealth) is based, and s. 51(xxix): 'External Affairs'. A number of pieces of Commonwealth legislation, such as the *Commonwealth Electoral Act 1918*, distinguish between citizens and non-citizens in the apportionment of rights and duties pertaining to voting, jury service, and permanent employment in the Commonwealth Public Service. Hence, the meaning of citizenship contained in legal texts is amorphous, with allusions scattered over various constitutional heads of power and legislative enactments (compare Rubenstein 1995). As with the Constitution, these acts are also subject to judicial interpretation. The preponderance of citizenship cases deal with disputes relating to entry permits and deportations. The plethora of such cases explains why the author of a book on Australian citizenship law has observed that the chief significance of Australian citizenship lies in the field of immigration (Pryles 1981, 41).

The hesitancy in acknowledging Australian citizenship is underscored by the fact that almost half a century elapsed after Federation before express legislation regulating citizenship was enacted. White Australians, whether born in Australia or naturalised, were not formally deemed to be citizens until 1948 when the *Nationality and Citizenship Act* was enacted. (The formal citizenship status of Aboriginal people remained ambiguous until 1962 when the vote was extended to all Aboriginal Australians.[7]) As with citizenship, no separate Australian nationality was recognised, as the High Court categorically asserted in the early years of Federation: 'We are not disposed to give any countenance to the novel doctrine that there is an Australian nationality as distinguished from a British nationality...'[8] The last vestiges of British subjecthood did not disappear until 1986.

Like the Constitution, and despite its title, the *Australian Citizenship Act* (which replaced the *Nationality and Citizenship Act* in 1973) does not attempt to define 'citizen', although 'Australia', 'child' and even 'responsible parent' are defined in the interpretation clause (s. 5). The act nevertheless proceeds to regulate citizenship by birth, adoption and descent. It also authorises citizenship to be granted to a person who is able to satisfy the minister regarding certain specified criteria, including whether he or she has been a permanent resident for two years, is over 18 years, is of good character, possesses a basic knowledge of English, and has an adequate knowledge of the responsibilities and privileges of Australian citizenship (s. 13(1)).

Until recently, the *Citizenship Act* was a paradigmatic illustration of the formalistic approach to citizenship, with no reference whatsoever to obligations, such as voting, serving on juries or defending the country against invasion. As a result of criticism that the act contained 'no comprehensive statement of who are citizens, nor of their rights and obligations, and because of the obscure drafting of the Act'(Australia, Parliament 1993, 5), amendments were effected in 1993 to acknowledge some of the ideals of citizenship. A preamble was added to the act, which referred to citizenship as a 'common bond, involving reciprocal rights and obligations, uniting all Australians, while respecting their diversity'. In addition, a pledge of commitment, based on a poem by Les Murray, was added:

> From this time forward [under God],
> I pledge my loyalty to Australia and its people,
> whose democratic beliefs I share,
> whose rights and liberties I respect, and
> whose laws I will uphold and obey.

Despite the inclusion of these more stirring and inspirational sentiments, the *Citizenship Act* falls far short of a code of the rights and responsibilities of citizenship. As the amendments referred to are not found in the body of the text, their significance is limited within the canons of judicial interpretation. Australian citizenship is therefore still perceived as somewhat narrow. It would seem that the shadow of subjecthood has not completely receded.

Active Citizenship and Legality

Even though a detailed citizenship code could be devised that enumerated the responsibilities of citizenship, the limits of the law have to be acknowledged. A legalistic approach to citizenship can identify only its passive or descriptive elements, it cannot capture the active elements, including the discrepancies in power between citizens that shape their ability to be good citizens (Thornton 1995, 1996, 1997). Power is invisible to the juridical gaze. Indeed, the universalism of citizenship, underpinned by the liberal myth that the citizenry constitutes a community of equals, masks differences between people. Those who do not fall into the category of benchmark men, that is, women, Aboriginal people, NESB people, religious and ethnic minorities, gays and lesbians, and poor people, have also been located within a 'marginal matrix of citizenship' (Evans 1993, 6).

Jocelyn Pixley argues compellingly that the opportunity to engage in employment is a basic condition of being a citizen (Pixley 1993). Indeed, it is apparent that economic worth and property enhance opportunities for producing active or 'good' citizenship. Unemployment and dependency may be devastating for those on welfare, particularly for many women, Aboriginal people, and people from non-English speaking backgrounds. A lack of social power may deny those without property a speaking voice. Legal formalism provides a convenient cloak of universalism so that crucial differences arising from property and power are rendered invisible. An appearance of equality for all is thereby maintained, while simultaneously privileging vested interests.

The facilitation of 'good' citizenship for benchmark men has enabled them to be seen as the indigenous inhabitants of the polity, whereas women have not properly been accepted as citizens, despite the significant gains of second wave feminism (e.g. Pateman 1988; Jones 1990; Gatens 1991; Lake 1994). Like Messrs Delacretaz and Kardamitsis, they have not been permitted to be 'good'citizens through participation in public affairs, other than at the local level (Phillips 1991, 60–1). Formal admission to the polity through enfranchisement has not guaranteed a corresponding right of representation. Indeed, it was deemed necessary for most Australian States to enact special legislation to permit women to be political representatives.[9] As recently as 1959, there was a formal (albeit unsuccessful) challenge to the nomination of two women to stand for the South Australian Legislative Council 65 years after the passage of legislation enfranchising South Australian women and conferring on them the right to be elected to Parliament.[10] Resistance to the idea of women as representatives of benchmark men continues, compounded by a history of masculinist authority in the public sphere (Phillips 1991; Jones 1993; Sawer and Simms 1993; Cass and Rubenstein 1995). The complementarity thesis, which avers that women can realise their good citizen potential by being good mothers in the private sphere has not disappeared, despite formal acceptance of the non-discrimination principle. Vestiges of the juridically unequal treatment of married women, rendering them less than legal persons in their own right, are still to be found in the toleration of domestic violence,[11] as well as in affirmations of indivisibility in financial and property transactions.

Aboriginal people have been constructed as subordinate by two centuries of violent practices, exclusion and paternalism, facilitated and legitimised by law. Enfranchisement certainly did not guarantee instantaneous admission to the community of equals. Aboriginal women may have been formally, albeit inadvertently, enfranchised along with white women in South Australia in 1894, but enfranchisement has not guaranteed social acceptance or an end to racism (e.g. McGrath 1993; Sykes 1997). Aboriginal people have been confined to a citizenship shadow land. However, positive initiatives, such as the *Racial Discrimination Act 1975* (Commonwealth), and the Mabo and Wik cases,[12] prefigure a more active conceptualisation of citizenship. Such initiatives are concerned with access to education and employment, and rights to land, which are key dimensions of civil society. These changing images contrast with the criminalised model of Aboriginality that typically prevailed within Anglo-Australian law for almost two centuries. While significant High Court cases, such as the Stolen Children[13] and Hindmarsh Island[14] did not succeed on the merits, their initiation by Aboriginal plaintiffs dramatically attests to the changing role of Aboriginal people in the assertion of legal rights. The acceptance by courts that such claims are justiciable corrodes the idea that civil courts are the preserve of benchmark men. This activity also supports the view that the status of the citizen is not fixed, and that reinvention is possible.

Conclusion

Deconstructing the legalised citizen exposes a number of characteristics not otherwise discernible. When we take a step backwards from the citizen and examine his or her averredly common national identity, we find a plethora of differences emanating from race, class, sex, sexuality, and so on, which affect his or her ability to participate in the community and be a good citizen. Historically, the opacity of citizenship within legal texts has permitted the polis to authorise benchmark men to invest it with a substance that has operated to their advantage. More recently, the concept has begun to acquire colour and shape, as Australia has gradually acquired more confidence in the wake of postcolonial subjecthood.

While citizenship invariably appears as an empty abstraction within legal texts because of the international law orientation, it is apparent that the currency of the concept within popular discourse is exerting an impact, and a shift is occurring away from the idea of an unproblematic universal. As substantive ideas of citizenship crystallise within popular discourse, a hazy reflection of this revisioning has begun to form within the legislative and juridical imagination. Although the elusiveness of the legal meaning of citizenship within liberalism has privileged benchmark men in the past, the indeterminacy also provides scope to facilitate reinvention in the future.

Notes

1 Only in the 1990s did the Australian High Court begin to 'discover' such rights within the Constitution, highlighting the importance of judicial interpretation. See, for example, *Nationwide News Pty Ltd v Wills* (1992) ALJR 658; *Australian Capital Television Pty Ltd v The Commonwealth* (1992) 66 ALJR 214; *Theophanous v Herald & Weekly Times Ltd* (1994) 182 CLR 104. In *Leeth v Commonwealth* (1992) 107 ALR 672, Deane, Toohey & Gaudron JJ (dissenting) were prepared to find a doctrine of legal equality underpinning the Constitution, a notion unknown at common law. For recognition of the interests of citizen children, see *Minister of State for Immigration and Ethnic Affairs v Ah Hin Teoh* (1995) 128 ALR 353. For commentary on constitutional developments, see Doyle 1993; Detmold 1994; Kennett 1994; Blackshield and Williams 1996.
2 *Immigration Restriction Act 1901* (Cwlth).
3 63 and 64 Victoria, ch. 12.
4 (1992) 109 ALR 577. The primary question was whether the first respondent, who was on leave from the Victorian Education Department, held an 'office of profit under the Crown' contrary to s. 44(iv) of the Constitution. This question was answered in the affirmative (per Mason CJ, Brennan, Dawson, Toohey, Gaudron and McHugh JJ; Deane J dissenting).
5 *Nottebohm Case (Liechtenstein v Guatemala)* ICJ Reports 1955.
6 In 1996, the validity of a House of Representatives election was challenged on the ground that (inter alia) the successful candidate held dual Australian and New Zealand citizenship contrary to Constitution s. 44(i). However, the focus of challenge was confined to the candidate's service as an RAAF officer at the time of nomination under Constitution s. 44(iv). It therefore cannot

be inferred that the citizenship issue was not pursued because the candidate was from New Zealand rather than from a non-English speaking background. See *Free v Kelly*, HCA sitting as Court of Disputed Returns, 11 September 1996 (unreported). In an earlier case, the petitioner challenged the election of the respondent on the ground that he was a professed member of the Roman Catholic Church and therefore under '"acknowledgement of Adherence, Obedience or Allegiance to a Foreign Power" – the Papal State' (Unpublished Judgment 1977, 171). The petitioner's argument was rejected as untenable. See *Crittenden v Anderson* (HCA 1950, unreported; Unpublished Judgment 1977, 171).
7 *Commonwealth Electoral Act 1962* (Cwth); Select Committee 1961.
8 *Attorney-General for Cth v Ah Sheung* (1906) 4 CLR 949, 951.
9 *Women's Legal Status Act 1918* (NSW); *Parliamentary Elections (Women Candidates) Act 1923* (Vic.); *Elections Act 1915* (Qld); *Parliament (Qualifications of Women) Act 1920* (WA); *Constitution Act 1921* (Tas.).
10 *The Queen v Hutchins; ex parte Chapman and Cockington* [1959] SASR 189.
11 As recently, as 1988, an Australia-wide survey revealed that 19 per cent of the population (17 per cent of women and 22 per cent of men) considered that the use of physical force by a man against his wife was acceptable (Office of Status of Women 1988, 2; Graycar 1996; Astor 1995; Thornton 1991).
12 *Mabo v The State of Queensland (No 2)* (1992) 66 ALJR 408; Bartlett 1993; *Wik Peoples v State of Queensland* 134 ALR 637.
13 *Kruger v The Commonwealth*, Matter No. M21 of 1995 (HCA).
14 *Kartinyeri v The Commonwealth* [1998] HCA 22 (1 April 1998).

Further Reading

Davidson, A. (1997). *From Subject to Citizen: Australian Citizenship in the Twentieth Century*. Cambridge: Cambridge University Press.
Lister, R. (1997). *Citizenship: Feminist Perspectives*. London: Macmillan Press.
Kymlicka, W. (1995). *Multicultural Citizenship: A Liberal Theory of Minority Rights*. Oxford: Clarendon Press.
Peterson, N. and W. Sanders (eds) (1998). *Citizenship and Indigenous Australians: Changing Conceptions and Possibilities*. New York: Cambridge University Press.

CHAPTER 12

Economic Citizenship

Jocelyn Pixley

Ours is a time of worldwide economic insecurity. Since economic life is one of those facets of existence over which most of us have little to no individual control, many people see only two economic options: more market liberalism or economic nationalism.[1] Australia's chronic unemployment has tainted the political landscape for a quarter of a century. Economic nationalism claims to recognise Australians' fears about global markets and, at its extreme, wants the state to rebuild tariff walls, stop immigration and reinvent the male breadwinner. But economic nationalism is inconsistent and opportunistic, an exclusionary strategy no more interested in defending losers from winners than is market liberalism's promotion of global competition, low wages and generalised austerity. Both approaches subscribe to the dominance of economics of one form or another over all other facets of life.

This chapter will argue for a different approach. It will offer economic citizenship as one concept among others that can orient a rethinking of the legacies of citizenship. The traditional left and feminism have long argued that the public and political values of citizenship were marred by a lofty neglect of economic exploitation, private ownership and the inequalities of family life in the private sphere (Plant 1988, 1992). Economic citizenship offers a corrective in the form of criteria to inform public debate and to foster democratic control from below over the 'whole economy'. It emphasises the connections between household and market production, and non-market work is not banished from public debate. Moreover, the exercise of consumer rights, on the one hand, and industrial rights, on the other, is defended as different, distinct citizen practices. Indeed tensions between consumer and industrial rights often arise through lack of public, mediating institutions that are a step removed from these practices. Such institutions could allow citizens to make democratic decisions about economic life.

For some, the general concept of citizenship has become a 'talisman', carrying a 'heavy load of expectation and promise' in its 'war' with the market (Norman 1992, 35; Barbalet 1996, 70). However, criticisms of a linear 'progress' to modern citizenship as depicted by T.H. Marshall are well rehearsed. It only occurred thus for white males, strikingly so in Australia where the term 'citizen' was less used than 'worker'. Postcolonial countries established citizen principles quite differently, and the modernist citizen model was neither accessible to women at all, in the first 'stages', nor proceeded along a set path paved by western men (Walby 1994). It is also fair to object that citizenship is an often contradictory ideal. It implies universality, but its embeddedness in nation-states is about particularity and exclusivity, if not chauvinism and national competitiveness, as liberal and Marxist internationalists have long argued. Certainly the Marshall 'national functionalist' assumptions are no longer adequate. With a continental–regional formation in the European Union, the sociology of citizenship has rapidly moved to 'post-national' formulations of citizenship (Roche 1995, 716). To a lesser extent, the move from the General Agreement on Tariffs and Trade (GATT) to the World Trade Organization and the impact of other public and private global institutions place all nations in increasingly post-national configurations. However, the erosion of nation-state capacities is uneven, and the Australian, Canadian, and New Zealand states are differently constrained even though relatively similar.

Against the background of these changes, there is widespread agreement in the literature on citizenship that the concept needs to be rethought. Norman points out that if citizenship means membership of a secular 'community' with a 'common system of political procedures', then the boundaries of inclusion are quite arbitrary. So when shared economic activities are no longer confined in a national economy by the authority of a nation-state but are influenced by international bodies, economic membership of a broader 'community' is a possibility (Norman 1992, 39). Moreover, the predominant national understanding of citizenship identity was never the only one available. Durkheim among others suggested that 'citizenship might develop as the moral framework of some larger social entities such as humanity itself' (Turner 1993, 4).

Nonetheless, although Marshall's understanding of modern citizenship is less relevant today, his lack of interest in the economic realm remains a legacy in more recent citizenship debates (Turner 1993, 7; Gersuny 1994, 211). Marshall claimed that social citizen rights were 'at war' with the market.[2] This was something of an overstatement, given the *economic* benefits of social infrastructure and regulations to the market (Barbalet 1988, 76–9). His view also neglected the political and moral climate of that time which made the extension of social rights both a political imperative *and* economically viable. Today, neglect of the economic realm in a world of recession-prone economies fosters pessimism.[3] In Australia and elsewhere, 'tax revolts', high unemployment and internationalised corporations able to evade national taxes have eroded the tax base that pays for the social rights of health, education and social security, while the numbers requiring security payments have massively expanded.

Reinventing Australian Economic Citizenship

On economic issues, the old and formerly dominant citizenship discourse has little to offer. One reason lies in a tendency to reduce economic security to social security, conventionally understood as welfare payments based on social rights of citizenship. Each is important, but quite distinct. Another is the suspicion in recent citizenship literature that market liberalism, for all its instrumentalism, is a more viable, 'tolerant' and internationalist alternative than a nationalist revival of repressive monoculturalism. Such criticism of economic nationalism often entails a principled 'realism' about globalism. Yet, the less well-informed global citizenship themes tend to dismiss environmentally sustainable industry policies (for example) – even when *committed* to multiculturalism – as too 'nationalistic'. They also give too much credence to orthodox economics which has failed to find even one viable answer to the world economic crisis of the last 20 years. Economic orthodoxy asserts that any proposals aiming for economic security and greater equality would undermine 'efficiency' and the 'free market'.[4] The opportunity to earn a living thus becomes increasingly tenuous and tension-ridden for many women and men, and more and more distant for young people. Deregulation of the labour market is a further step in internationalising Australia's economy.

As citizenship becomes redefined in a global framework, the citizenship literature has tended to sidestep the intractable problems of unemployment and economic exclusion. It has focused on the *supply-side* – seeking well-meaning 'solutions' to help the unemployed and working poor 'get by' – but has rarely looked at the *demand-side*, namely employers and the market in general. Of course, most writers deplore the impact of unemployment on citizenship, with its effect of further excluding and punishing the economically marginalised. However, to them economic exclusion seems no more resolvable than the vulnerability to international markets that is accepted by governments, legitimated by orthodox economics and dictated by international agencies. An earlier 'postindustrial' optimism for a radical alternative solution to employment – such as 'informal' economic activity, worker co-operatives or communes, buttressed by some nationally guaranteed subsistence income – has faded (Pixley 1993; 1995). While we remain so far from moving 'beyond employment society', such alternatives to the 'cash/work nexus' presently seem neither so radical nor desirable as they once did (Keane and Owens 1986, cf. Pixley 1993). With global movements of low wage labour, those already marginalised from national welfare 'support' must seek whatever insecure job they can get. Working conditions and occupational safety are deteriorating in those service and industrial sectors most open to competition from low wage countries.

Economic Citizenship in a 'Common wealth'

Any effort to reinvent Australian citizenship must acknowledge these worldwide economic developments.[5] As many contributors in this volume affirm, ethical criteria and new practices are needed that move beyond conventional discourses of citizenship. Many principles exist formally in international covenants and treaties. Conservative governments, however, often reject human rights articles or environmental agreements as an impertinence to national sovereignty, while those treaties and credit ratings that reduce national economic sovereignty most detrimentally have been blithely accepted (Alston 1995). The OECD's promotion of the Multilateral Agreement on Investment (MAI) has caused international public alarm only because it represents a blatant attack on democratic sovereignty by multinational corporations in contrast to other subtle, but equally damaging ones.

Economic citizenship in contrast is an ethical ideal promoting substantive and democratic challenges to conventional economic arrangements.

Economic citizenship builds on the ancient Greek meaning of *oikonomia*, 'householding' – that is, long-term management to increase the value for all members of the household over the long run. This concept of householding includes conserving resources for future generations and recognising that economic life – as householding – is as much the activity of the unpaid domestic sphere as it is of the paid workforce. Orthodox economics has little space for economics as householding. It focuses on manipulation of property and wealth to maximise short-term returns to the owner,[6] regardless of the human and ecological consequences. Degrading the environment, leaving young people and the women to sustain the costs of raising the future generation on the margins – such consequences in this view are mere 'externalities'. Economic policies are modelled on the premise of the rationality of short-term maximisation and the conviction that market economies have self-adjusting tendencies. These tendencies are said to be the only means of economic flourishing, and any long-term policy aiming to influence market outcomes is regarded as an 'impediment' to market equilibrium.

Keynes was possibly the most influential economist to argue against the orthodox view that short-term maximisation for the few always turns out for the best for everyone 'in the long run'. However, the demise of international Keynesianism means that there are now few challenges to orthodox economics' claim that there is no alternative to short-term manipulation. It seems we must wait until it is thoroughly discredited by events (Painter 1996, 297).[7]

On the other hand, there is no lack of democratically inspired ideas to inform economic citizenship in Australia coming from feminism and environmentalism, while the labour movement's defence of industrial rights worldwide cannot be underestimated.

Environmentalists and feminist economics have tackled demand-side problems by building or defending mediating institutions of national and international bodies. Likewise, the International Labour Organization has formulated global principles of a 'common standard' for paid employment rather like Australia's original arbitration and minimum wage-fixing institutions. The principles of human and environmental sustainability inspired and debated by these three social movements provide the initial content of economic citizenship, just as public mediating institutions supported by them may represent potential bases and models for formulating democratic procedures for economic citizenship.

Economic, Consumer and Industrial Citizenship

Reinventing economic citizenship entails acknowledging the distinct practices and rights claimed by workers and consumers. Market liberalism has debased many of these practices, on the grounds that they fetter the market. But even if economics needs to be put in its place, and even if social life must not be reduced to economic life (as both market liberalism and Marxism tend to do), any reinvented citizen discourse can hardly leave out the undeniable social fact that economic provision is a main prerequisite of all human societies. Leaving its co-ordination to the market, however, may well mean the loss of all democratic control to the power of global corporations and speculators, bringing more inequities in the division of labour.

Economic citizenship involves a range of democratic procedures and practices to extend the existing protective economic defences of industrial and consumer citizenship. In challenging economic orthodoxy, economic citizenship cannot be effective or democratic when it endorses and expands existing collective practices and claims of workers and consumers. In principle, this is difficult because industrial and consumer citizenship are distinct. Often the inherent tension between industrial and consumer citizenship undermines one or another practice because we have few mediating institutions to allow us all to step back from these separate practices and make democratic decisions about economic life as a whole. Workers become desperate for a secure job, but then consumers suffer in any resulting collusion. Historically, sabotage and strikes often hurt consumers first and consumer boycotts hurt workers. Again and again consumers denounced union rights, even though they were battling management prerogatives over the production of poor quality, unprofessional products and services. Today the prospects are improving. In contemporary Australia women increasingly participate in the labour market, men at least share the shopping,[8] the labour movement is influenced by feminism, while the consumer movement has been greatly affected by environmentalism. It may be possible then for more Australian citizens to take a long-term view of the demand side in judging different economic policies.

Economic citizenship, I said, concerns economic democracy from below over the 'whole economy'. In contrast, industrial democracy aims to democratise individual workplaces through collective decision-making and autonomy. Current enterprise jargon of flatter structures and flexible specialisation may offer a pseudo-industrial democracy of microeconomic reform. But industrial democracy *within* enterprises, even in the form of the purer worker co-operatives, could operate as competitive islands in a sea of economic exclusion, unemployment and inequity towards future generations. The broader 'common wealth' may be lost from view. In contrast, economic citizenship aims to democratise economic policy in general.

A 'common wealth' implies a responsibly shared *place* that is nurtured and democratically controlled by all citizens. In an ideal common wealth, policy decisions by experts could be scrutinised by the people through formally constituted citizen bodies. Democratic deliberation in a range of public institutions and mediating associations would ideally ensure that all voices are heard. This polity would create opportunities for economically marginalised people to put their views, and to prevent people from suffering undue private constraints.[9]

Civil, Political and Social Citizenship

Economic citizenship is not set in opposition to civil, political and social rights. Although it would moderate civil contractualism, the other rights would flourish better on their own terms. Economic citizenship is simply concerned with work and householding (or production and reproduction in household, market and public sectors). It is about democratising duties and obligations in the economic realm. Instead of work being defined and imposed as a duty by employers, government policies and other powerful market players, in a regime where unemployment, underemployment and overwork co-exist, economic citizenship requires that the opportunity to earn a living be readily available, as a freely chosen right and a fairly shared obligation. The types of employment, their human and environmental sustainability and the extent of unpaid work would be democratically decided for the long-term good of the 'common wealth'. Such opportunities to fulfil social obligations through work are also a means of gaining social recognition and thus are a part of identity-formation at the public 'citizen' level (Pixley 1993, 1997).

While civil, political and social rights have their own independent principles, the effectiveness of each obviously depends on political *and* economic circumstances. Social citizenship, in particular, is being subsumed to counter-productive, short-term economic ends like labour-market 'reform'. Political rights of voting may appear less liable to economic degradation than social citizenship, but even so, the different elements of social and political citizenship cannot be nurtured while economic imperatives swamp their distinctive goals.[10]

In contrast with Marshall's narrow focus on state redistribution, the initial Keynesian approach saw social security as also having an economic function, namely, to protect minimum wage levels and to maintain effective demand and employment (Rogers and Streeck 1994). This economic function of security payments was part of a confident, powerful social policy. High levels of employment and investment in social and physical infrastructure were the aims of an economic policy that served social policy ends and were profitable to business into the bargain. Adjustment, diversification and restructuring in expanding and contracting sectors were facilitated by the greater security of plentiful jobs (Quiggin 1996, 229). Although later international problems were foreshadowed quite early (Coombs 1994), this 'welfare all round' appealed to most prominent economic groups for several decades (Pixley 1996).

Today, economic policy is less concerned about consumer demand. For those pursuing an export-or-die approach, social security provision is even said to undermine the export goal, since wages are kept above those of overseas competitors, while the maintenance of domestic demand is fairly irrelevant to those seeking only to expand foreign demand (Cohen 1991). This promotion of low-wage 'competitive austerity' (Albo 1994) assumes that the very poorest countries, like Bangladesh, must be highly competitive (Weiss and Hobson 1995).

Industrial Citizenship

Civil rights to individual freedoms and free enjoyment of property are the classic liberal rights of the private individual. The treatment of labour as property is the most relevant for discussion in this chapter. Clearly, the freedom to sell the 'property' of one's capacity to labour (or human capital) to an employer of one's choosing is an advance on indentured labour or serfdom, servitude and forced labour. This freedom is violated by work-for-the-dole schemes (Pixley 1993, 210–18). Dole-work is a form of primitive state conscription which treats people like convicted criminals on community service orders, deprived of the right (of Article 23 of the Universal Declaration of Human Rights) to 'free choice of employment'.

The civil rights of free wage labour, however, focus on *exchange* of labour. The *conditions* of employment are a different matter which historically have led to workers claiming industrial rights in return for fulfilling their obligation to work. In many ways, industrial rights and industrial democracy overlap in economic citizenship, for the latter would be meaningless wherever workers are denied industrial rights. Nevertheless, industrial citizenship should be regarded as a discrete practice, neither analytically nor practically connected to social rights. It is not individualistic like civil rights, but a 'status limiting the commodification of persons in employment' (Barbalet 1988, 26).[11]

In the citizenship literature, surprisingly few critics emphasise that political and social rights are necessary but insufficient in regards to the treatment of labour as a commodity. Marshall only mentioned 'industrial citizenship' in passing, as 'parallel with and supplementary to the system of political citizenship' (1965, 104). The industrial rights of workers to influence the conditions of their employment, Gersuny argues, is a 'stunted category' in Marshall's work and remains so in contemporary citizenship debates (1994, 211). Barbalet describes them as the 'Cinderella rights of modern citizenship' (Barbalet 1996, 69). Likewise, despite the formative influence of the Webbs, industrial relations literature has rarely drawn on the relevance of human rights proclamations in major international agreements (Dabscheck 1997, 4).

Yet in 1897, the Webbs concluded their *Industrial Democracy* with the following argument:

> The framers of the United States constitution, like the various parties in the French Revolution of 1789, saw no resemblance or analogy between the personal power which they drove from the castle, the altar, and the throne, and that which they left unchecked in the farm, the factory, and the mine. Even at the present day ... 'Liberals' all over the world see no more inconsistency between democracy and unrestrained capitalist enterprise, than Washington or Jefferson did between democracy and slave-owning. ... [M]anual-working wage-earners have, from the outset, felt their way to a different view. To them, the uncontrolled power wielded by the owners of the means of production, able to withhold from the manual worker all chance of subsistence unless he accepted their terms, meant a far more genuine loss of liberty, and a far keener sense of personal subjection, than ... the far-off, impalpable role of the king ... Against this autocracy in industry, the manual workers have, during the century, made good their protest. The agitation for freedom of combination and factory legislation has been, in reality, a demand for a 'constitution' in the industrial realm. (S. and B. Webb 1902, 840–1)

The Webbs called for a 'living wage' and a universal standard of labour, citing the new arbitration courts then being established in Australia and New Zealand as leading the world. They insisted that unions relying on their 'strategic position' for a better bargain merely allowed employers to exploit further those with little leverage or bargaining skills, for example 'the great army of women' whose wages are fixed according to strategic position down to the 'barest possible subsistence' (Webb 1902, 582). Although, in practice, Australia's arbitration initially excluded women from its standards, women's wages and conditions became better, thanks to centralised arbitration, than nearly anywhere in the world.

Yet the situation today seems generally little better than in the Webbs' time. Industrial rights remain fragile. Across the world, strikes are legally constrained, unionists are sacked, some have been killed and child labour is employed in 'parasitic industries' (that is, enterprises which are parasitic on other social and political support structures).[12]

Corporate Citizenship

If industrial rights (and, separately, economic citizenship) can aid in democratising the economic sphere from the bottom up, one could argue that 'corporate citizenship' represents the responsibilities of powerful economic actors working from the top down. As an ethical ideal concerned with principles of duty and obligation, it is popularly used to criticise irresponsible and criminally negligent corporations.

The application of 'citizen' principles to organisations entails the important requirement that individual responsibility be upheld wherever relevant in corporate law enforcement, particularly when de facto immunity from individual criminal liability for corporate executives has become so prevalent (Fisse and Braithwaite 1993, 6). Nevertheless, corporate actions are not merely the sum of individual actions, and individual accountability for corporate wrong-doing can often lead to scapegoating and buck-passing. Therefore, as Fisse and Braithwaite point out, it is also important to hold 'corporations responsible as corporations' (1993, 135) and to seek organisational reforms as well.

Opinion is divided as to the extent that major transnational corporations (with more power than many nations) are taking seriously their responsibilities in advancing the human rights of their own employees and those of their suppliers. Corporations also have a patchy record in their relations with countries which abuse human rights: companies only stopped dealing with the white supremacist government in South Africa after years of worldwide opposition to apartheid (Smith 1994, 149–51). Corporate culpability for environmental and human disasters, such as the destruction in the Ok Tedi region of Papua New Guinea by BHP and the explosion at Union Carbide's plant in Bhopal, India, have led to public outcries. Other transnational corporations, such as Levi-Strauss, expect suppliers to abide by international labour standards. The Body Shop is committed to high environmental standards, to 'trade not aid' in its relations with indigenous and impoverished peoples. It also encourages employee civic activism.

Clearly many corporate enterprises will need to be forced to accept restrictive regulations on management decisions and employment practices by the legal system, international and national labour and human rights bodies, environmental and occupational safety agencies. Other corporations are willingly pursuing their 'citizen' obligations at a global level.

Consumer Citizenship

Consumption is another area where the civil rights of classic liberal doctrine, like consumer sovereignty and *caveat emptor* (buyer beware), have proved wanting. Consumer citizen practices also have their own logic for, whatever our other affiliations and interests, we are all consumers. The struggle to move beyond the liberal model of atomistic, perfectly informed customers has depended on the depth and strength of the public sphere to inform consumers and to 'shame' and boycott corporations. Consumers cannot exercise sovereignty against limited liability companies and cannot 'beware' of hidden dangers, price fixing and poor quality of products without national and international regulations.[13] The highly publicised examples of unsafe cars, thalidomide, salmonella and mad-cow disease are obvious cases where consumer sovereignty is no defence against death, disability and illness.

Instead, consumer citizenship entails guarantees by the state (or international agency) to maintain independent regulatory bodies open to public scrutiny, codes of labelling and expert inspectors. It depends on international and national laws, regulations and adequate policing. It is a necessary corrective to industrial citizenship, being primarily concerned with bringing managerial decisions to public account. Thus if workers should not hold jobs requiring them to produce cars 'unsafe at any speed', then so be it. There will always be tensions between consumer and industrial rights and practices. Yet, a safe car produced under less alienated conditions is more then a mere compromise.

Democratising Economics

The Keynesian argument that microeconomic action has perverse effects at the macroeconomic level provides an entry point for economic democracy. The claim of Keynesian technocrats to *know* the answers, however, left an undemocratic legacy. Today, criticism of neoclassical theory and of Keynesian empiricism presents an opening to broader debate on economic policy. On the one hand, facts do not 'speak for themselves' as Keynesian experts and social policy 'do-gooders' would have it (Panitch 1994, 38). On the other hand, the neoclassical theoretical model cannot speak to human needs and aspirations. Neither position's grounding assumptions could be considered democratic or participatory.

The first step towards democratising economic decisions is to discuss openly such grounding presuppositions. There are precedents for this. Many early Keynesians were committed to a less positivist epistemology, acknowledging that their assumptions about the nature of empirical evidence (and the direction of state intervention) were grounded in the need for political debate among the 'major players'. At the time these were labour, capital and the state, and many Australian Keynesians subscribed to this view. Keynes himself also rejected the neoclassical assumption that humans can have knowledge of the future, and instead drew on convention and emotion to explain how economic agents cope with uncertainty. Likewise, Marxian theory at its least positivist recognised that it should develop out of, and thus speak in concepts oriented to the changing needs of oppressed groups which today must incorporate ethnicity and gender as well as class. If the theory is rejected by oppressed groups, then *theory* must change.[14] Any approximate understanding of social needs that might democratically frame economic policy must accept a diversity of subject positions.

Mediating Institutions for Practising Economic Citizenship

A major problem for active citizenship in a large pluralistic society like Australia is the lack of public mediating institutions which actually confer political power on citizens. Nowhere is this more stark than in economic policy. In Norman's view (1992, 46), the only political associations 'which provide individuals with a point of entry into political life' are almost all adversarial ones, namely 'political parties, trade unions, protest groups and campaigning organisations'. Worse still, populists like Pauline Hanson and her One Nation party dangerously pretend that an allegedly unmediated relation (with a politician!) is credible (on grounds that populists 'listen'). The question for active citizenship remains, as Norman says, one of how to 'create the institutions of participatory democracy' (1992, 46–7). In the economic sphere, Australia has few obvious institutions of economic democracy to provide procedural mechanisms for open debate and responsible policy formulation from below. One can cite a few parliamentary committees, but land and environment courts were disbanded, institutionalised negotiations over native title were removed by the Howard government in 1998 and human rights commissions were run down.

Equally important is delineating some balance between a potential economic democracy at national and international levels. Although a 'national economy' should not be dismissed as an anachronism in Australia, few recognise that certain international agreements have actually expanded democracy from below. Meantime, the state remains the arena where, potentially, we may be able to debate the 'good life' (Emy and James 1996, 33). A 'better state' would be fostered, among other practices, by economic citizenship.

Conclusion

Reinventing Australian citizenship to democratise economic life requires open, public debate not only about the most efficient means of increasing production, but also about the ends of economic life itself. Economic citizenship protects all residents' access to the existing civil, political and social rights of citizenship, and urges the expansion of both industrial and consumer rights. It proposes that citizens in a democratic commonwealth should have access to the means, not just of economic survival, but of economic flourishing. But without institutional changes it will remain a utopian ideal. Hence, a major challenge for Australian citizenship is to build institutions to democratise economic life. Australia also needs to incorporate those international treaties and agreements that further the aims of economic citizenship worldwide.

But citizens also need to recognise that economic citizenship is in their interests. They need to experience the link between economic security and sharing employment more equitably. There is no shortage of *work*, given the overwork in employment and unpaid work, and of potential work to care for the young and old and the natural environment. There is only an inequitable division of work. Co-operative solutions to unemployment are only possible if workers do not fear losing rights. Ideas to improve the quality of marginal jobs and ideas for work-hour reform to give workers greater control over their life course are plentiful.[15] There are also numerous models, from feminism, environmentalism, unions and Australian Indigenous peoples, which aim for public, democratic control over the economy.[16] We have only to have the courage to move forward as democrats with real concern for one another.

Notes

1 In Australia, neoclassical economics and its political counterpart, economic or market liberalism, has been called 'economic rationalism', notably by Michael Pusey. Because I wish to draw attention to economic *nationalism*, I will use *market liberalism* as the contrasting term. Keynesian economics is too internationalist for the term economic nationalism, although it did foster national economic controls. The extent that Keynesian economics subscribes to tariff protection is a moot point. Certainly Australian Keynesians in the postwar period promoted UN trade agreements designed to support third world countries (see Coombs 1994). The Keynesian era was markedly different from the so-called 'settlement' of the 1900s when tariffs and White Australia were introduced, but this is ignored by Paul Kelly (1992), Ian Marsh (1995a) and many more. Kelly (1992) assumes 'certainty' as an Australian fixture since 1900 until the 1980s: what happened to the Depression?
2 Marshall (1965, 129), for example, assumes there is a 'duty to work' but did not consider the problems when economies do not generate full employment. See also Barbalet (1988, 1996) and Pixley (1993, 220–7).
3 Many defences of social citizenship lack the incisive understanding of economics that influences the work of Mishra (1984) and Gil (1992) in the social policy area. As Smyth (1994) points out, most Australian social policy assumes away the Keynesian era.
4 See Gordon (1994). The literature on citizenship rarely makes reference to problems that orthodox economics has often caused or exacerbated. Few draw on the extensive literature on the sociology of economic life.

5 Among intellectual debates in Australia, Melleuish (1995), Emy (1993), Stretton and Orchard (1994) criticise the ascendancy of market liberalism in diverse ways; taking heart from constructive alternatives (e.g. Langmore and Quiggin 1994), the churches and peak welfare lobbies have made strenuous public criticisms of the declining quality of many facets of Australian citizenship.

6 Aristotle defines two distinct forms of economics, *oikonomia* refers to house-holding, *chrematistics* refers to short-term manipulation: environmentalists are trying to revive his distinction (Burnett, undated paper). 'Household management..., not being money-making, has a limit, since money-making is not its function, but only a means to an end' said Aristotle (*The Politics*, Book I, Ch. 9, 1962, 44).

7 At the time of writing, the IMF's role in imposing austerity in South and East Asia in 1997–98 has been criticised heavily, not least by the World Bank, but economists there were bemused at the question of whether the World Bank could itself become a more democratic body. Personal interview with the Senior Adviser to Joseph Stiglitz, 5 August 1998, World Bank, Washington DC.

8 Men's time spent on shopping, cooking and childcare has risen but cleaning and laundry has 'stalled' (Bittman and Pixley 1997). Yet such improvements specifically reduce the gendered division of worker–consumer.

9 See Meehan (1994, 73–4). Also, while arbitration, for example, cannot be characterised as a democratic forum, it compares very favourably with the lack of any effective public institutional constraint on employers and enables unions to put forth a collectively devised log of claims (see Gersuny 1994).

10 See Quiggin (1996), who argues these reforms have not lived up to expectations of bringing increased living standards. The case of telecommunication reform, in particular, has made 'no economic sense' but seen the 'dissipation of billions of dollars' in duplication (1996, 123). In general, some inefficiencies were removed, but microeconomic reform has no means to prevent new inefficiencies, there is deeper insecurity with high unemployment and the 'intensification of work associated with it is unsustainable in the long run' (Quiggin 1996, 229).

11 Again, industrial rights are no more intrinsically 'at war' with the market than other rights. Hirschman (1970) shows how voicing complaints about poor performance is an important message that organisations are foolish to ignore. Thus, union rights give workers the freedom to exercise 'voice' and, potentially, to improve a moribund organisation before it is too late. In contrast, passive loyalty in an authoritarian enterprise prevents constructive criticism and innovation, creates stress and increases turnover – the 'exit' option in Hirschman's terms. Germany's strong unions are notable here, for as Weiss and Hobson (1995) argue about British industrial decline, a cheaper product is not always a more desirable one.

12 See Dabscheck (1997) who highlights the relation between international human rights and the Webbs' view, also Gersuny (1994).

13 Louise Sylvan cites how limited liability companies have significant privileges over the rest of us, only a few of which have been challenged, such as an Australian High Court decision that the privilege against self-incrimination is a 'human' privilege not a company one (1995, 111).

14 Marx (1977, 61–72). On early Keynesians in Australia, see Smyth (1994), and on Keynes and uncertainty, see Lekachman (1957).

15 See here Ormerod (1996, 14). For example, caps on overtime, effective banking of hours, sabbatical entitlements and parental leave all suggest 'time sovereignty' or 'elective-time work'. Also, partial retirement, an easing off from full-time work, is less threatening to older workers than early retirement and useful for the organisation (Buchanan and Bearfield 1997). Sweden is the furthest in reconstructing the old gendered working roles, with its extensive parental leave system, where men and women share earning and caring most equitably of all (Sainsbury 1996).

16 See Rogers and Streeck (1994); Also D. Brennan (1994) and Sawer (1995) on the mobilisation in Australia for the childcare accreditation scheme, to ensure quality, dependable childcare centres – this was a form of economic democracy. Seccombe (1993) proposes citizen environmental review boards with powers to tax offenders and to foster clean industries with the proceeds: i.e. bodies quite separate from 'slush-funds' run by politicians, as seems to be the case with proceeds from the partial sale of Telstra in 1997.

Further Reading

Alston, P. and M. Chiam (eds) (1995). *Treaty-Making and Australia: Globalisation Versus Sovereignty?* Sydney: The Federation Press.

Bittman, M. and J. Pixley (1997). *The Double Life of the Family.* Sydney: Allen & Unwin.

Cass, B. and P. Smyth (eds) (1998). *Contesting the Australian Way: States, Markets and Civil Society.* Cambridge: Cambridge University Press.

Roche, M. and R. van Berkel (eds) (1997). *European Citizenship and Social Exclusion.* Aldershot: Ashgate.

CHAPTER 13

Social Citizenship

Winton Higgins and Gaby Ramia

Current debate on citizenship reproduces a fundamental moral divide that has marked western political theory and western social thought in general, since early modern times. On the one side of this moral divide stands *instrumental rationality*, whereby a powerful group grants itself the privilege of calculating how elements in its natural and social environment, including various categories of people, can best be used or deployed to further this group's interests. In this way political actors and planners treat the environment and society as mere *objects* whose utility is to be exploited in a 'rational' way. The opposing moral view is to see all individuals as equally entitled to think, plan and act around their own chosen values and purposes. On this second view, all individuals are *subjects* or *moral agents*, whose value does not derive from their utility to the purposes of powerful others, but rather from the inherent dignity of conscious human life. This view emphasises moral understandings that govern relations between subjects of equal dignity, and is thus called *intersubjectivism*.

The first view underpins mainstream liberal thought, and its adherents in Australia include the major political parties. The second position is espoused by some welfare advocates, most environmentalists and virtually all feminists. Its most important supporting philosophical traditions are feminism, communitarianism (and these days the closely allied civic republicanism), and critical theory.

The divide between instrumental rationality and intersubjectivism finds expression in diverging notions of citizenship and of policies to promote it. Above all, the divide implies radically different *forms and principles of association* for civic life (see, for instance, Hirst 1994; Miller 1992; Frazer and Lacey 1993; Gray 1995). On the one hand, liberal individualism holds that each individual should rationally calculate her or his options and choose the most (materially) advantageous course of self-interested action. The isolated individual is 'disembedded' – abstracted from any essential social context. But s/he is nevertheless bound to behave in conformity with social expectations as expressed in (and enforced by) market mechanisms and public opinion. Individuals are formally equal and free, however radically unequal they may be in the substantive resources they would need to pursue real options. On the other hand, intersubjectivism constructs an opposing notion of individuality which presents the individual as 'embedded' in a specific social, familial and cultural context. The social contextualisation of the individual allows for an inquiry into the individual's real resources and options, her or his practical possibilities of pursuing a self-chosen life project. In this way a socially contextualised view leads to an inquiry into the basis of *social citizenship*.

The modern concept of citizenship imports the values of equality and inclusiveness. Either one is a citizen of a given nation or one is not – one cannot be more or less of a citizen than some other individual. And contemporary citizenship is usually inclusive, in that it shuns exclusions on the basis of ascriptive differences such as gender, race, age, religion, ethnicity, disability and sexual preference. *Social* citizenship, as a subset of citizenship in general, exists when a nation's laws and social provision override de facto disadvantage based on ascriptive difference and personal misfortune. It exists when they see to it that individuals have resources and options to pursue their life projects, no matter how they are socially embedded or personally embodied as women or men, young or old, able-bodied or disabled, indigenous or non-indigenous, and as members of cultural, racial and sexual minorities or majorities. The individual's life choices and moral evaluations become operative only if the social context supports their continuous development and pursuit throughout the individual's life cycle. In this chapter we use the term social citizenship to refer to the relative success of each western society in empowering its citizens in an equal and inclusive way throughout their lives, in their inevitable periods of material dependency as well as those of self-sufficiency.

Reinventing social citizenship is a fundamentally important part of the broader strategic program of overhauling citizenship in Australia. This chapter argues that social citizenship in contemporary Australia should be rethought in the light of recent policy and theoretical developments. Its political importance has been elevated by attacks on the welfare state and on other socially protective mechanisms in this country. The first section of the chapter outlines three suggested criteria for effective social citizenship. The second briefly reviews Australia's performance historically against these criteria. The third and final section identifies some key contemporary problems regarding social citizenship in Australia and proposes the policies likely to overcome them.

Three Criteria for Social Citizenship

Social citizenship establishes comparable life chances between citizens through provision for social entitlements based on membership of the political community known as the nation state. Analyses of the concept often begin with the legacy of T.H. Marshall's (1963) germinal essay, 'Citizenship and Social Class'.[1] However, though Marshall's work began the analysis of social citizenship, we need to look far beyond it. He wrote in a quite specific context (mid-twentieth-century Britain), and omitted some fundamental elements that occur in any study of social citizenship today, such as women and the family, racial and ethnic minorities, and individuals lacking the capacity for self-determination (see Bulmer and Rees 1996, 275; Lewis 1994). Marshall's conception of citizenship was largely statist and thereby underestimated the importance of individual and collective agency.

In this chapter we argue that social citizenship in Australia should not be conceived in wholly statist terms. Instead, we suggest that it is most appropriately viewed as part of a broader agenda for enhancing citizenship, one that brings together rights in various spheres of life, such as the economic, political and legal. This agenda needs to affirm the diversity of its citizens' ways of life that every contemporary western community – Australia above all – manifests (Tully 1995).

Social citizenship demands, among other things, a democratisation of society through substantive eradication of the blanket exclusions of individuals from disadvantaged groups: women, racial minorities, and the disabled among others (Benhabib 1989). While bearing in mind that social citizenship needs to be located within a broader citizenship program, we propose three closely related criteria for judging how far any given society has come in according its members social citizenship. A society has provided social citizenship, we suggest, if it has established conditions under which *all* adults within it are *autonomous*, in which they enjoy *justice and equality*, and in which they are supported by *democratic forms of association*. The challenge of social citizenship is to bring the project of universal rights to fruition for 'embedded and embodied' individuals: individuals in the context of their specific gender, race, age, ethnicity and so on. We will expand on these criteria in turn.

Individual Autonomy

Critics of liberalism have often pointed out that its negative freedoms –

whose social circumstances leave them with few real options anyway. While both sides agree on the importance of freedom from arbitrary interference, *individuality* demands forms of association that put real options about what personal projects to pursue in their lives and how to pursue them into the hands of all citizens. At base, this means that all enjoy social security so that unmet need, real or threatened, does not subvert their personal options in practice. To meet this criterion is to go beyond even progressive liberal perspectives, which contend that liberalism has the *potential* to provide the substantive conditions necessary for autonomy among all individuals. That potential can only be realised in the unfortunately rare case where voluntary associations harmonise their inputs with those of sympathetic governments (see, for example, Macedo 1988).[2]

If we are concerned with the autonomy of *embodied* individuals, we have to factor in our biologically conditioned *dependency*, especially in childhood, sickness and invalidity, and old age. Society has thus to provide for the autonomy of embodied individuals through both income transfers and high quality caring services, lest women, for example, continue to labour disproportionately under the burden of unpaid – and usually unacknowledged – care in the home. This is a burden which remains a major obstruction to their worklife and other civic participation. Beyond that, individual autonomy requires access for all to the amenities that the society in question can provide in the form of material amenities and quality of life, including health care, educational opportunities and leisure. At the present stage of socioeconomic development, such access depends chiefly on paid employment, but society must make this status available to all adults of working age who seek it (Pixley 1993), or compensate the individual for its absence.

Such rights are under threat from a growing trend in the English-speaking world (not least Australia) towards the 'contractualisation', and therefore the individualisation, of various relationships between individuals, and between individuals and the state. At the heart of this trend is an ethos of 'reciprocal obligations', whereby services and benefits once provided as of right (by the state or, say, employers) are now subject to 'negotiation' between parties who are formally equal but often substantively very unequal. In the sphere of social rights, contractualisation takes most conspicuous form in the individualisation of relations between employees and employers, and in the relationship between the state and recipients of many welfare services and benefits. Applicants for unemployment benefits, for example, have had a greater onus placed on them to demonstrate active attempts to find work before they qualify for benefits. And such demonstration usually requires the unemployed individual's consent to be 'case-managed.' Another condition of the 'welfare contract' typically requires her or him to undergo specified education and labour-market training programs, on pain of withdrawal of benefits (see especially Carney 1996, 1997; Eardley 1997).

In her analysis of such arrangements, Anna Yeatman (1995, 1997, 1998) argues that the 'new contractualism' is not necessarily antithetical to the cause of social citizenship, because unlike 'liberal' contractualism, it 'extends the status of individualised personhood to all, regardless of differences in marital status, race, ethnicity, sexuality, religion, ability and so on' (Yeatman 1998, 228). The 'status of individualised personhood' as Yeatman formulates it, however, remains an abstraction, and it abstracts precisely from the individual's embodied and socially embedded condition that threatens her or his personal autonomy in the first place.

Apart from liberalism, the other political tradition that cannot satisfy the criterion of individual autonomy is the conservative wing of communitarianism. This school exercises a growing influence on American conservative politics and enjoys niches of influence under official multiculturalism in Australia. Communitarians as a whole insist on the importance of community in supporting moral elements of personal identity. But as Benhabib (1989, 77–8) argues, the school breaks down into two opposing conceptions of community.

Whereas the progressive, 'participationist' wing sees community as a *process of interaction* that often involves intractably diverse groups and individuals – a matter we will return to under the third criterion – the conservative 'integrationist' wing affirms a static and homogeneous notion of community (an integrated 'community of virtue') around fixed (usually traditional) moral premises. These conservative communitarians thus often defend or hearken back to forms of association characterised by patriarchy, religious fundamentalism and other forms of authoritarianism, implying rigid roles, hierarchical organisation and intolerance of difference. In this way they deny individual autonomy, since the latter implies the freedom to abandon received roles in favour of self-chosen ones, and to creatively redefine moral meanings.

Equality and Justice

Patterns of social subordination and exclusion in societies like ours often follow lines of inescapable difference between people: differences related to sex, race, ethnicity, religion and so on. *A universalist project to establish equality and social justice must do so precisely across these lines of irreducible difference.* Both equality and justice are central promises of liberalism. But they have never been achieved in diverse societies under liberal auspices *because liberalism equates equality with sameness.* In a pure liberal model, it is assumed that if all individuals enjoy equal 'rights', the requirements of equality have been met. If everyone receives equal treatment and respect (is treated in the same way), everyone has also received justice. This conclusion would hold good for a homogeneous group whose members enjoy equal starting points.

But citizens of western countries do not answer to this description. It is only among the imaginary, disembedded and disembodied denizens of liberal theory – who are all the same and thereby enjoy equal starting points (for instance in Rawls 1972) – that liberalism delivers equality and justice. It signally fails embodied individuals whose very forms of embodiment (as women, say) carry social connotations of subordination and exclusion (Pateman 1988). Liberal notions of equality and justice thus fake the universalist project. They were designed only for interaction between well-to-do men in their 'public' (economic and political) roles – men who depended for their private needs on women's unpaid domestic care.

In the case of the equality and justice criterion, the real challenge is, similarly, to establish desirable relationships between embodied – and thus also heterogeneous – individuals without either trying to pour them into the same mould or ignoring the artificial boundary between the 'public' and the 'private' spheres. For example, anti-discrimination and equal employment opportunity measures do not take economic gender equality very far in the absence of immediately available, affordable and high-quality childcare, income-replacing parental benefits and strenuous attempts to get fathers to use them. These liberal measures merely invite women to become the same as men, to take on unreconstructed male roles at great personal cost.

Part of a real social citizenship agenda would be the establishment of a pattern of distribution of physical, cultural and social resources that equips each individual with the widest possible range of options and that minimises relative deprivation. This pattern would have to exclude a disproportionate accumulation of social endowments in the hands of a privileged few.

Community as Democratic Process

We have already indicated how both contractarian-liberal and conservative-communitarian forms of association obstruct the development of social citizenship. In insisting on sameness and conformity, they bear the seeds of intolerance and systemic inequality (Tully 1995). They focus on the legitimation of power and powerholders' decisions, not on *the process* of 'the democratic conversation': not, that is, on the quality of the interaction between diverse groups and individuals that make up any modern collectivity. To the extent that these schools of thought approve of a small range of representative or 'democratic' institutions, they see them as mere clearing houses where fixed sectional interests are reconciled in a 'legitimate' decisionmaking process. In them powerful groups strike enforceable deals and the obedience of all is secured to formally correctly taken decisions, as Joseph Schumpeter (1947) classically argued. Beyond that, liberals and conservative communitarians have no objection to elitist and authoritarian forms of association, above all ones that enshrine instrumental rationality.

The alternative view sees democracy as developmental for its participants. Social citizenship and its supportive community are *constantly generated* in ongoing, open dialogue, which ideally occurs in all settings in which people co-operate and interact – in national and local assemblies, in interest organisations and at the workplace. Topics, participants and modes of expression in this dialogue are in no way limited. In the process individuals and groups learn more about each other, possibly generate empathy across lines of irreducible difference, and so enlarge their sense of their own political and social agendas (Benhabib 1989, chs 3 and 4). There is no end point in this process, and it certainly ought not to end in a consensus, or in an 'integrated' community where difference and contention have no place.

The Australian Tradition

In theory, in liberal societies the market distributes wealth, income, life chances and access to education, culture and leisure to individuals and groups. But such distribution treats individuals as if they are commodities of drastically varying use value rather than as equal citizens with an equal call on society's resources (Esping-Andersen 1985, 1990). Australia has evolved as a market society informed by liberal ideals. Instrumentally rational individualism has formed our institutions more than have collectivist interventions that aim to 'protect society' (Polanyi 1944), that is, to ameliorate the inequalities and exclusions endemic in market-driven socioeconomic development.

The institutional pattern of social protection in Australia involved various strategies designed to defend the living standards of *wage-earners*, and not *citizens* (Castles 1985; Kenny 1997). Minimum wage standards provided through compulsory arbitration reflected attempts to secure the living standards of male workers. Women most often received lower wage rates because they, unlike men, were assumed not to be financially responsible for their families. This inequality reinforced the susceptibility of women in Australia to economic dependence and poverty. Female sole parents and their children were even more economically vulnerable. Aborigines and non-white immigrants were also largely excluded from the Australian system of social protection.

In both conception and execution, modern genocide in general has its roots in instrumental rationality (Bauman 1989). It was instrumentally rational for the white invaders of this country to regard it as uninhabited and available to their exclusive exploitation. On this pretext they subjected the Indigenous population to genocidal policies (HREOC 1997b, 270–5) and then to total marginalisation (including formal exclusion from citizenship until 1962) and social disruption, in the name of 'progress.' Other minorities fared little better. Under the White Australia Policy, immigration was severely restricted due to the cultivated fear of the 'yellow peril' to the north, and the concern that the wages of Australian workers would be undercut by the 'coolies' and the 'Kanakas.' Later, the activities of the Japanese during the Second World War caused similar fears (see, for example, Castles, Cope, Kalantzis and Morrissey 1992). These policies and attitudes excluded from social citizenship minorities already living here.

Against this background, the most effective means of achieving social citizenship lay in the welfare state. But as both overseas and Australian social policy researchers note (for instance Esping-Andersen 1990; Saunders 1994; Carney and Hanks 1994), the Australian welfare state has traditionally been, and remains, targeted toward the very poor and has performed badly as an egalitarian redistributor (Korpi and Palme 1996). Given its exceptionally 'targeted' approach and comparatively small budget, it offers a highly deficient basis for social citizenship. However, even if the welfare state treated the systematically exploited and excluded groups equally, this would not have reversed their maltreatment in the marketplace; for social citizenship also involves the market and not just the state sphere. This is a consideration we will address in the next section of the paper.

Towards Social Citizenship in Australia? Proposals for Reform

Though some important instances of progress can be seen in recent Australian history, fundamental change is required before Australia attains a degree of social citizenship comparable to most western nations. In this section we suggest four key policy directions: a more serious approach to gender equality in public policy formation; the establishment of an effective industry policy and a re-regulation of the economy; the expansion and integration of welfare and labour-market policies; and the fostering of more effective popular organisations, without which none of the first three can be achieved.

The Elevation of Gender-Equality

In recent times minor progress toward gender equality has been made, for instance in the criminalisation of rape in marriage, the improvement of access to apprehended violence orders, and campaigns against sexual discrimination and harassment at work. Nonetheless, law enforcement agencies of all kinds continue to support the subordination of women by failing to intervene in 'private' matters (for a recent illustration, see School of Social Science and Policy 1997). A clear example lies in the case of the judge in a South Australian Court who, in 1992, ruled that a man should be entitled to use force in his attempt to entice his wife to have sex.

As Australian feminists have often stressed (for example Pixley 1993; Cass 1995; Shaver 1995; Bryson 1995), women have yet to attain the requisite equality for social citizenship in their dealings with the labour market and the welfare state. Despite the official establishment of equal pay in the 1970s, in practice discrimination is still a reality. Pronounced gender segregation in the labour market remains, women's unionisation rates continue to be lower than those of men, and many unions often serve and represent their actual and potential female membership poorly (Pocock 1997). Given the historical salience of labour-market rewards in distributing income and life opportunities in this country (Castles 1985, 1996), and thus of the wages system in defining social citizenship, these issues are paramount. They are closely related as well to the inadequacies of childcare provision, and the niggardliness and restrictiveness of social security benefits have reinforced disadvantage among groups such as (overwhelmingly female) sole parents.

Industry Policy and Economic Re-Regulation

Our criteria for social citizenship can only be met in an economy capable of generating enough employment to make quality jobs and career paths available to all job seekers, and enough revenue to support the requisite income transfers and high-quality welfare and educational services. Economic performance depends principally on economic regulation, and in particular on the mix of 'political' regulation as against unregulated market allocation of resources. Every modern economy relies on both, but their importance in any given policy regime depends on the relative political dominance of economic liberalism (see Pusey 1991).

Australia has now had a quarter of a century of economic liberal revivalism in the management of our economy, under both Labor and coalition governments. This has been an era of a major trend increase in unemployment and a spectacular decline in the manufacturing sector (as measured, for example by contracting industrial employment and a chronic trade deficit in manufactured goods), of reduction of an already stunted welfare state, and of growing socioeconomic inequalities. Economic liberalism not only turns its face against policy interventions in aid of social citizenship, it also lays waste to the socioeconomic preconditions for it in economic performance.

Reversing these trends requires a national strategy of socioeconomic development to replace the present total abandonment of national economic sovereignty and correct the supine posture towards 'market forces.' An overarching and selective industry policy – hardly a novelty in other western countries – could rescue the country's industrial fortunes, and thereby restore the quality and quantity of work, not to mention national income (Higgins 1994).

The manufacturing sector is of critical significance here, because it is in this sector that most quality jobs and career paths are generated. It is also where technology is developed to constantly improve human productivity for the creation of real national wealth and income (that is, real goods and services, not simply the accounting profits of 'paper entrepreneurialism,' or purely financial activity).

Manufacturing failure frustrates the attempt to raise the quality of life (particularly worklife), and leads to deficits in the balance of payments that further diminish a country's policy choices in many areas, including social policy. And manufacturing is an area where market regulation has failed most spectacularly, both here and in other English-speaking countries, which as a group are particularly prone to an economic-liberal political culture. The winners in international industrial competition have been countries where public authorities have taken responsibility for the national manufacturing effort – a notion that is in itself anathema to liberals. This has been done through selective interventions to make good market failures, for instance, in forging essential linkages between interdependent technologies, and in ensuring a flow of investment funds to research and development and new high-growth and high-risk industries (Higgins 1994).

Expansion and Integration of Welfare and Labour Market Policies

Australia has one of the developed world's most niggardly welfare states. In Korpi and Palme's (1996, table 2) survey of 18 OECD countries, Australia spent least of all on social expenditure as a proportion of GDP. Australian welfare arrangements shore up market society by preventing (to some extent at least) visible social distress while at the same time forcing many to take paid work on any conditions. These people thus join 'the working poor', whose wages – even for full-time work in many cases – do not suffice to lift them and their dependants out of poverty. In other words, the nation has no egalitarian agenda.

Over the last two decades a tacit American model of 'full capitalism' has developed with bipartisan support in Australian public policy. Along with financial deregulation, there has occurred the progressive decentralisation of the industrial relations system, displacing collective bargaining from the national to the enterprise level largely with the consent of the trade union movement (Hampson 1996). As well, social security benefits have become ever more restrictively targeted. Finally, increased student–teacher ratios in schools and universities, and the increase in the costs for students of university education, have decreased the likelihood of many Australians attaining the equality inherent in any credible notion of social citizenship.

The ramifications of this agenda include the feminisation of poverty, particularly among single mothers (and consequently their children as well), and 'job creation' via labour-market deregulation, which produces a 'sub-proletariat' that gets by on badly paid, insecure, dead-end and often hazardous 'junk jobs'. This model powerfully subverts social citizenship. Fortunately, however, resistance from the women's movement, unions and welfare organisations (including churches) have so far managed to slow 'progress' towards this model in Australia.

We can contrast this American model with the Scandinavian ones which typically 'encompass' most households as both contributors and beneficiaries, and are designed for egalitarian redistribution of income and life chances among all citizens, both those in paid work and those outside it (Korpi and Palme 1996). In stark contrast to the Australian case they aim to eradicate relative deprivation. Many benefits (including paid parental leave claimable by both mothers and fathers) are earnings-related – that is, they seek to maintain the individual's standard of living when s/he drops out of the paid workforce because of parental responsibilities, illness, ageing or joblessness. They also begin the process of eroding gender inequities in worklife by partially socialising the caring activities that have traditionally tied women down to unpaid work in the home. A move to enlarge social citizenship in Australia should begin with the introduction of a welfare state of a similar kind.

As Günter Schmid (1995) has suggested, however, the welfare state's full contribution to social citizenship will not emerge until its operations mesh with the world of work. To integrate work and welfare is a particularly difficult task in a country such as Australia, which in contrast to Scandinavian countries has a strong historical legacy of a comparatively rigid separation of the two spheres. The social security system here mainly acts as a last-resort safety net for those 'deserving' citizens who cannot find work (Castles 1985; Esping-Andersen 1990). Schmid (1995) recognises that the old notion of male full-time full employment up to a prescibed retirement age is now an anachronism. A creative way to redistribute today's employment opportunities would be to give employees and employers much more flexibility in adjusting the former's engagement in paid work to meet changing needs, wants and circumstances.

'Transitional' arrangements that integrate welfare provision with labour-market regulation would allow employees to take leave or reduce their working week on earnings-related, publicly funded benefits in order to have children, look after dependants, retrain, or take an extended sabbatical, without prejudice to their permanent, full-time status. Employers would at the same time be able temporarily to reduce their workforce's cost and presence in the enterprise in order to ride out business cycle contractions and major restructuring. This integration of welfare and labour-market arrangements would give employees greater options to mesh their worklife with their other life projects, and could considerably undercut the dilemmas women face between careers and having children. It would also relieve the economy of the current unproductive irrationalities of labour hoarding in recession followed by recruitment problems in booms, and of growing unemployment often accompanied by steep increases in overtime worked and stress experienced by those who still have jobs (see for example Buchanan and Bearfield 1996).

More Effective Popular Organisations

In keeping with the argument that social citizenship is not wholly a statist project, trade unions and other forms of popular organisation need to flourish. Indeed, without popular movements the state cannot be compelled to fulfil the three criteria previously outlined. As Turner (1986, 89) argues, 'much of the conflict and political change of modern society is located in a number of diverse social movements which have a complex class composition but which clearly extend beyond a class basis.' This is precisely the secret of the Scandinavian countries: traditions of powerful popular mobilisation go back at least to the mid-nineteenth century in the forms – in order of appearance – of rural self-help organisations, the multi-faceted labour movement (with all its political, temperance, educational and cultural ramifications), consumer co-operation, the women's movement and other 'new social movements'. By contrast, in Australia an elitist political culture has consolidated itself in the absence of opposition from a similarly robust grassroots and communitarian associational life. A comparison of the styles of government in Australia and Scandinavia bears witness to these divergent historical legacies. Popular movements have little influence on the framing of legislation and the business of government in Australia, whereas most important policy developments have to go through an elaborate process of consultation in the Scandinavian countries.

We can reject fatalistic, culturally relativist explanations of the comparative weakness of Australian associational life ('Australians are basically conservative, apathetic', and so on) by referring to counter-examples such as the large and militant anti-war movement during the Vietnam war. The better explanation probably lies in this society's colonial and postcolonial origins, and the lack of far-reaching democratic and egalitarian organising principles and ideals in the labour movement, which is the most important form of associational life in our history. This movement still carries a malign legacy from its formative years, when it pursued a labourism that was masculinist, racist, factionalised, inward looking and jingoistic. Progressive elements within the union movement have tried in later years to break out of the mould, most recently in the election of a woman (and a feminist), Jennie George, to the presidency of the ACTU, a world 'first'.

At the same time, however, the union movement's political affiliate, the ALP, has acted in government as the vehicle of economic liberal politics par excellence and has campaigned for a 'minimalist' republic based on bread-and-circuses nationalism rather than on social citizenship. The road to social citizenship must pass through an invigorated grass roots associational life whose democratic inspiration is more pronounced and whose demands on government are more policy-oriented and strategically focused.

Conclusion

The development of post-liberal institutions and policies is fundamental to the reinvention of social citizenship. Only by looking beyond liberalism will we be able to create an inclusive, democratic society in which all adults enjoy autonomy, justice and equality, and democratic participation – alongside their often intractably different fellow citizens.

Social citizenship will only develop when present political and policy trends change dramatically. Though radical change is not likely in the foreseeable future, it is not necessarily out of the question in the longer term. But several preconditions would have to be met, preconditions which admittedly seem utopian to many at present. The rights accorded women would have to be raised by the establishment of policies which edge toward greater gender equality, both in the economic and social spheres. An effective program of economic regulation – one which is not informed by the ideology of economic liberalism – would need to be implemented. The welfare state and the labour market would need to be treated as interconnected spheres, facilitating a co-ordinated, and hence more purposeful approach to social protection and individual options. Finally, a renaissance of associational life would need to be achieved as part of a wide process of renewing social solidarity and trust. My conclusion here may seem visionary, but it is meant to underline the crucial point that we should not accept the restricted and damaging understanding of citizenship we are so often offered in Australia.

Notes

1 For recent analyses of social citizenship following Marshall see Turner (1986), Barbalet (1988), Roche (1992), Dean (1996), van Steenbergen (1994), and Bulmer and Rees (1996).
2 Macedo (1988, 111) suggests that 'combining liberal capitalism with intermediate associations like voluntary groups and state and local government helps to elevate and shape self-interest, promoting a citizenry capable of and insistent upon liberal self-government'.

Further Reading

Bryson, L. (1995). 'Two Welfare States: One for Women, One for Men.' In A. Edwards and S. Magarey (eds), *Women in a Restructuring Australia: Work and Welfare*. Sydney: Allen and Unwin.
Castles, F.G. (1996). 'Needs-Based Strategies of Social Protection in Australia and New Zealand.' In G. Esping-Anderson (ed.), *Welfare States in Transition: National Adaptations in Global Economies*. London: Sage, 88–115.
Davidson, A. (1997). *From Subject to Citizen: Australian Citizenship in the Twentieth Century*. Cambridge: Cambridge University Press.
Shaver, S. and P. Saunders (1995). *Two Papers on Citizenship and Basic Income*. Sydney: Social Policy Research Centre, University of New South Wales.

CHAPTER 14

Sexual Citizenship

Barbara Sullivan

Sexuality has recently come to assume an important – and controversial – role in the Australian polity. Sexual minority groups have called for equal citizenship rights and waged a range of campaigns around issues like the decriminalisation of prostitution and (male) homosexuality, the rights of prostitutes to equal treatment before the law, the participation of lesbians and gays in the armed forces, the rights of lesbians to access fertility programs, and the entitlement of homosexual couples to the social and welfare benefits presently available to (married or de facto) heterosexual couples. However, these campaigns have also generated opposition. A large proportion of the Australian community – and of our parliamentary representatives – would appear to believe that gays, lesbians, queers[1] and prostitutes should not be treated like other citizens.

In this chapter I argue that citizenship needs to be reconceptualised outside of normative assumptions about sexuality in order to prevent continuing discrimination against sexual minorities, and in order to ensure that richer conceptions of citizenship are available to all. This chapter is in two parts. I begin with a review of the small literature – emerging from gay and feminist sources – which has attempted to explore the ramifications of sexuality for citizenship theory and practice. I then examine the practical need for a reconceptualisation of citizenship in Australia via an analysis of the ongoing discrimination and disadvantage sustained by citizens who do not conform to sexual norms.

Theorising Sexuality and Citizenship

Feminist authors were the first to explore the relationship between sexuality and (women's) citizenship via a range of specific concerns with issues like marriage, abortion, prostitution, pornography and sexual harassment. Carole Pateman (1988), for example, has argued that there is a direct relationship between the maintenance of men's public and private power over women and the practice of heterosexual intercourse in both marriage and prostitution. For Pateman, women's citizenship is actively undermined by these 'normal' sexual practices. Another feminist author, Iris Marion Young (1987, 1989), has developed a critique of 'universal citizenship' and notions of a homogeneous public sphere. In her view, the deployment of arguments about universal citizenship produces the exclusion of racialised groups, women and homosexuals. These groups are 'culturally identified with the body, wildness, and irrationality' (1987, 107). In order to preserve an ideal of universal citizenship, an homogeneous public sphere is elaborated in which women, homosexuals and racialised groups can be offered only a compromised, second-class citizenship.

Much feminist work in the area of citizenship is, however, focused on the achievement of gender equality (see Lister 1997). Sexuality issues tend to be ignored, marginalised or dealt with as if they can be more or less completely mapped onto those of gender (so that sexual practice is always conceptualised as a consequence of gender). This strategy has been useful for locating many of the disadvantages which accrue to women from 'normal' heterosexual practices and, therefore, for advancing women's citizenship. For example, the argument that women are disadvantaged by 'normal' sexual practices has assisted the call for affirmative action programs by emphasising the connections between 'normal', private gender relations and broader patterns of discrimination against women in the public sphere. However, the conflation of gender and sexuality within much feminist work on citizenship renders it less than useful for understanding some of the particular issues facing sexual minorities such as lesbians, gays, queers and sex workers. It is not that an attention to gender is irrelevant for these groups; however, an important dimension of the oppression they encounter in their daily lives will relate to normative judgments about sexual practice (rather than gender).[2] Consequently, as Gayle Rubin (1984, 307) has argued, there is a need to:

> challenge the assumption that feminism is or should be the privileged site of a theory of sexuality. Feminism is the theory of gender oppression. To automatically assume that this makes it the theory of sexual oppression is to fail to distinguish between gender, on the one hand, and erotic desire, on the other.

Rubin and recent postmodern feminist theorists of sexuality (see for example Butler 1993; Sedgwick 1990) draw significantly on the work of the French philosopher, Michel Foucault, and his *History of Sexuality Volume 1* (1984 [1976]). They view sexuality not as a biological essence but as a social and political construct; for Butler (1993) this construction is forcibly produced through a daily and ritualised repetition of social/sexual norms. They also see sexuality, and in particular the deployment of sexual 'norms', as deeply implicated in the broader arrangement of power in modern western societies. So individuals and whole populations are governed or managed via an attention (scientific, medical, familial, legal, etc.) to sexual practice and sexual discourse.

Rubin (1984, 279–82), for example, explores the historical and contemporary operation of sexual norms in western societies. She argues that a sexual hierarchy – turning around a specific (hetero)norm – assigns value and privilege to some while justifying the punitive treatment of others. Heterosexual/married/reproducing couples are always seen as 'good' and virtuous. De facto heterosexual couples and some homosexual couples (particularly those who are monogamous) are moving in the direction of respectability. But most homosexual activity – together with sadomasochism, fetishism, transsexuality, commercial sex, etc. – remains demonised and subject to harsh legal and social sanctions. The problem is, Rubin argues, that our culture lacks a concept of 'benign sexual variation'; sexual activities and sexual minorities are judged according to narrow, heteronormative standards. Instead, she suggests: 'A democratic morality should judge sexual acts by the way partners treat one another, the level of mutual consideration, the presence or absence of coercion, and the quantity and quality of the pleasures they provide' (1984, 283). From this perspective the specific nature of the sexual activity – gay or straight, coupled or in groups, commercial or free (etc.) – is unimportant. If the sexual act is conducted with due consideration for 'democratic morality', then it should not be subject to legal and other sanctions. In western culture, however, sex is a major 'vector of oppression' with effects akin to racism (Rubin 1984, 292). Although Rubin's argument is not connected to a discussion of citizenship, it clearly suggests that the operation of sexual norms will undermine the citizenship status of many groups and individuals.

This argument has been explicitly addressed over the last five years by several authors (Evans 1993; Plummer 1995; Richardson 1998; Weeks 1998) who have developed the concept of sexual or intimate citizenship. David Evans (1993), for example, examined the 'sexual citizenship' of homosexuals, bisexuals, transsexuals and others in the British context. He concluded that homosexuals have gained some new rights over the last two decades, particularly as private consumers in an expanded gay marketplace offering the accoutrements of a gay 'lifestyle'. In the public sphere, however, there has been a mobilisation 'of core moral values' which reify particular (hetero)sexual 'norms' and family arrangements. In this process homosexuals have been effectively marked out as non-members of the citizenship community.

Ken Plummer (1995, 183) has argued against Evans' conceptualisation of 'sexual citizenship' because of its exaggerated concern with the erotic. While also concerned with the situation of sexual minorities, Plummer prefers the concept of an 'intimate citizenship' that is more broadly focused on 'the kinds of relations we choose to have, the gender we express, the feelings we explore, the body, identity and the imagery we construct and gaze at'. Clearly, this approach includes, but is not exclusively concerned with, the impact of sexual practice on citizenship status. Plummer grafts his concept of intimate citizenship onto T.H Marshall's (1950) influential account of citizenship. Marshall suggests that three main 'bundles' of citizenship rights – civil, political and social – have emerged over the last two centuries in Britain. Plummer argues that a fourth tier of citizenship rights – associated with the intimate realm of relations, gender and the body – should now be added to this.

Plummer's approach has recently been utilised by Jeffrey Weeks (1998, 39), who argues that the concept of sexual or intimate citizenship has certain commonalities with claims for citizenship being made by other groups, such as women and racial or ethnic minorities. All these claims are 'about enfranchisement, about inclusion, about belonging, about equity and justice, about rights balanced by new responsibilities'. However, intimate or sexual citizenship is also different and important in its own right (Weeks 1998, 39–40). Weeks argues that the figure of 'the sexual citizen' brings into central focus some of the powerful changes in personal and everyday life that have occurred in western societies over the last three decades. These changes include a democratisation of relationships, especially male/female relationships, and the development of radically new narratives of self, identity and community appropriate to the conditions of late or post-modernity (Weeks 1998, 39–48).

Sexuality and Citizenship in Australia

What evidence is there in Australia that sexual norms are operating to marginalise and/or exclude certain individuals and groups thus diminishing their citizenship status? It can be argued that much progress has been made in recent years in the extension of citizenship rights to sexual minorities like lesbians, gays, queers and prostitutes. Over the last 20 years several states and territories – notably New South Wales, Victoria, the Australian Capital Territory and the Northern

Territory – have legalised various prostitution-related activities (Sullivan 1997). This represents a significant enlargement of the space where commercial sex may legally be enacted. The main benefit is likely to be experienced by sex workers who, for more than a century, have been the target of punitive laws against prostitution. For sex workers, stigmatised by the sexual component of their work, prostitution law reform presents the possibility of a real improvement in working conditions.[3] It also enables sex workers to seek legal redress in cases of sexual assault. This should be seen as an extension to sex workers of the equal treatment before the law that is a basic right of citizenship.

Over the last 30 years Australian laws against homosexuality have also undergone significant change. Laws which criminalised private, consensual homosexual acts between adult males (private, consensual homosexual acts between females have never been against the law) have been repealed in all Australian jurisdictions. South Australia was the first state to do this (in 1972) followed by the ACT (1976), Victoria (1980), the Northern Territory (1983), New South Wales (1984), Western Australia (1989), Queensland (1991) and Tasmania (1997). Law reform in Tasmania occurred after an appeal to the international Human Rights Committee and after the Commonwealth government enacted the *Human Rights (Sexual Conduct) Act* of 1994. This act prohibited any Australian jurisdiction from making laws in relation to 'sexual conduct involving only consenting adults acting in private'.

There have also been recent significant additions to Australian anti-discrimination law in the realm of sexuality. Discrimination on the grounds of 'sexual orientation', 'lawful sexual activity', and 'homosexuality or transsexuality' (the terminology varies) has been outlawed in all jurisdictions except Western Australia. A bill to outlaw discrimination on the grounds of sexuality and transgender identity is presently before the Senate of the Commonwealth parliament.[4] Since 1990, however, the (Commonwealth) Human Rights and Equal Opportunity Commission has been empowered to investigate complaints of discrimination on the grounds of sexual preference. In 1993 the Australian government lifted the ban on homosexuals in the armed forces (see Wills 1995), a significant move given the historical association between citizenship and the duty to bear arms on behalf of one's country. In 1994 the ACT outlawed discrimination on the grounds of 'occupation', a provision specifically designed to address the needs of sex workers. New South Wales also recently legislated against homosexual vilification while the new Victorian *Prostitution Control Act* (1995) specifically outlaws 'intimidating, insulting or harassing a prostitute' in a public place. In the Australian Capital Territory the *Domestic Relations Act* of 1994 established, for the first time in Australia, a legal recognition of same-sex relationships and due process for the adjudication of property and other disputes when same-sex relationships end.

All this would seem to suggest a gradual extension of rights, and equality of citizenship, to two important sexual minorities: gays and sex workers. There are, however, grounds for significant scepticism. Despite some legalisation of prostitution, the range and scope of Australia's prostitution laws has significantly increased over the last 50 years (see Sullivan 1997). Since 1945, but particularly since 1970, many more activities have been defined in law as 'prostitution' or as 'prostitution-related'. Much higher penalties have been introduced for most prostitution offences, particularly street soliciting, and laws have been extended to encompass male prostitutes and the clients of prostitutes. Even where prostitution transactions are conducted in private and between consenting adults they have been targeted by law. In the Northern Territory and in South Australia, it is against the law to receive payment for sexual relations conducted by adults in the privacy of their own home. In the Australian Capital Territory and in Victoria those who engage in home-based prostitution sex must register or be licensed by the appropriate bureaucracy (Sullivan 1997). While the *Human Rights (Sexual Conduct) Act* of 1994 prohibited any Australian jurisdiction from making laws in relation to 'sexual conduct involving only consenting adults acting in private', this legislation was not seen to be applicable to prostitution sex (Australia, H of R, 12 October 1994, 1779). A clear distinction was drawn in parliamentary debate between the legitimacy of private sexual acts where money was overtly exchanged and those where this did not occur (at least overtly). The former were seen as rightfully subject to law while the latter were not. Such assessments clearly rely on moral judgements about prostitution sex and those who participate in it. They also rely on a denial of the extensive sexual economic exchange involved in most 'normal' heterosexual relations, particularly marriage.

A range of related problems arise in relation to the citizenship rights of gays, lesbians and queers. While there has been a significant amount of law reform in this area, Australian law and public policy continues to reinforce heteronormativity and to treat homosexuals and same-sex relationships in a discriminatory fashion (see HREOC 1997a; Australia, Parliament 1997). Despite the decriminalisation of homosexual sex, the age of consent is much higher for homosexual than for heterosexual sex in many Australian jurisdictions. Higher ages of consent for sex between men and/or for anal sex exist in New South Wales, Queensland, Western Australia and the Northern Territory (Morgan 1995, 145). In Western Australia, for example, a person must be 21 years of age to consent to homosexual activities but can consent to heterosexual activities at 16 years of age.

Significant problems also flow from the lack of legal status accorded same-sex relationships. Under Australian law, heterosexual relationships have virtually the same legal status if the couple marry or if they live together in a de facto relationship; various entitlements and obligations proceed from this legal status. However, neither marriage nor de facto recognition are available to those in lesbian and gay relationships in most Australian jurisdictions. This leads to discrimination and disadvantage in a wide range of areas including social security, taxation, superannuation, inheritance, adoption, guardianship and custody, family leave, immigration and worker's compensation (see Lesbian and Gay Legal Rights Service 1994; Australia, Parliament 1997).

The disadvantage and discrimination sustained by gay, lesbian and queer citizens has usually been justified in the public sphere by (moral) judgments about the 'unnaturalness' of same-sex relations and by (conservative) political arguments about the need to sustain heterosexual norms, particularly in relation to families and young people. Even those who visibly support the rights of homosexuals will normally view this in quite limited terms. They may, for example, argue for equal respect and non-discrimination against homosexual persons and support the decriminalisation of homosexual sex but argue against the extension of the right to marry for same-sex partners (see Brennan 1998). Wayne Morgan (1995) has demonstrated that Australian laws which purport to extend 'equality' to non-heterosexuals are also actively involved in the reiteration of heterosexual norms and the construction of homosexuals as deviant and dangerous individuals. The Victorian *Equal Opportunity Act 1995*, for example, prohibits discrimination on the grounds of 'lawful sexual activity' but allows for exemptions, that is, ongoing discrimination, where there is genuine religious belief or in situations involving the care and supervision of children. Similar exemptions are to be found in other Australian anti-discrimination law. As Morgan argues (1995, 124), exemptions like these 'more than negate' the protection from discrimination offered to sexual minorities. They reinforce existing structures of power which produce 'mythologised and sanitised heterosex as the only acceptable form of sexuality' (Morgan 1995, 135). They also help to construct, 'as reasonable', widespread social beliefs about the dangerousness of homosexuals particularly with regard to children. So Morgan concludes (1995, 121) that anti-discrimination law in Australia is 'currently, at worst, homophobic and, at best, irredeemably heterosexist'. It certainly does not ensure equal treatment – or equal citizenship – for sexual minorities.

Conclusion

This analysis clearly suggests that problems exist in the contemporary constitution of Australian citizenship in so far as judgments about 'unnatural' sexual practices are deployed in public political life. The main ramifications are likely to be experienced by those who live on the borders of existing sexual 'norms', most notably lesbians, gay men, queers and prostitutes. But there are important implications for everyone in the deployment of theories and practices of citizenship which are unable to deal with the diversity of the Australian population – in this case related to sexual practice. Citizenship needs to be rethought in order to eliminate heteronormative assumptions, prevent discrimination against sexual minorities and ensure that richer conceptions of citizenship are available to all Australians.

Notes

1 The concept of 'queer' has assumed some prominence in the 1990s. It has been adopted as a term of self-description by those who pursue a politics of opposition to heteronormativity and who are critical of lesbian and gay identity politics (see Jagose 1996). Those who describe themselves as 'queer' may, then, have sexual relations with opposite and/or same-gender partners; they may be celibate, transgender, sex workers, or sadomasochists etc.
2 For a useful review of debates about the relationship between sexuality and gender see Pringle (1992). Also Sedgwick (1990) and Butler (1993).
3 For example, many sex workers now work in businesses covered by occupational health and safety regulations.
4 The Sexuality Discrimination Bill of 1995 was developed by the Australian Democrats and referred to the Senate Legal and Constitutional Committee. The committee presented its report in December 1997 (see Australia, Parliament 1997).

Further Reading

Evans, D.T. (1993). *Sexual Citizenship. The Material Construction of Sexualities.* London: Routledge.
Morgan, W. (1995). 'Still in the Closet: The Heterosexism of Equal Opportunity Law.' *Critical Inquiries*, 1(2), 119–46.
Richardson, D. (1998). 'Sexuality and Citizenship.' *Sociology*, 32(1), 83–100.
Sullivan, B. (1997). *The Politics of Sex. Prostitution and Pornography in Australia.* Cambridge: Cambridge University Press.
Weeks, J. (1998). 'The Sexual Citizen.' *Theory, Culture and Society*, 15(3–4), 35–52.

CHAPTER 15

Educational Citizenship

David Hogan

In *The Spirit of Laws* (1748), the great French political theorist Montesquieu describes the 'spirit' of 'democratic' or 'republican' forms of government – the governments of ancient Athens, Sparta and Rome in which 'the people are sovereign' or 'supreme' – as 'virtue' or 'love for the republic'. Given that the function of education was to 'prepare us for civic life', the ancients assumed that education in a republic should focus on the cultivation of 'virtue' (1977, 127):

> It is in a republican government that the whole power of education is required. The fear of despotic government rises naturally of itself amidst threats and punishments; the honor of monarchies is favored by the passions, and favors them in turn: but virtue is a self-renunciation which is always arduous and painful.
> This virtue may be defined, as the love of laws and of our country. As this love requires a constant preference of public to private interest, it is the source of all particular virtues; ...
> This love is peculiar to democracies. In these alone the government is entrusted to private citizens. Now government is like everything else: to preserve it, we must love it. (1977, 130)

Montesquieu much admired the ancient republics and the classical ideals of active citizenship and civic virtue. But he was also convinced that the social and political conditions that sustained them were long gone. The emergence of large nation-states, centralised bureaucracies, the expansion of trade and commerce, the division of labour, the new legitimacy of ambition and self-interest, growing social inequality, and the preference for private enjoyments had destroyed the classical nexus between size, simplicity, frugality, equality, virtue, liberty and participation. Modern republics were far more interested in the liberty of the citizen – 'the right of doing whatever the law permits' (1977, 200) – than in the cultivation of civic virtue and active citizenship. But, while a constitutional regime based on the 'separation of powers' (202) and 'democratic representation' (204) could do much to protect the liberty of subjects, such institutional devices were far from sufficient. The liberty of citizens also depended, at least in part, on 'civic virtue'.

In this chapter I want to use Montesquieu's distinction between ancient 'virtue' and modern 'liberty' to develop an account of citizenship and education that I am going to term 'republican'.[1] I take it that the central challenge confronting a republican theory of education is to reconcile the demands of 'liberty' and 'virtue', both suitably redefined, and to do so within a normative framework that does not violate core liberal democratic principles of justice and democratic self-determination. Specifically, I will argue that a 'republican' education is one that pursues three key objectives. It:

- provides all students, and all students equally, with meaningful opportunities to make informed and deliberative choices about the nature of their civil and civic interests that they have as interdependent members of a liberal democratic society, broadly defined (discussed in the first part of the chapter);
- develops the capacities that enable citizens to pursue and protect their civil and civic interests within the institutions of a liberal democratic society (second part); and
- develops the capacities and commitments that prompt and enable citizens to engage in those social and civic practices and forms of civic agency that maintain, improve or alter liberal democratic institutions in line with the requirements of democratic self-determination or what Amy Gutmann (1987, chs 1, 2) terms 'conscious social reproduction' (third part).

We start with the key aspects of the normative framework from which these principles are derived.

Normative Framework: Republican Liberty and the Theory of Interests

At the heart of contemporary liberal democratic theory is a particular notion of individual autonomy embedded in a broader account of the fundamental moral interests that individuals have by virtue of their status as persons and citizens. Since it is not possible here to trace the intellectual history of these concepts or their relationship to other key liberal democratic principles, I will instead, in a highly schematic way, briefly outline some of the key normative principles that underpin a contemporary republican theory of liberal democratic education.

1. Individuals, other things being equal, are the best judges of their own interests. This is essentially an empirical claim that centres on what Robert Dahl (1989, 100) calls the 'presumption of personal autonomy' but has only found wide acceptance in western societies since the seventeenth century.
2. The highest order interest of an individual is to live a life of his or her own choosing. That is, we value autonomy because we generally yearn to live a life that is authentically our own – of being true to ourselves and our own particular way of being. Charles Taylor puts the matter thus.

> There is a certain way of being human that is my way. I am called to live my life in this way, and not in imitation of anyone else's. But this notion gives a new importance to being true to myself. If I am not, I miss the point of my life: I miss what being human is for me. (Taylor 1994, 28, 30)

Thus, John Stuart Mill, for example, in the middle of the nineteenth century, defined liberty in terms of 'framing the plan of our life to suit our own character' so long as we do not cause others 'harm' and 'of pursuing our own good in our own way, so long as we do not attempt to deprive others of theirs, or impede their efforts to obtain it' (Mill 1989 [1859], 14–16). John Rawls (1973) too argues that our highest order interest is to lead an autonomous life and that an autonomous life consists of the capacity to form, revise and pursue our conception of the good, where the good is defined in terms of 'the satisfaction of rational desire' so long as we do not deny others an equal liberty. '[F]ree persons', Will Kymlicka suggests, 'conceive of themselves as beings who can revise and alter their final ends and who give first priority to preserving their liberty in these matters' (1991, 12–14). Indeed, Joseph Raz goes so far as to argue that at least in western societies, individual well-being is identified with, and presupposes, 'the ideal of personal autonomy' (Raz 1986, 375–6, 369, 381–5).
3. The highest order interest that persons have in living a life of their own choosing is by no means equivalent to saying that a person's interests, in a moral sense, are what they are interested in, in a psychological sense. Individuals can be, and often are, mistaken about their interests and desire things that are contrary to their interests. Preferring an object does not make the object good; rather, we prefer it because we believe it to be good. Merely wanting or desiring something is not by itself a reason to have it: we can always ask whether it is in the person's interest to have it.
4. The ability of persons to live lives of their own choosing depends, in part, on their ability to live according to principles and values that

they have freely and reflectively chosen. As Joseph Raz (1986, 369) suggests,

> the ruling behind the ideal of personal autonomy is the idea that people should make their own lives. The autonomous person is a (part) author of his own life. The ideal of a personal autonomy is the vision of people controlling, to some degree, their own destiny, fashioning it through successive decisions throughout their lives.

But contemporary liberal democratic notions of autonomy go beyond the presumption that each person is the best judge of his or her own interests. They also draw upon much older, essentially Stoic notions of reason, self-government and moral agency. In this tradition, autonomous persons are moral agents who reflect upon and pass judgment on their desires, actions and practices and who habitually live their lives in accordance with their considered judgments (Kymlicka 1991; Raz 1986; Dagger 1997; Taylor 1989).

5. The capacity to be autonomous requires more than the ability to reflect and pass judgment on one's desires and to live one's life according to principles one has freely chosen. It also requires the absence of arbitrary coercion, interference or domination. This is a much stronger – and far more republican – notion of liberty than normally associated with liberal democratic theory. The conventional liberal democratic notion of liberty, derived from Hobbes and Bentham and valorised in our time by Isaiah Berlin as a purely 'negative' concept, assumes that liberty is the absence of coercion or what Hobbes termed the 'silence of the law' or 'the absence of opposition'. But as Philip Pettit argues, it is not so much the absence of opposition that is a necessary condition for liberty but the absence of domination:

> Being unfree does not consist in being unrestrained ... the restraint of a fair system of law – a non-arbitrary regime – does not make you unfree. Being unfree consists rather in being subject to arbitrary sway: being subject to the potentially capricious will or the potentially idiosyncratic judgement of another. (Pettit 1997, 5)

6. The principle of autonomy derives its moral (as opposed to its existential) appeal from broader moral principles. While, historically, the principle of autonomy or self-determination has been supported by a range of arguments, three have been especially influential. One suggests that individuals deserve moral autonomy because they possess natural rights derived from natural law. Utilitarians, on the other hand, typically derive the principle of autonomy from considerations of individual or social utility. For Immanuel Kant, the

principle of autonomy is derived from the nature of the self, and specifically, from the status of individuals as persons or moral agents capable of moral deliberation, choice and action. For a contemporary neo-Kantian like John Rawls, citizens are 'free and equal persons' (1993, 14) who are free and equal by:

> virtue of their two moral powers (a capacity for a sense of justice and for a conception of the good) and the powers of reason (of judgement, thought, and inference connected with these powers) ... Their having these powers to the requisite minimum degree to be fully cooperating members of society makes persons equal (1993, 18–20)

and secures the principle of equal liberty and mutual respect. Consequently, the right to autonomy and self-determination is both the highest order interest that individuals have and prior to all other rights.

7. The value of liberty or autonomy is not independent of the purposes or ends that persons have or develop. As Joseph Raz suggests, liberty is not valuable merely 'because it is wanted. On the contrary, those who desire it do so because they believe that it is valuable, and only on condition that it is valuable' (Raz 1986, 390). In effect, we value autonomy because we value our interests. The value we place on freedom is derived from the fact that we are purposive beings and that our fundamental interest lies in pursuing our interests or purposes.

8. Individual interests are interdependent with the interests of others and embedded in, and constituted by, patterns of sociability and community life. The human condition is fundamentally and unavoidably a social condition in both an ontological and existential sense. Ontologically, human beings, their conceptions of a good life, their interests, purposes and projects, are socially constituted and historically patterned. Existentially, individual interests are interdependent with the interests of others and embedded in patterns of institutional and organisational life. Persons cannot realistically hope to satisfy their interests (to be loved and respected by others, for example) without at the same time recognising the need of others to have their interests respected (to be loved and respected in turn).

9. Individual conceptions of interests must satisfy a range of normative standards or principles of justice that limit in various ways the kinds of conceptions of interests or the good that are morally permissible and defensible in a liberal democratic community. For utilitarians like Jeremy Bentham, conceptions of interest were morally permissible so long as they did not violate the utilitarian maxim of the greatest good of the greatest number. John Stuart Mill, far more

sensitive to the dangers to individual liberty of the utilitarian standard than Bentham, believed that conceptions of interest that resulted in 'harm' to others were not morally permissible. Immanuel Kant set an even more demanding standard: conceptions of interest should not violate the principle of mutual respect or respect for persons. For John Rawls, closer to Kant than to Mill, the pursuit by individuals of their interests is limited by the equal right of all other citizens to frame and pursue their own conceptions of the good. Rawls terms this the principle of 'equal liberty' (Rawls 1972, ch. 4). For Joseph Raz, even this standard is not demanding enough. For Raz, conceptions of the good must also be supported by reasons that the community finds valid and persuasive. Merely desiring something is not a good enough reason for a community to accept it as morally valuable (Raz 1986, chs 6, 12, 14). This is a persuasive argument. From a republican perspective, for example, social practices associated with conceptions of interest must be consistent with the ability of a liberal democratic political community to be self-determining.

Framing Interests

The first part presents a republican account of interests, autonomy and justice. The next step in the argument is to derive, in an equally schematic way, a republican theory of education from this normative framework.

1. Given that the value of autonomy or liberty depends on the purposes or ends that persons have or develop, it follows that the value of liberty is also dependent on the ability and opportunity of persons to frame, revise, pursue and protect informed and reasonable conceptions of their good or interests as interdependent members of a liberal democratic community. Since the middle of the nineteenth century, liberal democratic societies, including Australia, have generally entrusted a major part of the responsibility for the development of informed and reasonable conceptions of interests to schools, and to public schools especially, on the assumption that churches and families could not, and in many instances, would not, do so. An *informed* conception of our interests is necessary because the value of our liberty depends in part on the opportunity to make meaningful and knowing choices from a capacious set of choices. For this we require an extensive understanding of the range of choices that we might make and a developed understanding of the consequences of making one choice rather than another. Amy Gutmann usefully describes this kind of governing principle of a democratic education as the principle of 'non-repression' (Gutmann 1987, 44). A *reasonable*

conception of our interests is necessary because we can and should demand that conceptions of interests be publicly defensible, and not merely subjectively desirable. This can be best accomplished, I will argue shortly, when the process of framing interests is both public and deliberative and when interest claims are limited by the requirements of justice and collective self-determination.
2. A republican education is also committed to the provision of those learning opportunities and resources that permit students to develop *political* conceptions of the civil as well as the civic interests. Young people have a broad range of civil interests, including access to a good education, steady employment, meaningful work and a reasonable income, having meaningful and successful relationships with intimates and friends, possessing physical and emotional health, securing the respect and esteem of others, and so on. Young people have civic interests as well, including a recognition of their rights, access to political information, and the provision of expansive opportunities to participate in the public life of their communities and the democratic process. But on a republican view of education, the conceptions of interests that students form ought not just be private but political in character – the framing of interests ought to be a process in which students are helped to develop a political understanding of their interests as members of a political community. This can be done by helping students understand how their interests are situated in, and affected by, the broader political context. As Nie, Junn and Stehlik-Barry suggest: in 'order for democracy to function, individual citizens must first be able to identify and understand their preferences and political interests' and 'to formulate considered policy preferences' (1996, 15, 16). If students lack such a conception of their interests or how these are affected by institutional arrangements and political developments, their ability to pursue, protect and realise their projects and purposes as adults will be significantly compromised.
3. Given the account of interests and education developed above, the process of framing interests in schools should be public and deliberative in character. Specifically, the framing of interests should conform to the standards of what John Rawls terms 'deliberative rationality' and others have more recently described as 'deliberative democracy'.[2] Public deliberation is a necessary condition for framing interests appropriate to the demands of justice and democratic self-determination. Developing an informed and reasonable conception of one's civil and civic interests requires processes of 'public deliberation' during which individual preferences and conceptions of individual interest are transformed as the participants take into

account the interests and preferences of others. John Dewey conceived of the classroom as a deliberative and democratic community of learning. An education for democracy, he insisted, must be an education *in* democracy conceived as a form of social life, a 'mode of associated living', a community of full participation and 'conjoint communicated experience' necessary for the development for social understanding, sympathy and deliberative moral reason (1964 [1916], 93). Schools and classrooms should be organised as inclusive and deliberative democratic communities of learning, not merely in their administration and governance, but in the everyday life of their classrooms. But if classrooms are to be organised as deliberative and democratic communities of learning, they cannot be organised, as they currently are, as a *manufactory of instruction and discipline* preparing the young for the world of work, a *haven in a heartless world* focused on protecting the needs of children, an ambient *playground* centred on what children are interested in, or finally, a *competitive meritocratic marketplace* focused on identifying, developing and sorting the 'pool of talent' necessary to maximise aggregate social utility.

Protecting Interests

The first task then of a republican character is the provision to all students, and all students equally, of those opportunities, resources and learning experiences necessary to the development of informed conceptions of their interests, both civic and civil, as interdependent members of a liberal democratic community. But the responsibilities of a liberal democratic education of a republican cast do not stop there.

The task of education is also to develop the capacities that all students, and all students equally, need to *pursue* and *protect* their interests in civil and civic society, in ways that satisfy the requirements of democratic equality and democratic citizenship. We might term this commitment the 'protective' aspect of citizenship education, which stems from protective conceptions of citizenship dating back to the seventeenth century. Contemporary protectionist conceptions of democratic citizenship come in a variety of models: the disengaged consumer (the so-called 'democratic elitist' model of Pareto, Michels and Schumpeter), the rational consumer (rational choice theory), judicial, and participatory. The democratic elitist model assumes that the modal (and even model) citizen is a disengaged, uninformed, essentially apathetic consumer who shops around in the political market at election time, if at all, for a party to support as the whim of the day suggests. Over the past couple of decades, rational choice theorists have developed a variant of this model that grants the citizen greater information and rationality than would Schumpeter. Citizens, they argue, are rational consumers who make rational political choices in line with their underlying preferences about how they want to distribute their time and resources, about the cost and benefits of political or civic participation, and about which political party offers the most appealing range of benefits.

'Judicial' models of protective citizenship are far more demanding of the civic capacities of citizens than either the Schumpeterian or rational choice models. The judicial citizen evaluates and judges the intentions, character and performance of his or her representative and assesses whether that representative acts in a way consistent with the principles of a liberal democracy, including the protection of the interests of all citizens in a fair and measured way. The good citizen is a judge, a watchdog, an ombudsman, a probing, watchful inspector who makes a judgment at the end of every electoral cycle on the performance of the people's representatives. Locke's good citizen is very much a civic judge. In more recent times, Stephen Macedo, among others, suggests that model liberal democratic citizens, as the source of political authority rather than its subject, constantly engage in 'interpreting the law and reviewing the decisions' of the lawmakers and act as 'conscientious interpreters and enforcers' of public morality. In fact, they are 'the ultimate judges' of the compliance of other citizens and the state to the 'social contract'. They employ the canons of 'public reason' rather than private prejudice to critically assess the performance of their representatives. Consequently, the good liberal democratic citizen is one possessed of those 'liberal virtues' or 'traits of character' appropriate for a liberal democracy:

> critical reflectiveness on public principles ... a reflective, self critical attitude, tolerance, openness to change, self control, a willingness to engage in dialogue with others, and willingness to revise and shape projects in order to respect the rights of others or in response to fresh insight into one's own character and ideals. (Macedo 1991, 128–29)

The participatory model of protectionist citizenship focuses less on 'judicial' expressions of civic agency than on active forms of participation in political society. Although the forms of participation are a far cry from those exercised in models of direct or 'strong' democracies, disciples of civic participation argue that through their active participation in political society – by following political developments, by contacting government officials, by writing letters to the editor, by calling talk-back radio, by voting, by joining political organisations, by supporting social movements, by protesting, by contributing money to political parties or causes, by signing petitions and so on – citizens give voice to their political preferences and seek to ensure the more effective representation and consideration of their interests in the political process. Verba, Schlozman and Brady describe the model in the following terms:

> Citizen participation is at the heart of democracy. Indeed, democracy is unthinkable without the ability of citizens to participate freely in the governing process. Through their activity citizens in democracy seek to control who will hold public office and to influence what the government does. Political participation provides the mechanism by which citizens can communicate information about their interests, preferences, and needs and generates pressure to respond.
> Voice and equality are central to democratic participation. In a meaningful democracy, the people's voice must be loud and clear – clear so that policymakers understand citizen concerns and loud so that they have an incentive to pay attention to what is said. Since democracy implies not only government responsiveness to citizen interests but also equal consideration of interests, democratic participation must also be equal. (Verba et al. 1995, 1)

Verba, Schlozman and Brady emphasise that political equality requires equal voice or power defined in terms of the equal representation and consideration of interests. It is this idea, for instance, that underlies the assumption in Australia that all citizens can be required by law to vote (or at least make an appearance at a voting booth) and the more general principle that all citizens have an equal right to vote. Democracy rests on the notion of the equal worth of each citizen, Verba, Schlozman and Brady note.

> The needs and preferences of no individual should rank higher than those of any other. This principle under-girds the concept of one person, one vote as well as its corollary, equality of political voice among individuals. On the presumption that those who are excluded from participation will be unable to protect their own interests and, thus, will receive less favourable treatment from the government, any system that denies equal participatory rights violates a fundamental principle of democracy. (1995, 10)

It is noteworthy that while Australians have an equal right to vote, they do not have a right to a vote of equal value: we have an equal right to 'one person, one vote' but we do not have a right to 'one person, one vote, one value'. Of course, the rendering of the principle of democratic equality as the equal representation and consideration of interests does not necessarily mean that the interests of each and every citizen will be equally satisfied – it merely means that the interests of all citizens should be equally represented and considered alongside the interest claims of everyone else.

The assumption that democratic equality requires equal voice has not gone unchallenged. Charles Beitz, for example, questions whether political equality necessarily requires that democratic institutions should provide citizens with equal procedural opportunities to influence political decisions, and even whether the political preferences expressed by each citizen should receive equal weight in every decision-making process. Instead, he suggests, the institutional arrangements for participation should be justifiable to each citizen, taking into account their core 'regulative interests' that arise from their dual roles as both the subjects of the sovereign power and as the source, agents or 'makers' of sovereign power (Beitz 1989, 99).

Advocates of 'active' forms of democratic citizenship have advanced far more ambitious accounts of the scope and justification of political participation and/or abandon, in varying degrees, the protective model of citizenship altogether. Among the former group, advocates of 'developmental' models of participation, going back to Rousseau and J.S. Mill, argue that participation in the public life of a democratic community is not merely protective but educative and morally transformative and for this reason especially, political and civic institutions should be designed so as to maximise the opportunities for participation. Among the latter group, deliberationists, communitarians, and civic associationists have been the most prominent. Advocates of deliberation, for example, suggest that the good citizen is one who participates in the work of the public (*res-publica*) and does so by deliberating collectively and often. Public deliberation, they argue, nurtures the development of genuinely 'public' solutions to public policy problems rather than a politically negotiated compromise or aggregation of private or individual interests.

A republican education then will educate its citizens to develop not only an informed political conception of their civic and civil interests, but also the capacities necessary to defend them. In part this is a matter of 'engaging' students in the political process to the point where they are able to identify and protect their interests effectively. Citizens who are not engaged will have greater difficulty recognising how their interests might be affected by various political developments. In addition, citizens also need a range of dispositions, identities, understandings and skills that allow them to participate effectively in the political life of a representative democracy in order that they might protect their legitimate interests as persons and citizens.

Not the least of the challenges confronting republican education, however, is that there is ample evidence that existing patterns of social inequality undermine the ability of citizens to participate effectively on equal terms in the democratic political process. The interaction between family background social inequalities and unequal schooling results in highly stratified patterns of political engagement and empowerment. Furthermore, educationally generated inequalities stratify access to, and participation in, the political system. In *Education and Democratic Citizenship in America*, Norman Nie and his co-writers (1996) suggest, for example, that:

> formal education influences political engagement by allocating scarce social and political ranks that place citizens closer to or further from the centre of critical social and political networks that, in turn, affect levels of political engagement. The rank to which individuals are assigned is the result of the impact of education on a long train of life experiences, including occupational prominence, voluntary associational membership, and family wealth. For political engagement, formal education works as a sorting mechanism, assigning ranks on the basis of the citizen's relative educational engagement. Relative education is not the absolute number of years attained but the amount of education attained compared to those against whom the citizen competes. (1996, 6)

Nie et al. explain that access to politically influential social networks is important because it structures the social distribution of political information and influence:

> The cost of political information, the price of staying tuned to politics, the difficulty of getting heard, and the ability to influence political outcomes vary dramatically depending upon where one is located in the social network. Because the components of engagement are more instrumental and essentially competitive in nature, what is most affected is the cost of that political engagement. In other words, through its influence on network position, education creates engaged citizens by cutting the cost of pursuing and protecting interests in politics. Perhaps the best analogy to social network centrality is the location of one's seat in a large amphitheatre – those in the front rows have little trouble hearing or being heard, identifying the actors on stage, and being recognised by them. However, for those in the rows in the rear of the theatre, it takes substantial effort to hear and identify the players and even greater effort to be heard by those on the political stage. (1996, 59–60)

These findings are not encouraging for those who take political equality seriously or who look to schools to help establish the institutional basis of political equality. In particular, they suggest that the institutional consequences of schooling deepen or strengthen the unholy alliance between social inequality, meritocratic schooling and stratified forms and levels of political participation. In so doing, inequalities of educational attainment undermine the promise of political equality or 'equal voice'.

Protecting Protection: Common Interests and Political Community

In his metaphysically troubled account of 'sovereignty' and the 'general will' in *The Social Contract*, Jean-Jacques Rousseau (1967 [1762]) introduces a distinction between the 'will of all' and 'the general will' that presupposes a useful distinction between the particular interests that men [sic] have as individuals and the 'general' or 'common' interests that they have as citizens and members of a democratic political community (ch. 3). Now is not the time to pursue Rousseau's metaphysical speculations or devise a theoretical alchemy to resolve the difficulties he gets himself into, but I do want to make use of his distinction between the 'particular' and 'common' interests of citizens as a way of introducing the third major responsibility of a republican model of liberal democratic education. I speak of the responsibility to develop the capacities and commitments that prompt and enable citizens to engage in a range of social and civic practices and forms of agency necessary to maintain, improve or alter liberal democratic institutions in ways that protect and promote the highest order interests of all citizens within the limits of conscious social reproduction.

One of the standing charges levelled at conventional liberal democratic protective models of citizenship is that they lack an adequate understanding of the social and civic preconditions of a viable political community. Communitarians ask, for example, what the point of a culture of autonomy is if it fails to secure and protect the institutions that sustain it. More broadly, they suggest that a viable political community requires various kinds of 'common social goods' – a substantive and comprehensive notion of the common good, a particular ensemble of civic virtues, strong forms of civic identity, extensive participation in the civic life of the political community – that develop attachments, form identities, confer dignity, create disciplines of self-government, motivate social action, and inform conceptions of the good, interests and the self. A viable political community thus requires a form of citizenship that is different, or at least far broader, than a form of citizenship based on a rational calculus of the costs and benefits of social co-operation characteristic of merely protective forms of citizenship. It requires a conception of citizenship that emphasises a sense of attachment to, and identity with, a historically specific political community with its particular traditions and values. In addition, it requires a willingness to promote a kind of politics in which active citizens and duly constituted democratic majorities develop and pursue a particular substantive conception of the common good that is prior and superordinate to individual desires and interests. In effect, a viable political community requires a commitment to the development of forms of citizenship that jettison the liberal democratic model of protective citizenship in favour of communitarian forms of citizenship and citizenship education that enhance the attachment of citizens to the political community in order to promote 'social integration' and 'the common good'.

Contemporary civic republicans also worry about the thinness of liberal democratic conceptions of citizenship and political community, but they are generally not willing to abandon the liberal democratic commitment to individual autonomy and pluralism in favour of the communitarians' 'comprehensive' notions of the common good. Liberal democratic accounts of liberty as individual autonomy are rich and valuable. But liberal democratic theory fails to recognise that the protection of liberty involves protecting and improving the institutions that provide protection. The fantasy of the 'neutral state' that so beguiles some liberal democratic theorists would fail to secure the conditions that protect and secure autonomy. Others – Will Kymlicka, Joseph Raz to name two – have responded to these concerns by arguing for a 'perfectionist', but pluralist (or 'non-exclusionary'), state committed to supporting the cultural practices and institutional arrangements necessary for the exercise of individual autonomy. Republican theorists, however, argue that this concession doesn't go far enough and suggest that a 'republican' state is necessary to protect liberty and a culture of autonomy. The liberty of citizens not only depends on a state sympathetic to principles of autonomy, pluralism and equal liberty, it also requires their active involvement in the 'public life of the city'. Quentin Skinner and Philip Pettit, for example, endorse Rawls' account of the importance of individual autonomy and equal liberty, but insist that Rawls ignores a different conception of liberty in the civic republican tradition, and a civic republican argument going back to Cicero, that the security of liberty depends on the rule of law and the exercise of civic virtue understood in terms of public service, duty and devotion to the public good. The priority of liberty, Skinner (1990) concludes, cannot be absolute, for it necessarily presupposes a range of civic institutions and practices that promote a commitment to *res-publica* – the work of the public – and help protect liberty and secure 'a free way of life'.

How then might a republican education promote the 'common interests' of citizens without sacrificing their 'particular interests' or falling prey to the anti-pluralism of communitarianism? How might it simultaneously and without contradiction pursue individual liberty and civic virtue? In broad terms, it requires a form of education that is committed to the development of those social practices and forms of agency that promote an understanding of, and commitment to, republican and liberal democratic principles, strong but pluralistic forms of civic identity, and active and deliberative forms of civic agency. These objectives are recursively linked. Active forms of civic agency, for example, are both cause and effect of strong civic identities. Indeed, in my view, the development of appropriate forms of civic agency and civic identity provides the key to effective forms of republican education. A republican education should seek to foster forms of civic identity that acknowledge individual autonomy, social pluralism and civic membership. As Chantal Mouffe suggested,

> What we share and makes us fellow citizens in a liberal democratic regime is not a substantive idea of the good but a set of political principles specific to such a tradition: the principles of freedom and equality for all ... To be a citizen is to recognise the authority of such principles and the rules in which they are embodied, to have them informing our political judgement and our actions ... It implies seeing citizenship not as a legal status but as a form of identification, a type of political identity ... that is created through identification with the *respublica* [the work of the public]. (1993, 65–6)

She concludes that:

> what binds them together is their common recognition of a set of ethico-political values. In this case, citizenship is not just one identity among others, as in liberalism, or the dominant identity that overrides all others, as in civic republicanism. It is an articulating principle that affects the different subject positions of the social agent ... while allowing for a plurality of specific allegiances and for the respect of individual liberty. (69–70)

Similar views have been expressed in Australia by Donald Horne (1989) and Chandran Kukathas (1993) among others.

A republican educational strategy needs also to focus on the expansion of opportunities for participation in the life of the school as a political community, above all those forms of participation that permit and promote the development of deliberative forms of civic agency. It is here that the 'developmental' and 'deliberationist' models of democratic citizenship again come into their own in education, apart from their role in the framing of interests (see for example, Dewey 1927; Gutmann 1987).

Conclusion

I have sought in this chapter to develop a republican version of a liberal democratic education that reconciles, metaphorically speaking, 'virtue' with 'liberty'. I have suggested that 'liberty' understood as autonomy and self-determination constitutes the highest order good of individuals conceived as persons and members of liberal democratic communities. I have also argued that 'liberty' cannot flourish without 'virtue'; virtue is necessary to protect liberty within the institutions of a representative democracy, and to protect and improve the institutions that protect liberty and make possible 'conscious social reproduction'. Our children's liberty and the survival of a democratic political community depend on schools commited to both liberty and virtue.

Notes

1 This chapter is a contribution to the republican revival in education. In writing this chapter, I have drawn freely on a series of papers that I have published over the past several years. See, for example, Hogan, Fearnley-Sander, and Lamb (1996); Hogan (1996; 1997a, b, c).
2 On the theory of deliberative democracy, see Bohman and Rehg (1997).
3 For an exceptional discussion of the distinction between agency and practice, see Emirbayer and Mische (1998).

Further Reading

Callan, E. (1997). *Creating Citizens: Political Education and Liberal Democracy.* Oxford: Clarendon Press.
Nie, N., J. Junn and K. Stehlik-Barry (1996). *Education and Democratic Citizenship in America.* Chicago: University of Chicago Press.
Pettit, P. (1997). *Republicanism: A Theory of Freedom and Government.* Oxford: Clarendon Press.
Verba, S., K. Schlozman and H. Brady (1995). *Voice and Equality.* Cambridge, Mass.: Harvard University Press.

CHAPTER 16

Citizenship and Military Service

April Carter

Citizenship in its Greek and Roman origins was inextricably linked to the ability to bear arms to defend the city state, and the idea that citizens should be ready and able to fight has been central in countries such as France and Israel. But the renewed interest in citizenship in the 1990s, both in Australia and in the USA and Britain, has not included discussion of military service as a potentially central obligation of citizens. The purpose of this chapter is to examine some of the theoretical as well as immediate political reasons for this omission and to suggest that military service is still an important issue for examination in discussions of citizenship. A satisfactory interpretation of citizenship requires us to grasp both the symbolic and political significance of seeing military service as a citizen's central duty, and to consider what defence of the polity entails today.

There are a number of possible reasons why contemporary debates in countries like the USA and Australia are not concerned about the relationship between citizenship and the duty to bear arms. I have chosen here to focus on three possible theoretical explanations. The first is that a republican conception of citizenship, derived from the intense political life of the city-states, can now be seen as an anachronism, irrelevant to the world of nation-states and even more irrelevant in the increasingly interdependent world of the late twentieth century. Commentators today who are sympathetic to republicanism have tended to focus on the importance of people taking part in the public political sphere, not on the citizen as soldier. The second is that discussion of citizenship in Australia or North America has generally drawn on liberal ideas inherited originally from Britain, which understand citizenship almost exclusively in terms of individual rights or interests. The third is that the assumption that citizens share a common set of beliefs and values to be defended has been questioned by feminists and other theorists arguing for 'differentiated citizenship'. I examine briefly theories of citizenship drawing on republicanism, Anglo-American liberalism and a politics of difference, and argue that in each case there are arguments for a common responsibility for defence of the polity. I also note that in the past feminists have seen women's contribution to war as significant in demonstrating their citizenship and that since the 1970s some feminists have claimed the right and duty to bear arms.

In Australia, where debate about republicanism has become animated, intellectual energy has focused on the relationship with the Crown, constitutional implications and national identity, and on disentangling the various historical and contemporary strands in republican thought. But consideration of how Australia's experience of war has been interpreted, and in particular the 1995 commemoration of the fiftieth anniversary of the end of the Second World War, suggests not only that military myth is important in constructing Australian republicanism, but also that despite the hostility to conscription the ideal of the citizen soldier has a continuing resonance. It is therefore relevant to ask about the implications of that ideal for conceptions of citizenship in Australia.

Is the Ideal of the Citizen-Soldier an Anachronism?

Western debates about democracy and citizenship often look back to their origins in classical Greece and Rome, and it is therefore still of interest that citizenship originally entailed the automatic duty to defend the city. Hornblower argues: 'for Greeks and Romans political and military categorization were always close. Women did not fight, which helps to explain the automatic ancient assumption that they should not vote either' (Hornblower 1993, 7–8). That connection was maintained in the later evolution of the western republican tradition of thought: Machiavelli (1969) in *The Discourses* looked back to republican Rome and extolled the qualities of a citizen militia; Harrington grounded his ideal English republic on independent men of (landed) property ready to bear arms (Pocock 1975); and Rousseau applauded martial virtues, especially in his *Discourse on the Arts and Sciences*. By the eighteenth century the ideal of the citizen-soldier in a city-state, though still inspirational, might be seen as decreasingly relevant to the modern age of liberal individualism and the nation-state. The two great eighteenth-century revolutions, in America in 1776 and in France in 1789, nevertheless both embodied transmuted forms of republicanism. Springborg argues: '[m]ilitary effectiveness may also have been a primary motivation for the American and French republics which were self consciously modelled on classical forms. Once again the deal was struck: civil rights for military service' (Springborg 1993, 205). The republican heritage was more obvious in the French Revolution, which explicitly called its citizens to arms (as in the words of the 'Marseillaise'), but it has been argued that there is a republican strand within the American Revolution – for example, Jefferson's belief in the key role of small farmers bearing arms in upholding the republic (Rahe 1992). The inclusion of the famous clause in the United States constitution which guarantees the right to bear arms was intended to enshrine citizens' responsibility to defend the republic from internal or external enemies.

At the end of the twentieth century does a republican ideal drawing on a tradition originating in classical Greece and Rome still have any significance? It might well seem that the answer is 'no'. The country in Europe that comes closest to representing this republican ideal is Switzerland, which is often taken as an exemplar of participatory democracy and which relies heavily for its defence on a citizen army that undergoes periodic military training. Yet some of Switzerland's political and military arrangements, as opposed to its financial institutions, have a distinctly premodern cast. For example Swiss men did not grant women the vote at a national level until 1971 and one of its local cantons only agreed to let women vote in 1992.

There are, however, strands in contemporary political thought which connect with the inheritance of European republicanism. Feminist commentary on citizenship has suggested the continuing power of the image of the citizen-soldier (Hartsock 1982; Voet 1994, 61, 75), but this might be seen as a negative critique of historical baggage associated with citizenship rather than evidence that old-fashioned republicanism is still a positive force. Second, republicanism as a reassertion of the importance of the public sphere and of active political citizenship has been a significant element in North American communitarian critiques of excessive liberal individualism since the 1970s. Although contemporary republican formulations tend to emphasise political rather than military responsibility, a participatory democrat like Benjamin Barber is also prepared to argue the logic of compulsory citizen service, which could take the form of military training (Barber 1984). Amitai Etzioni's (1995) call in the 1990s for a new sense of communal solidarity and civic responsibility includes a proposal for compulsory service.

It should also be noted that in France and some other West European countries the tradition of citizens in arms and a willingness to accept the logic of conscription has been much more pronounced than in the liberal English-speaking world. Kymlicka and Norman suggest in a survey of citizenship theory that 'mandatory national service' on the European model could be one radical measure to promote a public-spirited citizenry (1994). The support for compulsory military service often represents not only a belief in the citizen-soldier but profound popular distrust of professional military elites. The fear that professional or 'mercenary' armies may be used to subvert the republic provides one strong argument for training citizens to fight. Another is the desire to avoid unnecessary wars. Since the end of the eighteenth century, republicanism has often been associated, not with celebration of war, but with a concern that citizens should ensure that only just wars are fought by their governments. This concern requires citizens to have some leverage on government decision-making on war and peace; the most effective leverage, republicans have believed, has been the refusal to fight in unjust wars. This was the position enunciated in *Perpetual Peace* (1795) by Kant, who saw citizen responsibility for the laws and for decisions on war and peace as the means to his cosmopolitan vision of a peaceful world based on a confederation of republics. (Belief that a citizen army will resist unnecessary or unjust wars, like the war in Vietnam, is a specific element in Barber's arguments for citizen military service.)

It might be argued therefore that the intense patriotism associated with the republicanism of the city-state is incompatible with contemporary trends towards a global society, but that a modern republicanism linking civic responsibility to internationalism may be a means of promoting such a society. The citizen-soldier has quite often been seen within this mode of thought not only as the most reliable defender of the republic, but as the best guarantor that states themselves will respect the rules of international society.

The idea embodied in the citizen-soldier can therefore be seen as still relevant to contemporary republicanism on two grounds. First, because it signifies willingness to subordinate self-interest to the public good and a conception of active citizenship, and because it entails a commitment to defend the republic against both internal and external enemies. Peacetime military training of citizens may seem unnecessary on military grounds, or may be seen as positively undesirable, because it invades personal liberty or because training of adults in use of arms could in some divided societies increase the potential for armed violence. The question then arises whether there are non-violent and political methods of achieving these goals. How far can citizens prevent the corruption of public life or the onset of tyranny, either through active political participation or by non-violent methods of resistance? The general strike for example has been a method used by citizens this century to resist coups d'état.

Second, a contemporary republicanism that incorporates the idea of democratic control over defence and foreign policy as a guarantee of international principles, and stresses that republics should fight only in genuinely just wars, requires political equivalents of the citizen bearing arms – for example, democratic devices to ensure some popular control over defence and foreign policy. Whether such popular control will necessarily lead to the results envisaged by republican theory is a question beyond the scope of this chapter.

Liberalism and Military Service

The liberal tradition that has been dominant in the English-speaking world has, because of its stress on individual freedom and constitutional limitations on government power, tended to treat democracy as a means of guaranteeing security for individual rights and interests and of curbing arbitrary power, rather than stressing individual responsibility to participate in formulating the public will or individual duty to the polity. English-speaking countries have also been free from the constant threat of military invasion – the navy has been more important than the army. So both ideological and military considerations have contributed to excluding serious discussion of military service in liberal versions of citizenship in the USA or Britain. Locke, the founding father of this kind of liberalism, mentions military service only to argue that even soldiers (who can be commanded to risk death) should not be subject to arbitrary power in their personal lives (Locke 1955 [1690], 188–9). From the seventeenth to the twentieth centuries the central issue in the English-speaking world has been the extension of civil and political rights. Since 1945 the major question has been how extensively or effectively social rights can be incorporated within the context of a market economy, and in Australia the extension of citizen rights of Aborigines has become crucial since the 1970s.

There is another strand in English liberalism that has also influenced the approach to military service, and that is a strong hostility to war as inhuman, wasteful of lives and resources and fundamentally irrational. War has been seen as the product of outdated aristocratic and military elites or the result of sinister interests operating behind the scenes of representative government. This line of thinking stretches from Bentham at the end of the eighteenth century to early twentieth century writers like Norman Angell who attacked arms manufacturers. So although liberals have generally accepted that the state has a necessary role in defending the population, English and American liberalism has also prompted anti-war sentiment.

There has been some discussion by contemporary liberal theorists in the USA of the obligation to fight, largely prompted by conscription for the Vietnam War. But it might be seen as typical of this kind of liberal approach to military service that the primary focus of the debate has been the individual's right to *refuse* to fight on conscientious grounds. This is the context in which the most important contemporary American theorist of liberalism, John Rawls, approaches military service (Rawls 1973, 380–81). The Vietnam War also focused attention on the importance of distinguishing between just and unjust wars.

Some English liberals have in the past taken a more positive approach. They have been willing not only to make a sharp distinction between a genuinely defensive war and other wars, but also to discriminate more broadly between just and unjust wars – for example, to support wars to end tyranny and suppression of rights. J.S. Mill falls into this latter category, criticising some of his pacifist liberal contemporaries and supporting war to curb aggression or to uphold just ends, including support for national self-determination. Mill was also prepared to endorse a citizen army on the Swiss model, both in order to avoid the dangers of internal despotism stemming from professional armies and to minimise the danger of unjust wars being fought (Mill 1963 [1866], vol. 16, 1224–5). Rawls is, if somewhat cursorily, prepared to suggest that international principles of justice should sometimes be upheld by going to war. He claims conscription, as a serious attack on individual liberty, is justified only 'if it is demanded for the defense of liberty itself' either of citizens of that society, or of individuals in other societies. He then goes on to argue that 'if a conscript army is less likely to be an instrument of unjustified foreign adventures, it may be justified on this basis alone' (Rawls 1973, 380).

Both J.S. Mill and Rawls are thus prepared to lean towards a modern republican view of citizen obligation to bear arms, not only to defend the country but to uphold international principles, and also to consider the argument that a citizen army is a bulwark against military or political elites embarking on unjust wars. Therefore even within British and American liberalism there are theorists who recognise the force of a republican case for a citizen army and popular control over the decision to go to war. In neither case is liberalism based on an extreme individualism; instead it entails a sense of reciprocal obligations within a society, and an international perspective based on a belief in just wars rather than pacifism.

To sum up, although mainstream English-speaking liberalism is in general either oblivious or hostile to the arguments for the responsibility of citizens to bear arms, there are significant exceptions. It can also be argued that liberal concepts of citizenship depend upon a usually implicit sense of a shared political community. Hindess has suggested that beneath T.H. Marshall's account of citizenship as the extension of civil, political and socioeconomic rights: 'it is not difficult to discern the model of the community as a democratic republic that

Western politial thought has inherited from the civic republicanism of early modern Europe' (Hindess 1993, 26–7). Rawls has indeed moved towards a sense of historically specific societies in which a concept of citizenship is embedded in existing institutions (Rawls 1993).

Common Citizenship or Differentiated Citizenship?

It is precisely the reality of such a shared political community, however, or the possibility of equal access to a public sphere, that has been questioned by the exponents of 'differentiated citizenship'. Although their approach links up with contemporary beliefs about multiculturalism, it stems from a more radical critique. Representatives of aboriginal peoples and other ethnic groups subjected to exclusion and discrimination, and many feminists, have questioned the ideal of 'universal' citizenship within the state, arguing that it implicitly privileges white and masculine definitions of the public sphere. One of the best-known theorists of an alternative ideal of differentiated citizenship is Iris Marion Young, who argues for specific group representation and veto rights to ensure a genuine voice to groups previously excluded from the dominant understanding of citizenship and political community (Young 1989). From this perspective a concept of citizenship based on common duties to the political community appears outdated, and belief in a citizen's duty to bear arms in the event of war particularly problematic.

One possible response is that even a concept of differentiated citizenship must presuppose some kind of shared public sphere where decisions affecting the whole society are made, and if so, there are common interests in maintaining a constitution acceptable to the different groups and defending that political sphere from internal and external attack. The only alternative is disintegration. Young's critique of 'universal citizenship' clearly springs from disillusionment with a republican conception of politics. Her aim is not to promote fragmentation but to ensure that a wider range of voices are heard in political debates and that groups can have a decisive say if theirs are the interests most affected by public decisions. Whether her definition of groups requiring special representation and veto rights is satisfactory, and whether her specific political proposals are realistic, can be debated. But in principle she appears to be trying to redefine the public sphere, not destroy it. Her approach is also consistent with trying to increase democratic input into decisions about defence or foreign policy.

A second possible response to the view that differentiated citizenship excludes common interests in defending the polity is that previously excluded groups may be highly motivated to defend a system that *does* recognise their rights, especially against threats to undermine or overthrow it. Moreover their experience of political organisation and protest to achieve their rights may provide a basis for future defence of the political system, *provided* they believe they are becoming full citizens and maintain a culture of activism. Both these provisos are major ones, as the present position of African-Americans in the USA suggests. Young's thought reflects the political protests of the 1960s and 1970s rather than American society today.

Third, it could also be argued that groups who have been excluded are predisposed to an internationalist perspective on citizen obligations, because they are especially sensitive to issues of injustice. Feminists, for example, have been willing to exert pressure to try to uphold justice for women at an international as well as a national level. African-Americans in the United States were particularly inclined to oppose the Vietnam War, not only because they were aware of injustice in the way the draft operated to throw many of them into the frontline, but also because they tended to see the war as a white man's imperialist war against an Asian country.

Differentiated citizenship may therefore in some instances strengthen a contemporary internationalist interpretation of republicanism, though internal divisions may also make agreement about the role of the state in international affairs more difficult.

Women As Soldiers

Although many feminists reject the citizen-soldier image, some (especially in the United States) have pressed for women to be allowed to enter the armed forces on the same basis as men. In most western countries women are now able to undertake almost all military tasks – the main exception is (usually) fighting in the front line in the infantry. The Gulf War of 1991 was arguably the first major war where a significant number of women were sent as soldiers into the area of operations (Muir 1993, 24, 47–8). Australia allowed women into combat-related roles in 1990, and since a 1992 review women are able to occupy 99 per cent of roles in the Air Force and to serve on most naval ships (Department of Defence 1991–92, 26–7). This new position of women in the armed services is in striking contrast to their supportive tasks in women's auxiliary services in the Second World War and to the dominant image of women as nurses. It contrasts even more strongly with maternal concepts of citizenship stressing women's contribution as mothers which feminists in Australia often projected before 1914.

The main arguments for allowing women into the armed services have been liberal arguments for equal rights and equal opportunities.

Since the question is the roles that women may play in the professional armed services, the focus has been primarily on job opportunities, not on citizenship duties. The American liberal feminist National Organization for Women (NOW) did raise the question of women's availability to be conscripted as a question of citizenship in 1981. NOW filed a legal brief (unsuccessfully) challenging the constitutionality of requiring only men to register for the draft (Elshtain 1987, 239). But women's right or duty to be conscripted has not been an issue in Australia, where conscription is not on the agenda. (In the Vietnam War there was no question of conscripting women to fight.)

Women who do not aspire to fight alongside men have, however, been sensitive to the significance of commemorating their contribution to the war effort in order to establish their claim to citizenship. Speck, in an examination of women's war memorials and citizenship in an Australian context, traces how women's groups commissioned war memorials after the First World War. She comments; 'commemoration was as important for the women citizens as it was for the men because it recognised how the women had responded patriotically to the call for war' (Speck 1996, 133).

Republicanism and the Second World War in Australia

The Australian celebrations of the fiftieth anniversary of the end of the Second World War in 1995 had much in common with those held in other western liberal democracies. The public ceremonies remembering those who fought in the war, in particular those who sacrificed life or health, were occasions for contrasting (if only implicitly) self-interested individualism and political apathy with the civic virtue of those who abandoned private concerns for necessary public duty. In fact, official ceremonies commemorating war in western liberal countries always draw on sentiments that still seem close to the republican view that those who die for their country deserve special honour. Remembering war is also an opportunity to praise qualities which are still needed for citizenship that may be notably absent in contemporary society.

The Second World War was used in Australia to promote a new sense of national and republican identity that also drew on the inspiration of citizens sacrificing themselves for a common good. For example, Paul Keating said in his speech at the Australia Remembers concert in Melbourne on Sunday, 13 August 1995: 'If we want to know what it means to be Australian we can turn to them' (ABC Television). The emphasis on common purpose was, however, combined in 1995 with awareness that excluded groups should be recognised. The most obvious way to do this was to stress their contribution to the war effort and their share of suffering. Hence media coverage and the ceremonies themselves gave prominence to the role of women, and recognised the role played by Aborigines. It was, of course, more difficult to incorporate immigrant communities who may not always have been on the same side.

Commemoration of the Second World War could also plausibly be combined with contemporary republican concerns about upholding international principles of justice. The Second World War was the only war Australia has fought that was clearly a just war in terms of two key criteria. First, it was a war to uphold the principles of democracy and liberty against fascism (whereas the First World War could more plausibly be seen as an imperialist war), and the Australians who volunteered to fight can therefore be seen as citizen-soldiers upholding universal principles of justice. Second, when Japan threatened Australia directly, the war was also unambiguously a defensive war, requiring citizens to take up arms to defend their territory and their political independence.

Implications for a Contemporary Concept of Citizenship

Although ceremonies in remembrance of old wars can be seen as exercises in nostalgia, or elite oversimplifications of a complex war experience for current political purposes, it seems reasonable to claim that they also have considerable symbolic and political significance for current understandings of citizenship. What is being celebrated is a sense that there should be more to political life than voting for the party which offers the lowest taxes. Indeed, focusing on the extreme model of citizen duty, risking death for one's country or for central political principles, can be used to highlight the importance of more commonplace but crucial citizen duties – voting responsibly and paying taxes willingly in order to promote what is understood to be the public interest.

But there is another reason for taking seriously the symbolism of the citizen-soldier. If this dimension to politics is ignored in mainstream political life (except when commemorating past wars), the urge to belong to a political community and to undertake heroic political action may be channelled into extremely illiberal forms. The rise of xenophobic nationalisms throughout Europe is ironically the obverse side of the historical triumph of liberalism and capitalism over Soviet-style communism. In the United States the growth of right-wing militias seems to signal a reassertion of old-fashioned republicanism in conjunction with an explicit racist and masculinist view of republican identity. Australia may be less vulnerable to either extreme, although

European nationalist antagonisms can provide a negative form of differentiated citizenship, and some Australians appear receptive to American right-wing appeals. If, then, the republican debate has created the possibility of reconceptualising what it means to be an Australian citizen, it might be wise to consider seriously the part that military service should play in any new definition.

Further Reading

Burk, J. (1995). 'Citizenship Status and Military Service: The Quest for Inclusion by Minorities and Conscientious Objection.' *Armed Forces and Society*, 21(4), 503–29.

Carter, A. (1998). 'Liberalism and the Obligation to Military Service.' *Political Studies*, 46(1), 68–81.

Pringle, H. (1997). 'The Making of an Australian Civic Identity: The Bodies of Men and the Memory of War.' In G. Stokes (ed.), *The Politics of Identity in Australia*. Cambridge: Cambridge University Press, 92–104.

Woolacott, A. (1996). 'Women Munitions Makers, War and Citizenship.' *Peace Review*, 8(3), 373–78. Special Issue on Women and War.

CHAPTER 17

Media Citizenship

Elizabeth van Acker

A well-known film actor used to say: 'The trouble with movies as art is that they're a business; and the trouble with movies as a business is they're an art'. The same could be said, *mutatis mutandis*, about the media and citizenship. The mass media have tried to serve both God (in this case the public God) and mammon, and suffered unavoidable confusion as a result. Private interest (the profit imperative) in this domain must struggle with and try to accommodate a presumed public function closely connected to an ideal of citizenship.

Traditional notions of citizenship presuppose that public discussion is essential to the political processes in which citizens engage. In liberal democratic countries like Australia, the organs of the mass media have always assumed particular importance as providers of the effective channels of communication that allow discussion to proceed: a free nation, it is said, requires a free press. The media, in fact, have been held to perform several vital citizenship functions: keeping citizens informed about their own nation and the world; supporting their (admittedly limited) participation in representative government through intensive political and electoral coverage; providing a forum for meaningful public debate by allowing access to the most diverse sets of opinions; acting as a watchdog on public and private wrong-doings detrimental to citizens' interests; defending the rights of citizens (individual or collective) by publicising encroachments upon them; and fostering and expressing 'public opinion' thereby turning it into effective 'public pressure'. The mass media assumed a certain leadership role in that they were expected not merely to reflect public opinion, but to mould it responsibly. A further expectation was that they would express the spirit and wield the symbols capable of creating a sense of regional and national identity among the citizen audience.

This, of course, was the ideal picture. Reality has naturally fallen short of it. Instead of informing, the media have too often misinformed (or diluted their messages under the rubric of 'infotainment'); instead of elevated debate they have given us down-market sensationalism; instead of pursuing investigative accountability they have often been either lax or politically servile; instead of expressing diverse views they have frequently been dogmatically mono-vocal; instead of defending rights they have tended to invade them; and instead of exerting a responsible leadership function they have too often merely pandered to popular prejudices. Much of this can be blamed on the aforementioned commercial imperatives which operate powerfully on media that are largely privately owned, distorting their presumed social functions. Some have even sought to repudiate the public role altogether. Rodney Tiffen provides an extreme quote from a former publisher of the *Wall Street Journal* that is worth repeating here:

> A newspaper is a private enterprise owing nothing whatever to the public, which grants it no franchise. It is therefore affected with no public interest. It is emphatically the property of the owner, who is selling a manufactured product at his own risk. (Tiffen 1994, 61)

Ownership and control of the traditional mass media, moreover, have tended over time to become intensely concentrated. It is composed of huge conglomerate enterprises (occasionally government owned) that are remote from, and difficult of access by, ordinary citizens. For these and other reasons, Tiffen concludes that the 'hero of democratic theory – the well-informed, rationally participating citizen – is thus revealed as something of a myth' (Tiffen 1994, 56). He also observes that, given the important link that the mass media represents between governors and governed in a liberal democracy, and given the anomalies mentioned, democratic theory has been strangely silent on the topic.

The theoretical question is now further complicated by profound alterations in the object of inspection. Julianne Schultz (1994, 32) writes that '[t]echnological innovation will collapse the boundaries between telecommunications, computing, broadcasting and print media, just as the boundaries between information and entertainment have already eroded'. She notes the relaxed attitude of the 1993 Commonwealth parliamentary inquiry into concentration of ownership of the media, which argued that technological innovation will permit an array of new services, reduce the barriers of entry, and increase diversity (1994, 32). Things have moved rapidly in this direction since then. People who in the past were totally dependent upon the mass media for access to and information about public and societal affairs are daily becoming much less so.

Some commentators have expressed expectations that citizenship will be radically enhanced by these innovations. Technology has in effect created a new public space that invites and enables infinite participation. It has changed forever the ways in which media producers and consumers relate to one another. Citizens are gaining the capacity to access debates and contribute to them to a far greater extent than previously, making opinion-forming a much more complex business than it used to be. Further, people may not only express their diverse opinions, but potentially create for themselves new and ever more diverse identities that could form the basis of new kinds of citizenship. Dahlgreen and Sparks (1991) speak of the development of 'netizens'. The new media, it is argued, will be able to perform more diverse and complex citizenship functions than the old media could even contemplate, much less fulfil.

This chapter affirms that the role of the media in citizenship needs to be reconsidered in the light of the new technologies. The subdivision and segmentation of formerly mass audiences and the increased capacity to participate may indeed have important effects on identities and on public knowledge. But it will also be argued that the real potential of the information and communication revolution with respect to citizenship is far from clear. It is debatable, for example, whether the proliferation of messages and the increasing opportunities for individuals to contribute to and initiate communications with others will necessarily lead to better-informed citizens. And some of the problems of the 'old' media are likely to persist, and to be augmented by new ones that are just as intractable. There may be increased opportunities for the expression of cultural diversity, for example, but there will also be problems of delivering access to new services and technologies to all who wish to use them.

I will first discuss the recent changes in communication technologies, and then examine the citizenship benefits that some have argued will result from them. After that I will present the counter-arguments offered by more sceptical observers. My conclusion it that it is too early to know exactly what benefits and disbenefits will accrue from the new media over time; the potentials seem real, but then so do the problems. If the information age carries the possibility of increased individual or community empowerment and therefore an enhanced and expanded citizenship, it also carries the potential for radical disempowerment. I will conclude by looking at the policy options and challenges for governments in a globalising world if they are, collectively and individually, to encourage the former and avert the latter.

New Communications Media

We are subject today to an insistent clamour about changing communications technology: we now live, we are constantly told, in the information society. The new technologies include computer hardware, software and services, satellites, the internet, pay television, video recorders, direct broadcast satellites, e-mail, polling, videoconferencing, teleconferencing, voice-mail, faxes, fibre optics, CD-ROMs, microelectronics, databases and bulletin boards. In 1996, the global telecommunications market was already worth more than US$650 billion dollars (More 1998 189). Though much of the new technology is controlled by a few global conglomerates that operate across nation-states, it has nevertheless made it easier and cheaper for smaller players to have their voices heard. We are rapidly becoming members of the 'wired society' with news, services and advice readily on tap.

In these circumstances, the borders between the old media – broadcast television, radio, newspapers, magazines, telephones and telegraphs – and the new technology have become unclear. The global 'superhighway', cyberspace, virtual reality and the internet challenge old ideas about the mass media and provide opportunities for new sender-receiver interactions. The latest outlets operate in influential ways, providing audiences with more personalised media, diverse information products and greater choices delivered to specialised markets in every part of the world. Geographical location has become less relevant as constraints of space and time diminish not only globally, but locally. These developments have created a global–local nexus whose impact on traditional notions of identity and citizenship is, at best, uncertain.

One of the more optimistic predictions on what the future holds envisions a communications-centred home where efficient families will work, play and learn through multiple telecommunications links.[1] Some commentators even argue that we are heading towards a revolutionary technological utopia. But as the traditional place of the media is transformed in this radically new environment, the identities of citizens are likely to become increasingly fragmented. Collective notions of citizenship may break down as rapidly changing technology helps to shape new and different identities. But questions arise as to whether these identities will be of the kind conducive to new notions of responsible citizenship. Whether the technological changes and increased access to information will lead finally to a better informed and more active public is a matter of ongoing debate. Let us look at some arguments for and against that have been presented recently.

Toward a Technological Utopia?

It was often argued that the old media stifled free communication because of expensive entry costs, lack of access to technical knowledge and monopolies on the production and circulation of ideas. New technologies, in contrast, could allow many people to play a more active role as citizens as well as consumers. Increasing numbers of them can now produce, edit and electronically publish their own projects, and in so doing create their own audiences. And these audiences, far from being passive consumers, are able to respond directly and instantly. The new and relatively cheap personal electronic media offer citizens diverse avenues and open up 'self-service windows' to the world. Anyone with a computer and a modem can transmit or receive messages across the globe. More people can be kept informed about a multitude of issues, discussions and debates. Direct messages and services can be aimed at particular audience segments along with high quality sound and visual images.

All this has potentially interesting effects on the relationship between politicians and their constituents. Through the new media, politicians can obtain quick responses about policies using feedback from polls and web sites, or the 'worms' that measure viewer reactions during election debates. If people can express their views quickly and easily, governments have a useful tool for gauging public opinion. Citing some popular response, a government could argue it had a mandate to take a specific course of action in its policies. The other side of the coin here is that it may prove harder for politicians to avoid giving specific answers to questions in the way they have become so skilled at doing in the old media. Using the new media, constituents can ask their parliamentarians particular questions about policies and will expect a detailed response (Petre and Harrington 1996, 76–7). Petre and Harrington (1996, 76) argue that, 'the online world can force the politician to give substantial answers, or risk being flamed by a million angry Net surfers'. A few 30-second 'grabs' for the evening news bulletins may no longer be enough. Even if politicians use an automatic response mechanism or staff to answer the message, the public can at least obtain immediate feedback about official government policy (Petre and Harrington 1996, 79). These strategies ought to improve the democratic process and give citizens a better opportunity to hold politicians accountable.

New technology also has the capacity to mobilise remote groups, generating publicity and putting pressure on powerful political players. Pressure groups can now quickly and cheaply relay their messages to a wide audience. Scattered peace activists, for example, no longer rely solely on organising rallies and street marches to gain public attention; they use videoconferencing and electronic mail functions to share information on matters of mutual concern, such as weapons control, toxicity and refugee rights (and see Peter Christoff's comments on environmentalists in this volume). This data also becomes available, of course, for use by political parties, bureaucrats and other pressure groups who may be addressing the problems discussed. Greater available information permits a more knowledgeable and more effectively mobilised public. Citizens have greater potential to make well-informed contributions regarding public policy thereby advancing their influence in the public domain.[2] Emerging technologies could thus support citizenship and lead to progressive political and social change.

The new media, of course, and the internet in particular, provide many other things not directly political: for example, counselling services, sex therapy, and intimate communication (finding a friend/lover in chat rooms) with people you have never met. Specific websites disseminate medical, dental and consumer protection information. Receivers of interactive technology can partake in a range of ways: playing in quiz shows, responding to news and current affairs polls, receiving fact sheets about lifestyle and health programs or booking holidays. There can thus be more intimacy and greater engagement with an audience. People are able genuinely to participate, rather than just 'taking away' the lessons of a program.

The mere process of interacting on the internet – sending and receiving encoded messages – has great appeal for many people. The expanding provision of information services, support and entertainment has a certain displacement effect on people's old identities, and enables the development of new subjectivities. The consequence may be a shift in traditional notions of identity. Poster (1995, 33) argues that the use of the internet to simulate communities far outstrips its function as retail store or reference work. People like being able to conduct ongoing relationships with a wide range of others. Citizens can connect with strangers without much of the social baggage that divides and alienates. Without visual cues about gender, age, ethnicity and social status, conversations open up in directions that otherwise might be avoided (Foster 1995, 35). Thus junior staff can communicate easily with their superiors in an informal way, and shy people can avoid difficult face-to-face meetings by communicating through e-mail. People are able to exchange ideas with others in different locations, cutting across barriers of income, ethnicity, political standing and lifestyle.

Bill Gates is (as one might expect) eulogistic on these egalitarian implications of the new technology (1995, 258–9). It is worth quoting him at length:

> [O]ne of the wonderful things about the information highway is that virtual equity is far easier to achieve than real-world equity. It would take a massive amount of money to give every grammar school in every poor area the same library resources as the schools in Beverly Hills. However, when you put schools on the on-line, they all get the same access to information, wherever it might be stored. We are all created equal in the virtual world, and we can

use this equality to help address some of the sociological problems that society has yet to solve in the physical world. The network will not eliminate barriers of prejudice or inequality, but it will be a powerful force in that direction.

The Technological Doubters

Bill Gates poses as a good corporate citizen of the world, fulfilling with technological miracles the dream of equal citizenship that politics has so long been unable to deliver. However, his assumption that 'we are all created equal in the virtual world' has not gone unchallenged. In fact, the generally rosy outlook painted by the 'technological utopists' has been seriously questioned by less sanguine observers of the new age.

Critics such as Herman and McChesney (1997) argue that citizens should be sceptical about modern visions that rely too heavily on technology to deliver revolutionary and utopian goals. Messages, they say, are developed in commercial ways to sell products rather than to encourage progressive thought and action. They argue that the convergence of global media and telecommunications systems implants, consolidates and concentrates advertisement-based commercial media. The global media system tends to: 'further centralize media control in a narrow business elite, whose offerings are shaped by advertiser interests; these in turn feature entertainment, the avoidance of controversy, minimal public participation, and the erosion of the public sphere' (1997, 189). It does not lead, they say, to a better-educated citizenry, an enhanced democratic process or to cultural diversity. Commercial media are accountable to owners and advertisers, not to the public, just as they have always been.

There are a number of other problems with the idea that the new media can enhance the access of ordinary people to politically useful information, therefore giving citizens greater opportunity to participate in public affairs. These can be grouped under five headings: first, the questionable impact on politics; second, the low quality of most messages; third, the danger of intrusion into private life; fourth, unevenness of access; and fifth, the nature of the new identities fostered.

There is no guarantee, given our present political system, that greater interaction with citizens via technology will have any real impact on the conduct of politics. Sardar (1996), for example, has strongly argued that 'electronic democracy' merely offers more of the same: more fragmented politics and more corrupt public life. He writes:

> citizens become no more responsible simply because they give instant opinion through cyberspace than when they decide to join a lynch mob. Cyberdemocracy is lynch law. It fosters the delusion of the frontier that you can get the laws you want – but laws are not products of individual clamour but of

collective and consultative acts that have to reflect the balance of the community. To be humane, just and protective of all segments of society, laws need the context of discussion, information and testing against the needs of all – the very things you can't get from an instant reflex in cyberspace. (1996, 32)

At any rate (and this is the second point), technology users seem mostly to have other things on their minds than the registering of political opinions. The general quality of the messages produced in the new technologies is highly questionable: abundant websites, chat rooms and pay television channels do not necessarily lead to an increase in knowledge. For example, the potential for good quality programs is negligible if familiar television shows and programming formats are carried out in a commercial framework (Herman and McChesney 1997). Further, even when politics is the subject, the content may be more voyeuristic than educational or participative. The affair between President Bill Clinton and Monica Lewinsky received enormous attention on the internet (in fact, it was the net that made the initial running on this story, leaving the regular media to catch up). Detailed evidence of their meetings, letters, sexual practices, 'the dress', etc., were made available. People may claim they do not want to know about such matters, yet millions of electronic users have accessed the various sites related to the affair.

The third strand of critique argues that, far from empowering ordinary citizens, the new information technology in fact gives more electronic power to the state and to other actors at citizens' expense. The capacity to collect, store, sort, analyse and retrieve data easily from a range of databases raises fears about increasing intrusion into people's personal lives (Lyon 1988, 102). Governments keep data ranging from voter registration, employment, incomes and tax, to Medicare details. Political parties collect an enormous amount of information about voters, while advertising corporations, banks, retail outlets, universities, insurance companies all collect personal details. Those who control the e-mail system can access people's private e-mails, intercept communications, read personal messages and re-route them (Sardar 1996, 32).

The fourth problem that has been raised is that of unevenness of access to the new technology. In the days of television and radio, equality of access to information was fairly easy to sustain. But people in lower socioeconomic groups – the unemployed, low income earners, senior citizens and welfare recipients – may not be able to afford a computer, modem and other hardware.[3] This can lead to a knowledge gap, as information itself becomes a commodity. Even if the costs decline, the very quick rate of development of new applications may permanently sustain a knowledge gap between the 'information rich' and the 'information poor'. Moreover, not all new technologies are 'user-friendly'. Some technical skill and knowledge are necessary to use e-mail, to search on-line databases, or to access bulletin boards. Even where cost is not an issue, not everyone will have the training to use the new media to full advantage. Motivation and confidence might also be lacking. Little is done to enhance positive notions of citizenship if people simply do not have the time, desire or expertise to access and digest the daily doses of new information, or to join in ongoing public discussions.

Developments in television provide another example of the way in which access may be skewed by the new technology. Those with subscriber television may eventually enjoy a superior product to those who are left using traditional free-to-air broadcast news. Advertisers might be less interested in the latter as the higher earning audiences move to subscriptions. Commercial television channels may move down-market towards 'infotainment' as they try to hold their audience share, and reduce the quality of their news coverage to cut costs (Ward 1995, 288). Wealthy and better-educated citizens will thus increase their advantage by being more involved and better informed about the world.

Because fewer women than men are among the information rich, there are also concerns about gender bias in the developing knowledge gap. Spender (1995) states that the typical users of the new media are well-educated, affluent, white men. Women, particularly those not in the paid labour force, tend to lag behind because they do not have the same access as men. This might change, however, if the expansion of new technologies from the workplace into the home continues. An optimistic scenario has women in the private sphere enjoying greater access and gaining a wider range of choices and opportunities to participate in different social activities. A more pessimistic scenario sees new technology merely increasing these women's isolation, as home banking or home shopping robs them of face-to-face contact with others. An even wider point is made by some who argue the gendered nature of technology itself. Feminists such as Wajcman (1991) claim that men construct and secure the masculine culture of technology which then embodies a predominantly masculine view of the world. Accordingly, women are denied the practical experience of operating modern systems of knowledge or contributing to technological innovation. New technology thus reproduces old patterns of power and privilege in the social distribution of knowledge (see Jansen 1989; Dietrich 1997).

Access may also be a growing problem for rural and remote Australians, condemning whole communities to a technologically induced second-class citizenship. Molnar (1998) argues that national identity and national networking are emphasised in the mainstream media at the expense of local information and cultural diversity. The opportunity for regional audience interaction is lacking, and the particular identities of communities living in rural and remote Australia fail to gain expression and recognition. Despite some public funding of projects for farmers (a telecentre to deliver education and government services, regional radio and television, or a new media facility to produce Indigenous material), country people continue to feel neglected. Molnar claims 'there is considerable evidence that ... communities in rural and remote Australia want to use communications technology to increase access to metropolitan information and services, while creating services that further define how they are different from metropolitan Australia' (1998, 9).

Then there is the question of the impact of the new media upon Indigenous Australians. Meadows and Morris (1998) have analysed the potential of new technologies to improve services for Indigenous people. They argue that videoconferencing, the internet and CD-ROM offer numerous opportunities to advance Indigenous cultural production, particularly in remote and rural Australia, but that this raises serious issues about cultural identity and the ownership of material. Their plea is to incorporate new media into community structures in ways that acknowledge the particular learning and training needs of Indigenous practitioners.

All these are access issues. The final doubt raised is not about access but about the claim that participating in new media practices leads to more fluid forms of identity. This may indeed be so, but does it follow that the identities created will form the basis for a more active citizenship or for valuable communities? Much communication on the net is undertaken by marginal groups communicating with other isolated groups from similar backgrounds and with similar interests. Sardar (1996) criticises this 'cyberspace community' as self-selecting, contingent and transient. He asks:

> what responsibilities does the 'electronic neighbourhood' place on its members? Can one simply resign one's membership from a community? And is identity simply a matter of which electronic newsgroup one belongs to? Communities are shaped by a sense of belonging to a place, a geographical location, by shared values, by common struggles, by tradition and history of a location – not by joining a group of people with common interests. (1996, 29)

It must be acknowledged that considerable uncertainty exists about the multiple forms of identity one can expect in the information age. People's lived experience as well as their ideas and emotions are being shaped and manipulated in as yet uncharted ways as technology continues its rapid transformation. We simply do not know, and cannot know, exactly what impact this will ultimately have on forms of citizenship and on citizenship practice.

Policy Issues Posed by the New Media

The two main players in the Australian media, Rupert Murdoch and Kerry Packer, whose companies own very large chunks of the print, television and pay television media, have jostled for the dominant position since the 1986 changes in media ownership laws. Their ambitions have been somewhat hampered by cross-media restrictions that presently limit newspaper and television ownership, but it seems that these may soon be rendered irrelevant by the proliferation of new media. And both Packer and Murdoch, though their fortunes were grounded in the old media, have been active in exploring the profit potential of the new, thereby hastening their development.

In the future, there will probably be a mere handful of powerful global players in the new media, and Australia will be fortunate to have one or two leaders among them. Since 1987, there have been several federal ministers with responsibility for telecommunications in this country, but it is possible that governments are being left behind and losing control as the global players override nation-level decisions and legislation. The need to encourage foreigners to invest in Australia may mean that foreign ownership laws will in time become redundant, resulting in the abolition of bodies like the Foreign Investment Review Board. Global corporate citizens, rather than politicians or national governments, are likely to drive the media agenda in the new world of universal communications, a state of affairs being hastened on by government policy itself.

Former Prime Minister Paul Keating liked to see the 'information economy' as enhancing cultural diversity, but Prime Minister John Howard approaches it on the basis of privatised communications infrastructures (Spurgeon 1998, 32). Federal governments have promised to remove barriers to full and open competition in the telecommunications industry, encouraging the expansion of the privatised market. The proposed sale of Telstra is a logical extension of this policy. Like his Labor predecessors, Howard's minister for Communications, the Information Economy and the Arts, Richard Alston, acknowledges that the information economy could lead to a widening of the division between the 'information haves' and 'have-nots'. He argues that government can help to prevent such divisions through the education system, and by providing on-line access to government information and services (Johnson 1998, 398). However, economic development and the perceived need to engage in free-market, deregulatory policies remains the dominant issue for the government. There has been little attempt to challenge the inequities already present in the design, production and usage of new technology. Moreover their policy positions are quite liable to be swayed by the new multi-media conglomerates. It was a sign of the times, no doubt, that Bill Gates should be invited to brief federal Cabinet in March 1998, an honour normally reserved for visiting heads of state.

Let us suppose, nevertheless, that governments are serious about inculcating stronger civic values and improving the quality of citizenship. What can they realistically do? And what problems must they address? For one thing, they will need to look carefully at the role and effects of the new media on identities and capacities and this means giving thought to the shape and content of the media themselves. Rheingold (1993) argues:

> we need a clear citizens' vision of the way the Net ought to grow, a firm idea of the kind of media environment we would like to see in the future. If we do not develop such a vision for ourselves, the future will be shaped for us by large commercial and political powerholders. (1993, 6)

Given the traditional role of the mass media in supporting functioning institutions of citizenship, their (partial) displacement represents a political challenge to find ways of making real the potentialities in the new technologies for genuine empowerment of citizens, and even for a reinvention of citizenship itself.

We have already discussed the problem of universal access, which is only one of the many questions currently being posed about life in the wired community that political elites need to face. Some others are: how can innovative services be regulated or policed, both at the global and local levels? Can specific codes of conduct be developed, and if so how can compliance be adequately monitored? Should the internet – given the many available hate and militia sites, not to mention pornographic ones – be censored?[4] What will constitute best practice? How can sensitive information be protected against theft or intrusion and how can it be adequately monitored? How is copyright and intellectual property to be legally protected in the age of free-flow information? What new difficulties does the era bring for traditional concerns with protecting freedom of speech and preventing defamation? What happens to workers who lose their jobs by virtue of the same technology that offers so many new horizons? What will happen to older, less flexible workers and less educated ones? What should government's role be in providing the infrastructure that will support the development and operation of the new media in ways that might enhance rather than undermine citizenship capacities? How can people be helped to cope with an unceasing flood of messages of highly variable quality, some from dubious sources, so as to realise the benefits promised and avoid being drowned in meaningless information?

What is obvious is that many of these questions cannot be answered by one government acting alone. The information age is truly global, and many of its challenges, whatever their local effects, can only be globally met. This points clearly in the direction of greater co-ordination of national governments and a corresponding increase in the importance of international law. It therefore points also to a more significant global element entering into the concept of citizenship, even as identities are encouraged to become more plural locally.

Conclusion

An important part of citizenship is about belonging, and the responsibilities that go with genuine belonging. The question is: to what or to whom do we feel we really belong any more, and what responsibilities do we perceive ourselves as having and to whom? A colleague at university often starts his class by asking how many students have spoken to one of their immediate residential neighbours in the preceding week (a couple of hands go up). Then he asks how many have communicated with someone overseas by e-mail (many more hands go up). His next question is: who then is your neighbour? It is a neat way of illustrating the changes to our sense of self and community that the new technologies enable and encourage. From the citizenship perspective, it holds the promise that individuals might develop much wider citizenship horizons along with enhanced capacities to fulfil broader citizenship responsibilities.

At the same time, as the criticisms rehearsed in this chapter remind us, thinking about media and citizenship requires acknowledging that technology is not neutral or independent of society's broader political and social biases. The new technology both amplifies and reduces our possibilities for social well-being and enhanced citizenship. Clearly, there are many contradictions in the disembodied realm of communication it creates. On the one hand, citizens may have greater control because they can select the particular information they wish to receive and transmit, and also begin to create new types of collective or individual identities. On the other, these opportunities depend on the citizen's capacity to access information in an environment where the provision of market-determined services is on a user-pays basis. Again on the one hand, the power relationships and structures implicated in the ownership of new information technology are fairly tight and closed.

And on the other, this technology creates public spaces that appear to be beyond the strict control of anyone, even of owners and governments.

Apart from profit and a multitude of particular utilities, there is no clear overall sense of what is delivered by the new media and why. There is little oversight of how the new technology is used, by whom and for what. Indeed, by the nature of the beast, this is extremely difficult to accomplish. But there are dangers in the disjuncture between the increased facility that communications technology provides and the lack of controls upon its functions. Some people, after all, are communicating money, trillions of dollars of it, all around the globe, with the sort of destabilising effects that we saw in South East Asia, effects that were rapidly communicated globally in our economically integrated world. An uncontrolled global communications network may be subject to unpredictabilities, and even prone to catastrophes, that will leave us all helplessly floundering. If the liberties and capacities delivered by the new media are contained within a realm whose effects can render them irrelevant, then the possibility that they may be used to create more effective forms of citizenship is seriously diminished.

Yet to call something a challenge is to eschew both naive optimism and self-fulfilling pessimism and to confront perceived difficulties and dangers with an attitude of realistic but determined aspiration. The new media age should thus be regarded by concerned citizens as a genuine and exciting challenge. As with any new thing, the dangers (not to mention the inconveniences and irritations) are real but so are the opportunities and possibilities, and the latter will undoubtedly grow as technology advances and comes within the reach of more people. The coming era will be marked by an unprecedented ease and freedom of communication on a global scale, and the communications generated will not be wholly controllable by any centralised power. Certainly, the dangers noted at the macro level point up the need for the continuing establishment of sensitive, flexible but effective global political controls on the new environment, but of necessity these will be of the consensual rather than authoritarian kind.

The political challenge is to ensure, moreover, that any such controls have the effect of securing rather than undermining whatever new forms of diverse citizenship may be emerging. For we should be in no doubt that the new freedom of communication, even if it inevitably spawns much vile and meretricious trash, also provides the means for innovative social, cultural and political action and participation by ordinary people the world over. It is a potentially democratic order that affords a level playing field on which good can confront or compete with evil. As more and more people take up the challenge of the good, the complex and interlocking networks formed can be expected to produce positive political effects at many levels and in many places, and to alter the way we think about active citizenship in the twenty-first century.

Notes

1 See Benedickt (1991), Rheingold (1993), Poster (1995), Herman and McChesney (1997) and Pavlik (1998) for discussions about the new media and emerging technologies.
2 Warnick (1998) surveyed web postings relevant to the 1996 American presidential race. She found two types of sites. First, serious sites emulated traditional news products like newspapers, periodicals and television documentaries. Second, sites which sought to entertain and to expose candidates' practices. One could participate in pseudo polls and sign bogus petitions. These activities provided the illusion of political participation and maintained public cynicism about politics.
3 In 1995, 1.4 million personal computers were sold in Australia. Approximately 15 per cent of households had modems. In 2000 there are approximately 3 million on-line users in Australia (Petre and Harrington, 1996, 20).
4 Some forms of Cyber Patrol and Net Nanny filter out undesirable material. Some service providers take measures to ensure that no offensive material goes through their network.

Further Reading

Dahlgreen, T. and C. Sparks (1991). *Communication and Citizenship*. London: Routledge.
Jones, S. (ed.) (1997). *Virtual Culture: Identity and Communication in Cybersociety*. London: Sage.
Petre, D. and D. Harrington (1996). *The Clever Country? Australia's Digital Future*. Sydney: Lansdowne.
Sardar, Z. and J.R. Ravetz (eds) (1996). *Cyberfutures: Culture and Politics on the Information Superhighway*. New York: New York University Press.
Servaes, J. and R. Lie (eds) (1997). *Media and Politics in Transition: Cultural Identity in The Age of Globalization*. Leuven: Acco.
'Superhighway Blues.' (1994) *Media Information Australia* 74, November. This edition covers a range of relevant topics.

CHAPTER 18

Environmental Citizenship

Peter Christoff

In this chapter I argue that social recognition of environmental problems has extended the scale and scope of citizenship in unique ways.[1] It is commonly observed that transboundary and global ecological impacts and risks, along with the processes and pressures of economic and cultural globalisation, have placed new demands on the state and eroded, or redefined, its capacity for relatively autonomous social, economic and environmental planning and regulation. As a consequence, transnational economic processes, transcontinental cultural links and transboundary environmental impacts have generated a new democratic deficit – the remedy of which requires new forms and institutions for democratic participation which extend beyond the borders of the nation-state. Indeed, the creation of international institutions has already begun to reshape the ways in which nation-states are structured and how transnational political communities and their inhabitants behave in relation to these states. In particular, environmental issues have led to demands for recognition of a new bundle of rights and responsibilities in relation to those living outside territorial borders, nature and the needs of future generations. This has constituted, I will suggest, a specific, new and distinctive type of citizenship – ecological citizenship – which champions these concerns both intra- and trans-nationally and is therefore not merely an adjunct to the forms of state-centric social citizenship which have preceded it. Finally, I discuss ways in which these changes challenge existing practices and institutions of citizenship in Australia.

Extending Citizenship

Globalisation, broadly described, is generating new deficits of democratic representation and participation within and beyond the borders of nation-states, and these deficits have implications for citizenship.

Transnational movements of workers and refugees have transformed the ethnic composition of most nation-states and thereby challenged mystical and exclusionary ways of constituting national identity and formal citizenship on the basis of 'blood and soil' – race and birth within territorial borders. At the end of the twentieth century, few countries remain ethnically homogeneous. Settler states such as Australia, Canada, United States – which have been largely constituted by such immigration along with the violent subjugation of their indigenous peoples – have offered immigrants the opportunity of full citizenship, of being 'naturalised'.[2] However European (and some Asian) countries, which sought to accelerate economic growth during the 1960s and 1970s by attracting substantial and permanent populations[3] of immigrant labourers – *Gastarbeiter* (guest workers) – and their families have continued to exclude these groups from citizenship.

The globalisation of economic activity and technology transfer, and the potentially catastrophic effects of the expansion of industrial technology also have implications for citizenship and democracy. There is a growing tendency for critical economic and military decisions to be made at great distance from, and without consultation with or the participation of, those whom they affect. The impacts of currency speculation on Asian economies and societies, of nuclear testing, and of the emission of ozone-depleting substances are examples in point. The capacity of individual nation-states to develop and implement domestic welfare, economic and environmental policies has been increasingly constrained[4] by international forces which have undermined the political value of 'domestic enfranchisement', and increased pressure for the construction of international regimes for economic, social and environmental governance.

These forms of disenfranchisement have generated their own political responses. In recent times, the permanent presence of immigrant communities has led to political tension and violence in parts of Western Europe. It has also generated intense debate over the need to extend formal citizenship by constitutionally embedding inclusive, republican notions of 'national belonging' which are dependent upon acceptance of the laws and civic institutions of the country of choice (Habermas 1991, 1994).

In addition, technological innovation, particularly the development of global, almost instantaneous, technologies of communication, has expanded the bounds of social awareness and political concern, and changed the potential scope of civic or active citizenship. These innovations have constituted communities which are combinations of abstract and face-to-face relations between individuals with multicultural identities and plural political loyalties and responsibilities (sometimes including dual citizenship) which extend beyond national borders. Such communities include those 'locals' who adopt the language of 'universal' rights to pressure their own governments to adopt policies which help oppressed 'distant' others – be they East Timorese, Kurds, Somalians, Tibetans, child labourers or Chinese dissidents. Here, the political manifestation of such citizenship primarily occurs through the formal and informal institutions of the residents' nation-state.

However, a vital complementary development has been the emergence of 'virtual' political communities constituted through the new communication technologies. Alerted by the global media, and using phones, the internet, and cheap air travel to gather information, create alliances, compare and co-ordinate strategies, mobilise others within alien states and lobby to change policy or practice, their inhabitants act out a citizenship which operates on several levels simultaneously and is equally intent on action in international as well as national civil society as in the formal institutions of local, national and international governance.[5]

As a result, 'the role of the state has been transformed and the military, economic and cultural [and, I would add, ecological] self-sufficiency, indeed self-sustainability of the state – any state – has ceased to be a viable prospect' (Bauman 1998, 64). Increasingly, political action for economic, social and ecological regulation also works the international domain. The evolution of a range of international institutions and regimes has created a truly cosmopolitan realm for political action, as well as a new range of problems associated with democratic representation in this realm (Archibugi and Held 1995; Falk 1992). Rosenau and Der Derian (1993) rightly see a trend here toward the 'bifurcation of world politics', with the traditional state-centred structure of the international system now co-existing with a (weaker), more decentralised, multi-centric system comprised of non-governmental organisations and other transnational actors. In other words, the transnational impacts of 'decisions made elsewhere' have led to pressure for new cosmopolitan institutions for democratic representation and participation and to a form or aspect of citizenship which is not dependent on the nation-state for its definition[6] or its effects.

These trends and outcomes are further accentuated by the environmental problematique. Since the 1960s, the revealed extent, intensity and multidimensional nature of environmental risk and destruction – and a global environmental awareness fostered by mass media and mass education – have magnified existing problems for democracy and for citizenship, while also adding dimensions unique to environmental concerns. We are aware of and concerned about the fate of previously unheard of places and species. It is often said that the birth of the new environmentalism was provoked by the first image of our planet floating in space, from Apollo 12. David Attenborough has filled our lounge rooms with penguins, whales, elephants, hummingbirds and Galapagos iguanas, and 'attached' us to endangered but rarely visited places like the Brazilian rainforests, the ice shelves of the Antarctic and the Patagonian high country. We now recognise that environmental problems such as acid rain and climate change are both transboundary in scope and may take decades or hundreds of years first to manifest and then to resolve. We may be profoundly uncertain of the environmental risks associated with new technologies or practices, such as genetic engineering.

How then are we to make informed democratic decisions which have consequences for people distant in space and time, and which also affect non-human species and ecosystems? Citizenship and democracy have to date only been formally institutionalised at the level of the sovereign state, enfranchising intellectually competent adults living within the bounds of the nation-state. How then can we include those humans with a 'vital interest' in decisions made beyond 'their' national borders? Who ought to participate in those decisions? And how are the rights or needs of future generations of humans, and of other species to be recognised?

These developments all reconstitute the definition of the 'relevant community' and the 'relevant actors' for democratic participation and representation of environmental issues. They emphasise the growing disjuncture or dislocation observed earlier between citizenship (as individual and 'community' action and moral responsibility) and the nation-state, and between democratic accountability and the actions of states and industries. They force a redefinition of what constitutes political and global action, operating as they do on several levels simultaneously. And they press for more universalistic, inclusive constitutional guarantees of rights and definitions of ecological responsibility.

From Social to Environmental to Ecological Rights and Citizens

Although there is some disagreement in green circles about the wisdom of doing so, environmental issues have in recent times often been addressed through the language of rights, which in turn has played a significant role in articulating environmental claims for institutional change and the extension of citizenship. In discussions of the links between citizenship and rights, it is sometimes suggested that several categories of rights have emerged in several historical stages, each of which in turn (re)defined the parameters of citizenship. These bundles of rights are usually described as civil rights: the rights of the individual against the state; political rights: the rights to participation in politics and representation in the legislature; social rights: rights to education, employment, sustenance, housing and so on; and environmental rights.

Alternatively, some writers prefer to talk about three 'generations' of rights. For instance, Waks (1996, 138) comments:

> while Anglo-American thinkers have used [and frequently critiqued] Marshall's formulations, an alternative terminology associated with Karel Vasak has recently been employed in international studies and the international legal community. This framework groups civil and political rights as 'first generation' rights as defining a sphere of activity which government may not enter, and of political participation. Economic and social rights then form a 'second generation' requiring direct governmental action. Environmental rights are now considered as belonging to a new 'third generation' of citizen rights.

However, such an evolutionary description of the emergence of the rights discourse is misleadingly simple and historically inaccurate: for example, one can point to the institutional articulation of certain environmental rights (such as legal protection of species from hunting) in the late nineteenth century, at a time when social and economic rights were barely recognised. Indeed, despite the relative novelty of global environmental issues, the ecological precursors of a more inclusive basis for citizenship have emerged over the past century.

At any rate, neither description resolves the conflicts which may exist between each bundle of rights nor provides guidance as to which set of rights should prevail in practice. Claims relating to environmental rights potentially conflict with social and economic rights. Consider, for instance, the struggle over the fate of Australia's old growth forests. On the one hand, timber companies want to harvest 'their' logs[7] (property rights), while timber workers want to preserve their jobs and resource managers want to be able to manage the forests for products such as timber and water for immediate human use (social rights to employment, culture, and development). On the other hand, environmentalists want to preserve forests for their wilderness values (reflecting social rights to meet 'abstract' aesthetic and spiritual needs) and biodiversity (reflecting environmental rights protecting an unquantifiable asset benefiting present and future humans, and intrinsic values relating to the existence of species and ecosystems). It is the presence of such – at their most fundamental – irreconcilable value conflicts which makes the relationship between social, environmental and ecological rights (and citizens) so problematic in practice.

Matters are further complicated by the existence of different and competing notions of environmental rights. Some writers regard environmental rights as an extension of human or social rights, because they see the goal as one of enhancing the quality of human life. In this sense, these are human rights to the environment (access to clean air, water, space, and a sustainable supply of natural resources valued in relation to human health and amenity). A second view,

> which best reflects current law and policy, sees human rights and environmental protection as each representing different but overlapping social values. The two fields share a core of common interests and objectives, although obviously not all human rights are necessarily linked to environmental degradation. (Shelton 1991, 105)[8]

Finally, a third view suggests that human beings are merely one component of complex ecosystems that should be preserved for their own sake. Rights here may be described as the rights of the environment.

Clearly the commonly used notion of environmental rights requires further refinement. Perhaps it is better to speak of two sets of rights: environmental rights (which are predominantly oriented towards the betterment of conditions for presently existing humans and therefore are merely a subset of extended social rights) and ecological rights (which redefine human rights and obligations in the context of a strong 'recognition' of the autonomous needs and claims – the 'rights' of nature and of future generations, and which therefore do not automatically give priority to human needs).

If this distinction is accepted, it becomes possible to describe some of the essential characteristics of the types of citizens who are the bearers and guardians of environmental and ecological rights, respectively. Characteristically, both environmental and ecological citizens 'extend' citizenship through their non-exclusive allegiances to a sovereign state – they constitute a transnational political community – through their consideration of the temporal consequences of their actions, and also through their boundary-blurring demands for ecologically informed behaviour in both the public and private spheres (individuals in the domestic sphere, are still consumers, polluters and despoilers: as for feminists, 'the personal is political'). They articulate an emancipatory project which seeks to enlist the state as a persistent regulatory force in both domestic and international environmental-political affairs, but also seeks to reform that state and give it moral purpose (Christoff 1996; van Steenbergen 1994). Such citizens 'act locally' but, equally, they move globally beyond and reflexively back upon the nation-state through the institutions of global environmental governance (Lipschutz 1996), and also the sub-politics of transnational cultural transformation. And they challenge the liberal-individualistic conception of citizenship (van Gunsteren 1994) by behaving in ways that altruistically benefit absent or future or non-human Others.

However, while environmental citizens characteristically attempt to extend and reconstitute social welfare discourse and related institutions in ways that recognise and protect the environment, they do so primarily, or in the final instance, for human benefit. They express concern about the impacts of pollution on human health, the availability and quality of open space for amenity, and aesthetic and spiritual considerations relating to the preservation of landscapes and species. But they remain resolutely anthropocentric in their claims for legal standing and protection of their interests, and biased towards the concerns of 'present' (actually existing, as opposed to future generations of) humans.

By contrast, ecological citizens are centrally defined by their attempt to radically transform social and environmental welfare discourse and the discourse of human (including environmental) rights in general, to extend recognition to the needs and claims ('rights') of other species as well as future human generations. They are ecocentric and seek to rework notions of citizenship to include custodial responsibility for, and representation of, these 'significant others'. Consequently there can be tension or even conflict between the claims of ecological citizens and those more territorially and temporally bounded claims of 'other' (sometimes including environmental) citizens and the state – as the former attempt to remodel and force open the boundaries of moral responsibility and engagement of the latter.

Naturalised Australians?

Feminists have argued that to portray citizenship as gender-neutral confirms an unacknowledged discursive bias. Similarly, green theorists can claim that while citizenship discourse remains 'denatured', it remains covertly and oppressively anthropocentric, denying the moral imperative and custodial responsibility to consider our impacts on defenceless and absent others. We need to become truly naturalised citizens. In this final section, I want to comment briefly on how interlocking local and global environmental and ecological claims have edged Australians towards such a 'naturalisation' as contests over resource use, pollution, and the preservation of endangered species and ecosystems, have provoked the creation of a cluster of political, administrative and legal institutions, which in turn has expanded the political space for environmental and ecological citizenship.

The Australian environment movement has evolved from the work of prominent individuals and a handful of small, authoritative but weakly integrated interest groups in the nineteenth and early twentieth centuries, to become the collective proponent and defender of ecological values. Between the late eighteenth and the start of the twentieth centuries, scientists and artists such as Banks, Gould and von Mueller, colonial administrators and local forums for the study of the natural sciences – the Linnean Society, the Natural History Association, colonial Royal Societies, the Zoological Society, the Field Naturalists' Clubs of Victoria and New South Wales – educated colonial and international audiences about Australian environments and species and established the cultural foundations for environmentalism in Australia (Moyal 1986; Finney 1993; Hutton and Connors 1999). Popular appreciation of Australia's natural environment was fostered in art and literature and through the mass media, and public concern for native species in general was developed through awareness of the 'loss of nature': the extinction of the Tasmanian tiger saw the species elevated in status, from the mid-1930s onward, from vermin to an iconic victim of Antipodean colonisation.

The establishment, in 1909, of the Wildlife Preservation Society of Australia, pressing specifically for the legislative protection of native species, best marks the emergence of a politically oriented environmentalist presence. This shift was also visible in the campaigns for preservation of 'wild areas'. From the creation of the first national park in 1879, land was being set aside to provide for human amenity. However it was not until the heyday of the Mountain Trails Clubs of the 1930s that bushwalking and field naturalist groups began to display the features (shared networks, unifying discourse, collective and sometimes co-ordinated approach to political action) of a nature-oriented social movement.

Then, in the 1960s and 1970s, media attention to works like *Silent Spring* (Carson 1962) and *Limits to Growth* (Meadows et al. 1970) raised public awareness internationally about population growth, resource overconsumption and depletion, pollution and urban environmental health. In Australia, these issues led to the formation of a large number of small, local, single-interest environmental groups that in most states federated into conservation councils to maximise their collective political presence. These councils and the Australian Conservation Foundation (ACF) (established in 1965), the Wilderness Society and Greenpeace (Australia) (established in the late 1980s), together now form the Australian environment movement's organisational core. Simultaneously, the international rise of new social movements (see Offe 1985) transformed the political style of environmental campaigning here and abroad into one more directly confrontational and media-oriented, while the utilitarian and anthropocentric environmentalism which had predominated up until the late 1970s[9] was displaced as Australian scientists and activists began to champion an internationally defined ecological consciousness which stressed the integrated relationship of species and habitat and the need to preserve nature 'for itself'. These shifts are evident in the Australian movement's overwhelming emphasis, since the early 1980s, on protecting wilderness and biological diversity, and its symbolically charged campaigns to preserve the Franklin River, the Daintree rainforest, Kakadu, and the old-growth forests of western and south-eastern Australia.

In turn, Australian environmentalists and their organisations have 'greened' the policies of Australia's established political parties and helped establish the Australian Greens, offering parliamentary representation of an ecological world-view. At times, they have helped determine electoral outcomes (for instance, in the 1983 and 1990 federal elections; see Bean, McAllister and Warhurst (1990)). Established Australian political parties have adopted environmental policies as part of their electoral platforms and new parties have emerged with (broadly defined) ecological principles as their raison d'être.

In addition, the state has become a significant site of contest over its contradictory roles in both supporting ecologically destructive activities and regulating for ecological sustainability. It has been transformed by administrative innovations which give partial expression to, and partially meet demands for, environmental and ecological welfare. Administrative responses and innovations include the creation of state and federal departments of environment and environment protection agencies (following the American model), advisory and deliberative bodies such as the Victorian Land Conservation Council and the Resource Assessment Commission (both now defunct), aimed at resolution of conflicts over land and resource use, and short-lived policy forums such as the federal Ecologically Sustainable Development process (Papadakis 1993, 1996; Christoff 1994, 1999).

> The Federal Government risks legal action under Commonwealth laws protecting endangered species if it does not order sufficient water to be returned to the dying Snowy River to revive its ecology. Native Fish Australia, a national organisation representing recreational anglers, scientists and others dedicated to protecting native species, warned yesterday that Federal Court action was likely unless the Government fulfilled its obligations under the legislation. (Miller 1999)

This example introduces my second major point, about the evolution of Australian environmental law. Over the past century, often highly contested legal reforms have defined and sometimes confined the space for environmental action, and formally articulated a set of (weakly recognised) environmental and ecological rights. These reforms – increasingly informed and influenced by international regimes and by overseas legal developments – have included both substantive changes affecting social behaviour in the private sphere (by prohibiting the destruction of native species and their habitat, preserving part or whole ecosystems, and regulating and limiting pollution and environmental impacts on human health), and procedural innovations that have facilitated the public representation of ecological interests.

The evolution of laws protecting native species and ecosystems is especially important in relation to my claims for the evolution of ecological citizenship. European astonishment at the uniqueness of the 'lost world' of Antipodean flora and fauna soon invoked imperial protection. During the latter part of the nineteenth and the early twentieth centuries, concern about the increasing scarcity of formerly abundant native game species and rising local interest in protecting agriculturally useful native species combined with growing social pressure to regulate against cruelty to animals and growing international 'sympathy' for wildlife in general, and the 'revaluation' of a handful of native species to generate unifying emblematic national symbols. Together, these factors led to public pressure for laws protecting certain 'named' native species first from hunting, and then in a generalised sense as 'endangered species'. In 1860s, colonial legislation protecting wildlife began to appear: in 1861, Tasmania passed an act prohibiting the taking of black swans – the first Australian statute to provide limited protection for a native species; in 1866, New South Wales passed its *Game Protection Act.* Other colonies followed suit. Wildlife protection laws emerged in several phases: before 1900, they provided sporadic (and ineffectual) protection for hunted species; from about 1900 to 1920, reflecting greater public concern for the environment, statutes offered continuous protection in limited areas; and from 1920 onwards more comprehensive legislation was articulated first at state-level (see for instance, Walker 1991), and then, from 1972 onwards, nationally, in response to pressure from the modern environment movement. A wave of legislative reform in the late 1980s, occurring in the context of the evolution of related international environmental regimes has further acknowledged increasing domestic and international demands for protection of endangered species, their habitat, whole ecosystems and biodiversity in general.

Laws and regulations protecting species and ecosystems are in the main still formulated and administered by the states. They continue to be uneven in their scope and offer little real protection for all except the most endangered species, habitat and ecosystems, despite Australia's formal acceptance of international obligations for the protection of biodiversity and the existence of related national strategies and legislation. This failure in part reflects the existence of deeply embedded institutional impediments (including the states' apparent power over resource and land use planning and successive national governments' reluctance to realise their potential for determining environmental capacities and responsibilities (Toyne 1994)) to the creation of nationally effective and uniform environmental laws.[10] Similar problems affect the creation and implementation of nationally uniform standards for urban environmental quality and health. Even with the creation of EPAs in most states urban environmental standards remain uneven between states – a problem only partially addressed since 1992 through the workings of the Inter-Governmental Agreement on the Environment (IGAE). Despite the growing influence of international environmental regimes on domestic environmental governance, including legislation, policy and state and corporate behaviour, the basis for environmental justice through legislative uniformity is only slowly and unevenly being realised (Christoff 1999).

An additional group of legal innovations is important because of its implications for the scope for citizens' action on environmental issues. During the 1970s, most states and the Commonwealth enacted laws (such as the Commonwealth *Environmental Protection (Impact of Proposals) Act 1974*) which can require developers to provide a preliminary assessment of the environmental impacts of their proposal. These laws offer a limited increase in the capacity of some citizens to participate in decision-making and to challenge specific development projects and processes on environmental grounds. This capacity has been further extended through the creation of a national network of (poorly funded and understaffed) Environmental Defenders' Offices (Willcox 1996; Robinson 1996; Stein 1996) and, in New South Wales alone, the Land and Environment Court. The legal recognition of third party rights, rights to public participation and the 'right to know' in processes and decisions relating to resource development, and standing for environment groups,[11] remains incomplete, repeatedly contested and is unevenly realised between states (Pain 1989; Robinson 1993; Gunningham and Cornwall 1994; Taberner, Brunton and Mather 1996). More recently, the concepts of 'ecologically sustainable development' and of the precautionary principle, which is central to the recognition of the rights and needs of future generations, and other species, have also been acknowledged in legislation and as part of common law doctrine (Gullett 1997; Barton 1998).

In all, these legal reforms reframe, transform and constrain what individuals can do 'to nature' and expect 'from nature'. Property rights have been recast. The rights of species have been partially recognised. Reforms have also given slight recognition to the political/civic role of individuals and organisations seeking to 'represent nature'. However, these positive changes are still strongly outweighed by the deeply embedded developmental bias of legal institutions overall.

Finally, there has been a cultural shift in favour of ecological claims: it is now as socially unacceptable to hunt and slaughter large mobs of native animals, or to dump toxic waste in a hole on some foreshore, as it is to send children down the mines. In the 1990s, there has been an ongoing (perhaps growing) emphasis on the environmental politics of lifestyle – bringing ecological concerns into the realm of everyday life, politicising and creating issues of general moral responsibility out of previously private, individual actions. Environmentalists have also extended their challenge into the economic sphere. Protests on industrial sites, in forests and in shareholders' meetings have focused attention on the activities and responsibilities of ecologically threatening industries as well as of those state departments which facilitate resource development, the 'developmentalist' components of major parties. And they have provoked 'counter-movements' (including in the labour movement, and those new grass roots and representative industry lobby groups such as the Australian Industries Greenhouse Network (AIGN) established in response to the 'green threat' to conventional economic growth and social organisation) which vigorously combat their influence in each of the arenas mentioned above.

Throughout, in considering these developments, it is essential to recognise the long-evident influence of a globalised ecological political discourse and of the actions of 'distant' ecological citizens on these domestic transformations. For example, developments such as the UN Conference on Humans and the Environment in Stockholm in 1972 and the Earth Summit in Rio in 1992, the United States' *Environment Protection Act 1969* which established the US EPA and the basis for mandatory environmental impact assessment and provided an internationally recognised template for institutional reform, a new generation of international environmental conventions, the World Conservation Strategy in 1980 and Our Common Future in 1987 (which together put the discourses of sustainable development on the international agenda), and the local tours of environmental sages and mega-stars like Paul Ehrlich, David Suzuki, David Bellamy and Stephen Schneider, and Greenpeace's *Rainbow Warrior*, each have helped articulate Australian environmental awareness and shift policies, political agendas and institutions since 1970 (Boardman 1990; Christoff 1999).

Conclusion

This chapter has argued that the ecological redefinition of citizenship is an evolving, conflict-ridden and incomplete process in Australia and that the process of establishing the conceptions and practices of ecological citizenship is as much transnational as it is national if one looks to the range of discursive and institutional changes which have constituted it.

Demands for the extension of representation and responsibility to other species, future generations and non-territorial humans and ecosystems – the establishment of the forms and practices of ecological citizenship – have been countered and, increasingly, bitterly resisted in recent times both by governments and sectoral social and economic interests, in some cases using the language of social and political rights to defend their own claims.

Nevertheless, we can see a slow and uneven transformation of the Australian state which, as an actor or an aggregated multiplicity of actors with a range of environmental potentials, is being pushed into becoming a moral guardian of the ecological claims of a larger community pressing for cultural change. It is one layer in the articulation of a new discourse as well as an instrument for regulation. Similarly a weak web of laws and regulations now sustains attempts at ecological protection and empowers those who would act as ecological custodians, and cultural transformations evident in the media, in the sphere of economic activity, in the realm of the private, encourage us to 'act green'. And alongside the work of individuals, the environment movement – as the organisational focus of ecological and environmental citizens' activities, constituted by their activities, membership, subscriptions and donations – serves as the collective actor which most effectively promotes the concerns and claims of this new citizenship.

The present challenge is to see the marginal and uneven recognition of ecological citizenship, and ecological rights and claims, further extended and institutionalised. However, as green theorists and activists observe, the 'universal' claims of environmental and ecological rights also raise unresolved problems for liberal democracy. How can ecological rights be guaranteed and the needs of other species adequately represented given the uncertainties of majoritarian democratic systems? How can 'distant' interests, the interests of those living outside the territorial bounds of our nation-state, best be included or represented in 'domestic' decision-making processes over policies with extensive environmental impacts? Do these problems collectively indicate that liberal democracy – and therefore the Australian system of government – is inadequate to meet the ecological challenge or, indeed, that it is 'anti-ecological' in its institutional bias, being both unable to respond promptly to emerging threats and resistant to their effective recognition? Do we need a Bill of Ecological – as well as Human – Rights? What might be the next steps towards a Green Republic?

Notes

1 Particularly global concerns which have become prominent since the 1980s, such as climate change, ozone depletion, nuclear proliferation, transboundary pollution, and the loss of biodiversity.
2 Notably, from 1901 until 1972, Australia invoked a series of policies and practices aimed at manufacturing ethnic and cultural homogeneity – most infamously, its White Australia Policy, and also cultural pressure for all immigrants to assimilate into its predominantly Anglo-Irish culture.
3 By 1990, foreigners in Western Europe made up between 3 and 16 per cent of their host country's population: in France, immigrants comprised 6.4 per cent of the total; Germany 8.2 per cent and Switzerland 16.3 per cent in 1990, with less than 4 per cent only in Denmark and Britain (Soysal 1994, 22).
4 To an extent often overstated by global pessimists – see Weiss (1998). See also Capling, Considine and Crozier (1998); Horsman and Marshall (1994); Strange (1996); and Wiseman (1998).
5 Such political communities represent an extension and transformation of the essentially state-centric discursive networks which preceded them.
6 And therefore does not accord with the bounded, formal and legalistic definition of citizenship as merely 'the full and responsible membership of an individual in the state' (Kuhnle 1987, 94).
7 In cases where the forests are owned by the state, property rights are usually ceded by way of a licence giving access to the resource.
8 Shelton (1991) details the many international conventions and instruments which have enshrined these rights – particularly those reflecting the intrinsic value of nature – over the two decades until 1991.
9 Garfield Barwick, as first president of the ACF, in the 1960s, writes fondly of the foundation's early policy to solve ecological imbalance: 'The proper solution was to use the kangaroo, particularly the red kangaroo, as a resource and devise a system of controlled culling. The meat and the pelt both had commercial value' (Barwick 1995, 261). See also Webb, Whitelock and Brereton (1969).
10 The Franklin River dispute in 1983 – when the Commonwealth government successfully used its constitutional powers, and *The World Heritage Properties Conservation Act 1983*, to preserve that area despite strenuous opposition and a High Court appeal by the Tasmanian government – showed that these obstacles are more political and administrative than constitutional. It is now widely accepted that the Commonwealth has the legal potential to determine national standards and to require uniformity of environmental performance, in most areas, from the states through its Constitutional power to enter into treaties and to make laws with respect to external affairs, and its corporate affairs and trade powers; the demands of most international environmental treaties for nationally uniform regulation and performance; and the preeminence of any federal laws implementing these treaties domestically. See Holland, Morton and Galligan (1996).
11 Environmental advocacy groups have failed repeatedly in their attempts to secure national and state legal reform which would give them standing on ecological issues in which they cannot show direct cause or interest.

Further Reading

Hutton, D. and Connors, L. (1999). *A History of the Australian Environment Movement*. Cambridge: Cambridge University Press.

Lipschutz, R. D. with Mayer, J. (1996). *Global Civil Society and Global Environmental Governance*. New York: State University of New York Press.

Papadakis, E. (1996). *Environmental Politics and Institutional Change*. Cambridge: Cambridge University Press.

Toyne, P. (1994). *The Reluctant Nation: Environment, Law and Politics in Australia*. Sydney: ABC Books.

CHAPTER 19

Communitarianism and Citizenship

John Kane

In March 1999, in the lead-up to the Republican referendum, Prime Minister John Howard released a draft preamble for a new Australian Constitution. Its only possible purpose was to represent symbolically the spirit, values and aspirations of the whole nation at the dawn of a new century. The challenge it represented was to provide contemporary Australia with an elevated image of itself in which all citizens could find themselves suitably reflected and ennobled. The authors[1] might therefore have been expected to rise above the social and political discords of the day and put partisanship aside, but this they failed to do. The government found itself embarrassed as the draft became the object of universal ridicule – though one man said he loved it because it offended every group in Australia that he hated.[2] Those offended included women, Aborigines, Labor politicians, media commentators, academic elites, and (presumably) anyone with an ear for language, none of whom found themselves, their values, their aspirations, or their aesthetic sensibilities satisfactorily accommodated. What might have been a community-creating opportunity was therefore squandered.

Various people rushed into the void, offering competing versions of the preamble that tried to be (and usually were) more inspirational and inclusive than the prime minister's (and Howard himself would later respond with a revised version). But the whole episode had raised anew the question of what exactly it means today to belong to, or to feel one belongs to, a national community, and even whether such a thing is any longer possible or desirable. These are issues I will address in this chapter by looking first at the problems of liberal individualism in a changing world and then at the various communitarian critiques of liberalism of recent years. A central question concerns the relationship between community and citizenship, and whether any definite sense can be given to the idea of a communitarian citizenship that might have implications for Australia.

Beyond Mateship

It was perhaps significant that the item that drew the most fire in John Howard's reviled draft preamble was a reference to 'mateship', an Australian tradition that emphasises a form of communal solidarity – though apparently not one now universally admired. Some objected to its inclusion on the grounds that the term was too colloquial, others that it was too passé, and many women, most vociferously, on the grounds that it was an essentially masculinist concept that excluded from its purview half the population of Australia. What was not generally noted, however, was that 'mateship' occurred in the text in significant opposition to the word 'independence': 'We value excellence as well as fairness, independence as dearly as mateship.' This sentence in fact expressed the dominant sentiment of the draft (aside from the desire to put Aborigines in their place – we are all immigrants in Australia, apparently, whether we arrived 40 000 years ago or yesterday). Another phrase emphasised our freedom to 'realise' ourselves as individuals, and another issued a warning about invoking equality against achievement. This was, in short, a very *liberal*,[3] as well as a Liberal, document. Moreover, the liberalism appealed to was arraigned *against* traditional Australian values and habits rather than enlisted on their behalf. The solidarity, egalitarianism and fairness enshrined in the idea of mateship do not, after all, conduce to a progressively enterprising spirit; they encourage rather an enforced mediocrity, anti-competitiveness, and a defensive if grumbling passivity in everything save sport where the spirit of ambition and competition is allowed free reign. The subtext here was the need to put aside our old ways and to replace them with an aggressive economic individualism that acclaims and rewards achievement.

The trouble with the liberal individualism expressed in Howard's draft preamble is that it offers no comfort to those whose sense of belonging has been fractured. Quite the opposite, it requires the continual retreat of the state from those supportive functions that underwrote membership of a national, caring community, and encourages individual winners at the expense, inevitably, of individual losers, thereby widening the gap between rich and poor. The hope, of course, is that a vibrant entrepreneurial individualism will create such economic prosperity that none of this will be a problem, but that is a hope that can be tested only in the long run. In the meantime, the political problems of radical change have to be negotiated, and the question to be asked is whether a renascent liberal individualism is the best ideological tool for negotiating them.

Liberalism and Community

Liberal individualism, in its purest form, has never served as a theoretical basis for community. Liberals are not against communities as such, provided these are voluntary associations that individuals may enter or leave at will; but they harbour an instinctive distrust of 'community' in a strong sense because it smacks of collective checks on an individual's liberty to pursue whatever version of the good life he or she chooses.[4] In the past, liberalism was gratuitously complemented and supported by the communitarian spirit of nationalism. It was a matter of historical contingency that liberalism and nationalism arose together to form a fortuitous union that enabled wealth creation within cohesive national boundaries (Meyer 1998, 63). Liberals saw themselves as freely pursuing their individual economic goals within a national political culture that accorded to all the status of equal citizenship.

Moreover, it was assumed that, for the union of liberalism and nationalism to succeed, nation and state must coincide. Free liberal institutions would survive, according to John Stuart Mill, only in a nation characterised by 'fellow feeling' and a common language that could encourage a 'united public opinion' (Mill 1958 [1861], 230; Meyer 1998, 63). That is, the national community underpinning liberalism had to be in some sense 'natural', and characterised by substantial homogeneity. Certainly, this was the assumption upon which the Australian state was founded in 1901. No doubt the homogeneity alleged by nineteenth century liberal states was overstated – and one of them, the United States, based its nationalism precisely on a premise of *heterogeneity*;[5] nevertheless, it is impossible to deny the intense cohesion and allegiance achieved by nation-states, often at the cost of destructive inter-state conflict, and always at the expense of competing, non-national forms of belonging, particularly of class solidarity – to the intense frustration of international socialists.

It has become increasingly hard, however, to contain the centrifugal tendencies of the liberal individualist ideal within the confines of the nation-state. Many of the conditions for creating a strong, unifying sense of a national community no longer obtain. Though nationalism remains a significant force, the nations now in question are as likely to be a threat to the integrity of the state or states within which they reside as a support to it. Even states that do not have significant problems with disaffected nationalities are increasingly likely to have problems with immigrant minorities, imperfectly absorbed into or accepted by the dominant culture and liable to assert a right to retain their ethnic distinctiveness. Insisting on the maintenance of a nation-state nexus in the late twentieth century has led, at the extreme, to the excesses of 'ethnic cleansing' – which in Kosovo in 1999 became 'citizenship cleansing' as ethnic-Albanian refugees were stripped by Serbian police of their passports, number plates, and other forms of identity at the borders across which they were being driven. But this is an unpalatable and unavailable option for most developed states, including Australia, which must strive to solve the problem of politically salient heterogeneity in more liberal-democratic fashion.

This is made difficult by the rise of groups who claim that the old liberal egalitarian ideal of universal citizenship masked the suppression of 'unequal' groups that did not fall under the category of white, middle-class, heterosexual males. The consequent clamour of 'other voices' has produced a politics of recognition (Taylor 1992; Honneth 1995) that in turn underpins demands for a 'differentiated citizenship' (Young 1989, 1990). While most of those arguing in this way are in reality demanding greater *inclusion* in the national community – for the fulfilment, in effect, of the liberal ideal of equal citizenship – the problem they present is how to re-imagine the nation as a 'community of communities' that can contain and sustain the collection of particular groups and communities into which the state seems to have fragmented.

The problem is further compounded by the fact that the conception of the state as a natural locus of political community appears to be undergoing a critical shift. States are relinquishing more and more of their economic control to transnational players, and transferring elements of their traditional sovereignty to international or supranational organisations. The communities that seem to matter most nowadays are economic ones formed by conventions of states in South East Asia, the Americas and the former Soviet bloc. In Europe, an economic community is being transformed into a genuinely political European Union; while a portion of authority is passed upwards, another portion is being devolved on a principle of 'subsidiarity' to regions that are not coincident with state boundaries. All of this inevitably makes more complex the relations of citizens to their relevant political communities.

Finally, a resurgent liberal individualism in a globalising market often undermines national communitarian sentiment. In other words, economic liberalism and nationalism are no longer mutually supportive, and company owners and managers are forced to look beyond national borders for both markets and production facilities if they are to compete in the global economy.

'Community' in Political Theory

All these interconnected and interacting developments have rendered the link between the citizen and his or her political community highly problematical, it has also prompted much theoretical reflection. In some of this the idea of community itself has been mooted as a partial answer to the problems raised. This 'communitarian response' offers a critique of liberal individualism in its purest, and allegedly dominant, form.

A couple of decades ago, in reaction to the influential theories about justice provided by John Rawls and Robert Nozick, writers labelled communitarians[6] argued that the liberal conception of 'atomistic' and 'autonomous' individuals informing these theories was unrealistic about the nature of human beings. It failed to consider, they said, our necessary sociality, the extent to which we are inevitably and beneficially dependent upon one another, unable to achieve or even conceive of individual goods outside of the communities and traditions which both form us and provide the context of our meaningful action (MacIntyre 1984; Walzer 1983). Communities are 'constitutive' of our very selves (Sandel 1982), and are therefore prior to individuality and to individual liberty (Taylor 1977, 1992). These communitarians, rather than destroying liberal values,[7] mostly sought to apply a corrective by pointing out that 'the social fabric sustains, nourishes, and enables individuality rather than diminishes it' (Etzioni 1996, 26; see also Bellah 1996; Barber 1984).

Others emphasised the importance of civil society to the healthy functioning of both the economy and the democratic polity. 'Civil society' was an 'adjectival community' (Novak 1982) between state and individual comprised of innumerable voluntary associations in which people learnt responsible social action and cooperation. Well-developed civil societies were characterised by dense, interconnecting networks of active association and large amounts of social trust. These together formed the 'social capital' of the society, and purportedly enabled it to perform well politically and economically (Becker 1975; Putnam 1993; Cox 1995; Latham 1998).

Another group, the 'associational democrats', advocated a modified socialism. Whereas the civil societarians do not necessarily include the corporate associations of the 'private' economy within the sphere of civil society, associational democrats insist on it. They propose a program for radical political and social change, opposed to both pure free-market individualism and state collectivism, in which as many affairs of society as possible, including economic and political affairs, are devolved to and managed by voluntary, self-governing associations of citizens (Giddens 1998). The state is to be reduced to a secondary, supportive role, mostly confined to the essential tasks of ensuring peace between associations, protecting individual rights and providing the public finance to fund voluntary associations (Hain 1983; Hirst 1993).

The idea of community is also central to the arguments of those who adopt a 'multiculturalist' perspective. Some of these are liberal theorists who take seriously the communitarian charge that individuals are not *sui generis*, but are formed by, or form themselves within, various communities and 'cultures'. Liberal tolerance, respect and rights, then, must arguably be extended from individuals to the particular communities to which they belong and which support them in their being (Raz 1994; Taylor 1992; Kymlicka 1989, 1995).

A still more radical stance came from various 'postmodernist' writers, who offered a thorough-going critique of the idea of liberal individual autonomy. In the work of some, the individual subject of liberalism is seen as not at all self-choosing but rather as created by a totalising political system that purposefully individuates its subjects (that is, determines them *as* individuals) who then require state interference for their protection (Foucault 1983; Connolly 1988).[8] Others argued the virtual dissolution of the individual self within a fabric of determinative social relations – the necessarily social individual is reduced to a 'subject position' within various 'language games', 'narratives' or 'discourses'.[9] Critics of postmodernism argue that, because its attack on all metaphysical foundations renders every position forever uncertain, it can found no clear political position, far less a communitarian one; in fact, its frequent stress on the importance of 'difference' might seem to preclude a communitarian politics. Some writers, however, have seen postmodernism as a liberating force providing a way to transcend the 'sterile debate' between communitarians and liberals and raising hopes of a healthier conception of community (Corlett 1989). Others point to the essential incommensurability alleged of the narratives and discourses in which human beings are embedded, and say this argues for the impropriety of imperialistically imposing the standards inherent in one of them (including supposedly universal standards of justice and conduct) upon any of the others. The way is thus carved for a 'politics of difference' which can include a defence of community (or rather communities): such a politics insists on the need for mutual tolerance and/or respect of different groups, and constant vigilance to expose unwarranted exclusions created and disguised by imperialistically imposed norms.[10]

Finally, it should be noted that an emphasis on community is also found in those conservative forms of politics that try to defend 'traditional' family and community values and structures.

Apart from an emphasis on the individual-in-community rather than on liberalism's radically autonomous and socially 'unencumbered' individual,[11] the common ground between all the perspectives noted is very uncertain. Each is, in addition, internally very complex, exhibiting little solid agreement about the nature of the individual–community relationship or its normative consequences. Indeed, it is not even clear what is meant by 'community' in any particular case.

Problems of Definition

Considering the array of associations sometimes given the title 'community' – cultural, ethnic or religious associations, legal, professional or sporting fraternities, social, political collectivities, economic communities – one might suspect it of being one of those concepts identified by Wittgenstein as indicating 'family resemblances' but having no essential core meaning (Wittgenstein 1997). Indeed, it has been argued in the past that the term is so ill-defined as to be virtually meaningless (Stacey 1973, 49). Amitai Etzioni, however, argues that it can be defined 'with reasonable precision' using two characteristics: 'a web of affect-laden relationships among a group of individuals ... and, second, a measure of commitment to a set of shared values, norms, and meanings, and a shared history and identity – in short, to a particular culture' (Etzioni 1996, 127). If the commitment be extended to include 'interests' and 'goals', this characterisation might serve to cover such things as golfing or sailing communities, scientific or legal communities, even criminal communities, as well as those that are more to the purpose of our subject here. Indeed it extends so far as to be perhaps too inclusive, a point I will return to shortly.

Marc Stier notes that the communities that matter in political discussion today are essentially moral communities, 'constituted by a particular vision of the good', and that the more solidaristic these groups the more exclusive they are (Stier 1998, 60). At the extreme, a community organised around a very strong conception of the good (say, religious or political) may try to organise and control all aspects of the lives of those included, and will treat as anathema the values of those outside. They are what Etzioni calls 'total communities' which reveal, some liberals argue, the darker side of community that communitarians tend to forget (Gutmann 1985; Phillips, D.L. 1993). Communities may confer meaning, identity, status, rights and roles upon those they recognise as members, but they must also impose disciplinary constraints to ensure compliance with norms and the fulfilment of necessary roles (Connolly 1983; Pearson 1995). Enduring communities, too, generally require rules of recognition, admission and exit that also require some means of enforcement. This applies as much to wholly voluntary communities that permit easy exit as to those unchosen communities into which we are born or conscripted – and no individual can utterly avoid membership in the latter unless, as Aristotle says, they are a beast or a god. Certainly those communities we call nation-states, however allegedly eroded their powers or however committed to individual freedoms, continue to hold the potential power of life, death and liberty over their members, and membership in them can never be regarded as wholly voluntary.

Some groupings to which we give the name 'communities' are rather anarchic and undisciplined (for example, business communities), or not characterised by either shared values or affective relations (for example, local communities). But let us ignore these for the moment and say, for the sake of argument, that communities can be broadly characterised as enduring human associations ('webs of affect-laden relationships') organised around sets of common goals, meanings, values, or beliefs, which have some way of recognising and policing membership and at least minimal means of enforcing compliance with norms and roles. The problem with this 'definition' is that it also fits organisations such as political parties and business enterprises – in fact, practically any co-operative human organisation from a tribe to a tennis club. But does referring to all these as 'communities' serve any useful purpose or does it merely mask important differences and promote confusion, particularly when we are considering the issue of citizenship?

As a matter of fact, the relationship between community and citizenship is usually taken to be one of entailment. T.H. Marshall, in his seminal work on modern citizenship (1950), defined it exactly as 'full membership of a community'. A contemporary proponent of civic republican citizenship argues that 'if one creates citizens, one also, and at the same time, creates community' (Oldfield 1990a, 88). The question is, what *kind* of community are we talking about? The obvious answer is, of course, a *political* community. In classical times, a citizen's membership of a central political community allowed common direction and defence of a polity that enclosed numerous particular communities of family, clan, tribe and locality, and also mitigated the sometimes dangerous rivalries they generated (Riesenberg 1992).[12] In modern times, as we have seen, the homogeneous nature of the national community was taken for granted and citizenship was universalised in a regime of political equality. The postwar work of Marshall aimed at extending this equality in social and economic directions but did not disturb the assumption of citizenship as equal membership of a national community. Today, however, the purported equality of the national political community has been questioned, while the relevance, rights and even priority of particular communities[13] have been forcefully asserted. In the process, not only the proper site of citizenship but the meaning of the term itself has been thrown into dispute.

Citizenship and Community

Communitarian critics of liberalism diagnose a sense of loss, even of pathology, in societies that promote the liberal ideal of individual autonomy. It is a loss of psychic connection to others, a loss of mutuality, and of a type of relationship that transcends the liberal's contractarian notion of mutual exchange for benefit. It is a form of relating to others which constitutes part of one's individual identity, and which makes up an essential part of any coherent notion of the good life. William Corlett (1989, 18–21) has characterised the difference by saying that communitarians aim at *communion* while liberals aim at *remunity* (from 'remuneration' implying reciprocal voluntary exchange by 'unencumbered' individuals).[14]

In current discourse community and citizenship overlap in the areas of *belonging* and *responsibility*, which can be equated, in citizenship discourse, with *inclusion* and *political participation*. To be a member of a community is to belong to something larger than oneself and also to have community responsibilities that one is expected to fulfil. Belonging brings responsibility and the fulfilment of responsibility promotes a sense of belonging. Though belonging generally connotes some responsibilities, one gets a different picture of community depending on which side is emphasised. In citizenship discourse, inclusion is an essentially passive concept and participation is an active one. People who argue the politics of difference or recognition are, generally speaking, approaching citizenship from the angle of *inclusion*, or more properly the failure of adequate inclusion of particular groups. Likewise for people who talk about such categories as multicultural citizenship, sexual citizenship, economic citizenship, or social citizenship. The main emphasis in such discussions is usually on citizenship rights and status and on matters of identity. If capacities enter the argument, it is generally for the sake of assessing the capacities that different categories of citizens need to acquire to make their equal status – and equal inclusion – a reality.

On the other hand, people who talk about such things as democratic citizenship, military citizenship, environmental citizenship or corporate citizenship are generally emphasising the active side of citizenship. They are less concerned with rights and status and more with public responsibility and action – less with inclusion and belonging, that is, and more with active participation. The capacities that matter here are those that one can draw upon or create for the pursuit of valued public goals. Indeed, in the cases of environmental citizenship and global citizenship, the status and inclusion aspects of citizenship may be largely irrelevant. One is an environmental or global citizen not by virtue of being a bearer of rights but rather a bearer of responsibilities, and therefore by acting morally and politically on matters of global public concern. It is this aspect of responsible public action that makes the language of citizenship applicable here despite the fact that status and belonging are at best subsidiary considerations, and despite the fact that the relevant public arena is not exclusively the nation-state but the whole world.

Of course, the roles and responsibilities that attach to membership of particular sociocultural communities are not equivalent, and may sometimes be incompatible with, political roles of citizenship responsibility. The concept of citizenship may be stretched very far, but it becomes meaningless if reduced simply to functional membership of any community.

To try to bring some clarity to the field, therefore, I want to offer the following grid. This classifies political positions along two dimensions: one on whether they advocate thin or thick conceptions of community, the other on whether they advocate passive or active conceptions of citizenship. Note that the position I have labelled 'moral citizenship' is intended to cover citizenships of the global and environmental (or ecological) sort. The position labelled 'strong communitarianism' indicates those who put their prime emphasis on the preservation of particular sociocultural communities as distinct from those whose main emphasis is on civil communities.

	Thin community	*Thick community*
Active citizenship	Moral citizenship	Civil communitarianism
Passive citizenship	Liberal individualism	Strong communitarianism

In the upper-left quadrant, moral citizenship combines active citizenship with a thin account of community. Moral citizens may constitute themselves as a political community as they combine to pursue common purposes, but this creation is an instrumental means toward their object and not the object itself. Moral citizens generally have some strong notion of a good to be attained that founds their active commitment, and they may pursue this good in not just one, but in multiple, public arenas. Liberal individualism also has a thin account of community but combines it with a passive notion of citizenship. The liberal view of individual liberty as non-interference in making life-choices goes naturally with the idea of a citizen as primarily a rights-bearer. Radical autonomy implies no commitment to a common good save that of the conditions for autonomy itself, and thus no necessary active commitment to some individual-transcending public interest. The liberal state, mechanically imposed on these individuals by their own agreement, exists to preserve the private realm, not to provide a public forum in which individuals might pursue non-self-interested goals.[15] The citizen, however active in the pursuit of private goals and preferences, is relatively passive *qua* the public order. Citizenship thus reduces to a status that guarantees rights and imposes minimal responsibilities – voting in elections, jury service, defending the state in times of threat. Even welfare liberalism's addition of social and economic rights to political ones does nothing to alter the essential passivity of liberal citizenship.

In the upper-right quadrant we find the communitarian critics of liberalism who combine a thick view of community with a commitment to active citizenship. Rather than the autonomous pursuit of self-interested choices, civil communitarians talk about the inculcation and practice of civic virtues informed by some definite conception of the public good. Society does not represent a *modus vivendi* of discrete individuals but is rather a moral order, and citizens engage in moral action in a strongly defined public realm. The psychic connectedness of people in community is for civil communitarians more than a fact of existence; it is a value-in-itself, an essential constituent of the good for human beings. Virtuous communal activity arises as a result of these intrinsic connections, and simultaneously reinforces them. In the lower-right quadrant are the strong communitarians who also value such intrinsic connections, but for whom communal solidarity within their particular communities is the highest virtue. The notion of active civic virtue as advocated by the civil communitarians may be quite absent here. Advocates may be so engaged or obsessed with the defence of particular communities that any notion of a good common to all communities is absent or lost (see Etzioni 1996, 198).

This grid is intended as an heuristic device, not as an exhaustive classification. Each quadrant might, indeed, contain quite distinct and opposed political positions. Social conservatives, for example, with their stress on family values and obedience to authority might find themselves in the lower-right quadrant cheek-by-jowl with multicultural extremists. The New Right perspective of the Thatcher–Reagan era (continued by the Howard government in Australia) that combines social conservatism with ideological liberalism, and interprets 'active citizenship' as 'standing on one's own feet' without state assistance, would have to be located in the upper left next to ecological citizens (Heywood 1994, 162–3). Totalitarian fascists, who fuse state and society in a singular political community in which citizens' responsibilities are unlimited, would cohabit in the upper right with civil communitarians whose temper is, at base, quite liberal.

There is also a danger that emphasising certain values will cause an unintended slide from one quadrant into another. Liberals, for example, have faced the tricky task of strongly asserting the importance of individual autonomy while extending tolerance and respect to groups who may not hold this as a value. Pushing liberal tolerance and neutrality with respect to values to its extreme, as for instance Kukathas (1997) does, can result in an effectual affirmation of values and practices that liberals find abhorrent. The result is a movement from the lower-left quadrant to the lower-right, where an already thin citizenship may be virtually extinguished and the values of liberalism itself frustrated.

Note, similarly, the dilemma faced by communitarian critics of liberalism. Their critiques work best when they presuppose, like liberalism, a unified social culture underpinning the political community in which active citizenship is practised. Their stress on belonging and attachment, however, tends to the validation of the plurality of constitutive linguistic and cultural communities in which people are embedded and which allegedly constitute them as the people they are. Thus Charles Taylor recommends 'that we recognize the equal value of different cultures; that we not only let them survive, but acknowledge their worth' (Taylor 1992, 64). But strong communities do not necessarily encourage, and may positively discourage, the kind of active civic participation dear to the hearts of civil communitarians. The trouble with stressing community as a value *per se*, and therefore encouraging it everywhere, is that it takes an act of considerable faith to presume that the multitude of communities within a particular state will blend spontaneously and harmoniously within a 'community of communities' that can afford them a common public realm.[16] Civil communitarians run the risk, therefore, of being pulled into the lower-right quadrant at the expense of civic republican values.

Thus liberals by stressing a neutrality about values and communitarians by stressing one particular value can both end by jeopardising the very things they most want to preserve or attain. The point I want to draw here is that putting a value on community as such – whether by way of liberal tolerance or of communitarian argument – can push us directly up against the problem of diversity without providing any clear answers. On the other hand, taking the other liberal route of neglecting community and stressing individual values courts the political problems that I noted at the start of this chapter. These problems must be politically addressed and negotiated if we are seriously to rethink contemporary notions of citizenship, but this requires that sociocultural values of community and civic-political values of citizenship be rendered somehow congruent.

Community and Citizenship in Australia

What lessons might we draw from all of this for thinking about our national Australian community? First I would argue that the belonging/inclusion dimension of community and citizenship continues to be psychologically and politically important. Here the relevance of particular communities, and thus of multicultural policy, to questions of national citizenship needs to be considered. Given that the national government will remain for a long while yet a significant focus of citizenship, it is important that multicultural demands continue to be interpreted as demands for greater inclusion and not for the anarchistic fragmentation of the polity into a set of strong and perhaps mutually antipathetic communities. Similarly, it is not in the interest of a polity to encourage strong communalism when strong communities can be hostile, not just to each other, but to the values and virtues of democratic citizenship itself.

To say this is to agree with Brian Galligan that multiculturalism is good social policy but bad citizenship policy (Galligan 1998). As a social policy it assures respect for people whatever their linguistic, cultural, ethnic, racial, sexual and so on background, and also a guarantee of the assistance they may need to make them fully and equally members of the citizen community. This is to recognise that inclusion requires more than just formal citizenship status. The necessary corollary is, of course, that the citizenship community cannot be founded on a thick sense of common identity – linguistic, racial, cultural – as Australia's once was. Difference can be no ground for exclusion (of either subtle or explicit forms), and the identification and elimination of exclusions based on difference should be seen as the goal of the politics of recognition. The common civic identity must transcend all particular identities while affirming people's right to maintain the particular identities they have inherited/developed – insofar as these are not incompatible with that civic identity. The fulfilment of rights of economic and social citizenship will continue to be an important indicator of the status and respect the national community affords.

What though of the other dimension of citizenship and community, that which stresses not rights and belonging but responsibility and participation? In Australia the main political issue is neither the danger that strong communities will compromise the individual autonomy of their members, nor the risk that intercommunal passions will lead to serious conflict, but rather a general apathy about, and alienation from, the whole political process. The forces of modernity, material and intellectual, are inexorably individuating, a universal solvent of traditional communities of all kinds. The political problem is not how to re-attach inevitably individuated people to their particular communities, but about how to attach them to a political community or communities in ways that will give their citizenship meaning and bite. If we must be individuals then let us be more thoroughly individualistic, not just in the thin liberal sense of learning how best to pursue our own advantage, but in the sense of facing up squarely to the necessity of moral and political choice. We should define and commit ourselves to the values that seem most important at the dawn of a new century, and found communities of moral citizens around these values. This may mean being less concerned with *to whom we* belong and more concerned with *to what we* belong. This, of course, raises the stakes in any attempt to rethink Australian citizenship. A communitarian citizenship for Australia will have to be forward, rather than backward, looking, emphasising open-ended, widely inclusive forms of belonging and participation that are adapted and adaptive to a rapidly changing world.

Notes

1 The original draft was by poet, Les Murray, who later disclaimed the greater part of it, saying that Howard and his Cabinet had effectively dismembered and rewritten it. Certainly, it read like something created by a badly steered committee. Paul Kelly described it as 'too bad to be true', noting that 'it wanders about like a tipsy journalist on a merry night into prejudice, fashion, ideology, achievement, excellence and mateship' (*Australian*, 24 March 1999, 1). More astonishing than its literary failings was its political ineptness, raising serious questions about the sureness of Howard's grasp of the national temper.
2 Letter to the *Australian*, 26 March 1999, 12.
3 Really a liberal-conservative document, which is how the Howard regime has defined itself on the Thatcherite model.

4 A famous statement of the liberal position was Robert Nozick's *Anarchy, State and Utopia* in which he claimed that there is no such thing as 'a *social entity*' only 'individual people, different individual people, with their own individual lives' (Nozick 1974, 32–3). Rawls' whole theory of justice as fairness was predicated on the possibility of a 'well-ordered society' which imposes no 'thick' conception of the good, but permits individuals to pursue their own life-plans (Rawls 1972). Ronald Dworkin, similarly, argued that 'political decisions must be, so far as possible, independent of any particular conception of the good life, or of what gives value to life' (Dworkin 1978, 127).
5 American heterogeneity, though real, was significantly qualified by the maintenance of racial and linguistic homogeneity among citizens generally and among the ruling elites in particular. Roger Smith has argued that, as well as the two ideological traditions of liberalism and republicanism usually said to characterise United States history, there was also a third that he calls 'American ascriptivism' often in tension with both the other two. This was the maintenance of different classes of citizenship based on race, traceable in the legislative and judicial decisions of all the state and federal governments (Smith 1997). This should be compared with the case of Australia which, not bound by an inconvenient founding declaration of human equality, felt free to proclaim and maintain itself proudly as White Australia.
6 Not all the theorists in question identified with this label. Alasdair MacIntyre, whose *After Virtue* (1984) was an early inspiration to communitarians, later denied that it could properly be applied to him.
7 They have in fact been described as 'interpretive liberals' (Corlett 1989, 32–6).
8 Foucault calls this simultaneous individualisation and totalisation of modern power structures a 'double bind' that ensures a subtle form of state dominance. It also produces certain cruel ironies: for example, when oppressed people stand up for their right to be the different individuals they are, free from the domination of others, they attack the very structures that have broken up community structures and made them the individuals tied to the identities they have (Foucault 1983, 211–12).
9 J-F. Lyotard (1985, 36) writes that '[H]uman beings are never the authors of what they tell, that is, of what they do.' This is because they are already embedded within narrative structures which are the condition of their saying anything. Thus 'we are always in the hands of some narrative or other: someone has already said something to us, and we have already been spoken' (Lyotard 1977, 47). According to Richard Rorty, the self is centreless, contingent through and through, a network of beliefs, desires, emotions with nothing behind it (Rorty 1989, 37–8).
10 Otherwise it issues in a politics, not necessarily incompatible with communitarianism, of highly differentiated citizenship or of radical democratisation. Thus Jacques Derrida in *Specters of Marx* recommends a perpetual orientation towards a democratic future which must, to avoid corruption, remain forever unrealisable (Derrida 1994). John Keane has argued that fulfilment of the democratic project is also the logical normative conclusion of the postmodern analyses of J-F. Lyotard (Keane 1992). See also Ernesto Laclau and Chantal Mouffe, *Hegemony and Socialist Strategy: Towards a Radical Democratic Politics* (1985). Iris Marion Young, who has been centrally involved in arguing for a politics of difference in the United States (1989, 1990a) has also drawn on the work of Derrida to defend her positions

(see Young 1997), though the Marxist roots of her work are quite clear (see, for example, Young 1989, 264). Indeed, the spectre of Marx can be said to haunt most of the literature in this area.

11 Sandel (1982, 175) described the liberal individual as an 'unencumbered subject of possession' independent not just of others but of its own attachments, aims and interests of the moment.

12 In the words of J.G.A. Pocock, 'Stated as an ideal, the community of citizens is one in which speech takes the place of blood, and acts of decision take the place of acts of vengeance' (Pocock 1998, 32).

13 The leading American theorist of difference politics, Iris Marion Young, speaks of 'groups' rather than 'communities' (Young 1990a, 1997). The relevant groups she mentions – blacks, Hispanics, gays, women, etc. – are defined by their dominated and excluded social positions. Obviously, being black or a woman does not by itself necessarily constitute one as part of a community, but it is notable that, when members of such groups become politically conscious and active they immediately do claim for themselves the status of community, stressing shared identity, oppression, resistance and goals and forging the necessary interpersonal linkages needed to pursue them.

14 Corlett wishes to go beyond this stale dichotomy of polar terms in order to 'supplement' (not replace) the current political debate with a vision of 'community without unity' (Corlett 1989, 210–15).

15 In fact, for all the critique in recent years of liberalism's public/private distinction, liberalism has a remarkably thin theory of the public realm in which such interests might be expressed (Meyer 1998, 74).

16 Marc Stier writes that one of the most unsatisfactory features of communitarian political thought is this failure to specify the exact location of the more communal political and social life it recommends. 'Too often, communitarians assume that we should aim at a greater sense of solidarity everywhere, from the neighbourhood to the country as a whole, or even beyond. And they expect that communities at each level will encompass and meld together [an] incredible diversity of people ... The vision has its appeal. But it flies in the face of everything we know about what real, solidaristic communities look like' (Stier 1998, 60).

Further Reading

Delaney, C.F. (ed.) (1994). *The Liberalism-Communitarianism Debate: Liberty and Community Values*. Lanham, MD: Rowman & Littlefield.

Lawler, Peter A. and Dale McConkey (eds) (1998). *Community and Political Thought Today*. Westport, CT: Praeger.

Oldfield, Adrian (1990). *Citizenship and Community: Republicanism and the Modern World*. London: Routledge.

Slawner, Karen and Mark E. Denham (eds) (1998). *Citizenship after Liberalism*. New York: Peter Lang Publishing.

CHAPTER 20

Global Citizenship

Geoffrey Stokes

Determining citizenship claims involves asking questions about which communities we belong to, what values we ought to uphold, how and where we may exercise our civic rights and responsibilities. Various conflicting answers have been given to such questions by Australian governments and those who are, or would become, Australian citizens. A recurring political tension is evident between two groups we may classify broadly as 'nationalists' and 'internationalists'. The nationalists tend to advocate a distinctive Australian citizenship community with sole loyalty to what they regard as particular Australian civic values. Internationalists tend to see Australians as holding rights and responsibilities within larger transnational communities. This chapter examines a number of the issues arising from transnational claims to citizenship and civic identity. In particular, it considers arguments about the possibilities for global citizenship.

The term 'global citizen' designates a type of civic identity and practice that transcends the concerns of national citizenship and the boundaries of the nation-state. In both the ancient world and in modern times, the title of 'world citizen' has been used to commend men and women whose work was not limited by the narrow interests of their nation. These terms have also increasingly come into popular use to describe those who seek to identify, publicise and overcome widespread problems such as war, mass poverty and starvation. A world or global citizen is one who considers such problems to be the responsibility of all people and nations. There is, however, more to the concept of a world citizen than international good works. The broader concept of global citizenship or cosmopolitanism may comprise a range of universal moral aspirations and political prescriptions that encompass both rights and obligations toward the whole of humanity. Such rights and responsibilities have sometimes extended beyond human beings to include the whole natural environment of the earth, and even the cosmos.

Despite their ethical appeal, such ideas have attracted a diverse array of criticisms. At a time when the tasks of governance have become more complex and the demands of national citizenship more difficult, the concept of global citizenship may seem naive and impractical. It is also widely presumed that an individual can be a citizen of only one polity. Hannah Arendt (1968, 81), for example, expressed the view: 'Nobody can be a citizen of the world as he is the citizen of his own country.' For many social and political theorists, multiple forms of citizenship appear to introduce too many difficulties about divided loyalties and conflicting political priorities. Other critics raise serious objections against any project that seeks to articulate universal values. It is claimed that universalist ethics do not take sufficient account of key social, cultural and sexual differences. On this argument, global citizenship is simply another version of the discredited ideology of universal citizenship that reproduces and imposes the values of masculinism and European civilisation.

This chapter outlines the general characteristics of global citizenship and distinguishes it from other kinds of transnational citizenship identities, such as multinational and international citizenship. It is suggested that, not only are global civic values supported by a developing range of philosophical arguments, but they are also evident in certain kinds of defensible global institutions and political practices. It is contended further that the concept of global citizenship offers a valuable contribution to the project of rethinking Australian citizenship. That is, an Australian civic identity can and ought to include commitments to world or global citizenship. But this shift requires us to understand citizenship as an ethico-political practice and not just as a legal or administrative status.

Historical Background – Theory and Practice

Philosophical precedents for global or world citizenship may be found in the ancient European world. Since the time of Diogenes the Cynic (412?–323 BC), a Greek who called himself a 'citizen of the world', European philosophers have argued in support of the idea of a political identity that extends beyond one's immediate polity, whether local community, city or nation-state (see Linklater 1992a). Universalist and cosmopolitan ideals were evident among the Stoics of Hellenistic Greece and Rome (see Heater 1990, 8–13).[1] At the heart of the Stoic ideal was the 'cosmopolis' or cosmic *polis*, a city of the universe or world in which all human beings could live in peace with each other under a universal natural law (Tinder 1986, 42–3). The Stoics argued for a common humanity uniting the different peoples of the earth, and as citizens of the world regarded themselves as having an obligation to put universal principles above loyalties to their particular state. It was understood that, as a citizen, one had dual civic rights and duties, both as a citizen of a state and as a citizen of the world. Versions of this ideal recur from the seventeenth century onwards in the writings of thinkers like Montaigne and Kant (Heater 1990, 13–15). Derek Heater (1996, x) tells us that the idea of a world state is also evident in the religions of China and India.

Today there is a growing multidisciplinary literature that discusses cosmopolitan ideals and the possibility of global citizenship. Significant contributions have been made by historians of ideas (e.g. Hirsch and Hirsch 1990; Weale 1991), sociologists (Turner 1993) and experts on international law (Falk 1994; Green 1987). Falk (e.g. 1994; 1995a; 1995b) has written extensively on issues related to globalisation and global citizenship. From the perspective of international relations, Linklater has argued for a Kantian cosmopolitanism (1992b) and written on global and international citizenship (1992a; 1996). Heater (1990, 139–60; 1996) has completed historical accounts of concepts of citizenship including the idea of world or global citizenship, and the way in which world citizenship relates to ideas of world government. The political theorists Bobbio (Italy) and Held (1993, 1995) are strong proponents of cosmopolitan democracy. Ackerman (1994) and Cohen (1992) have deployed the term 'rooted cosmopolitanism' to describe plural allegiances to national as well as transnational values. The philosopher Martha Nussbaum (1996) advocates a moral concept of global citizenship which does not depend upon global political institutions.

In the realm of political practice, various groups and individuals throughout ancient, medieval and modern times – both in Europe and beyond it – have explicitly drawn upon cosmopolitan ideas to justify their actions. Since the 1960s, such ideas are evident in the names and guiding principles of global ecological and humanitarian movements such as Friends of the Earth (FOE), Greenpeace, or Amnesty International. For certain kinds of international, non-governmental organisations (NGOs) – such as the International Red Cross – the ethics of global citizenship are often implicit. Rudimentary and possibly unreflective commitments to such values are also distinguishable in the relatively spontaneous practices of donating time and money to humanitarian public appeals and fundraising events such as the Bandaid concert, 'Walk for Want' or 'Forty-hour Famine'. Widespread concern for the global environment, the dangers of war and military weapons, and also for issues of poverty, health and human rights throughout the world indicate a growing sense of transnational and global responsibility among governmental institutions, non-governmental organisations and social movements.

Cosmopolitan ideas have gained greater prominence with the growth of institutions for regional and international coordination and governance. The processes of globalisation, evident, for example, in the development of international law, have changed the relations between citizens and their nation states. The increasing legal, moral and symbolic recourse to UN declarations and covenants world-wide have effectively created a new category of 'world citizen' who has certain identifiable rights and obligations toward others. Held (1995) argues further that, with increasing political and economic interdependence of nation-states as well as growing transnational institutional collaborations, we are witnessing the emergence of a global or 'cosmopolitan' democracy. The globalising tendencies in economic markets, communication and culture make the ideal of global citizenship more relevant as a rationale for engaging in transnational collective action. Such historical circumstances require us to reorient the focus on national citizenship characteristic of much contemporary political theory (see also Richmond 1994).

Multiple Citizenship – Sub-national and National

Certainly, the most familiar category of citizenship is that conferred by one's membership of, and allegiance to, the nation state or even empire. National citizenship is often a highly prized status that grants a number of political, legal and social welfare benefits and that also requires the exercise of a limited number of civic roles, rights and responsibilities. In part because of controversies over migration, political asylum and refugees, political attention is often focused on citizenship as a legal and administrative status. Yet, even within the nation, individuals have often held and managed multiple forms of citizenship.

In federated national states, such as Australia, there are a number of overlapping levels of citizenship jurisdiction based upon membership of not only the nation but also of other political and administrative units such as 'states', 'territories' and 'municipalities'. States in federations have commonly offered different rights and required different obligations from other states or sub-national units within the federation. At times, these differences are the subject of judicial or administrative dispute and even violent conflict between national and subnational forms of government. There is, however, no reason in principle for rejecting the idea of multiple citizenship. The relevant question remains one of practical effectiveness. National citizenship in a sovereign state therefore does not necessarily exhaust one's citizenship allegiances, rights and obligations. Similar arguments about multiple citizenship are possible for civic rights and responsibilities outside the nation state. Our next task is to differentiate between the different kinds of transnational citizenship.

Categories of Transnational Citizenship

It is possible to distinguish three main types of transnational citizenship: multinational, international, and global or world citizenship.

Multinational Citizenship

Raymond Aron (1974, 638) once asked: 'How could a citizen possibly belong to several political entities at once?' Indeed, Aron claimed that multinational citizenship was a 'contradiction in terms'. Yet, citizenship need not be confined to individual membership of one country. Many nations make formal provision for individuals to claim dual citizenship with other nations. One type of multinational citizenship therefore is where the nation-state allows for, and in some cases requires, dual citizenship with other sovereign countries (see e.g. Betts 1995). Here, however, we are concerned with multinational citizenship in the sense of citizens being members both of their nation and of a larger political federation or multinational legal union, such as in the European Union. Despite the political conflict that has occurred over the issue, such forms of dual citizenship status have a determinate, legal and political existence.[2]

In responding to Aron's claims about Europe, Elizabeth Meehan (1993b, 185) has concluded that, despite the many difficulties of loyalty and policy, 'a new kind of citizenship is emerging that is neither national nor cosmopolitan but which is multiple in enabling the various identities that we all possess to be expressed'. She notes (1993b, 186) a growing awareness of common issues arising from the many 'social' identities that individuals have and the problems they confront that transcend national borders. Such problems require common institutions for their resolution and these provide the framework for multinational citizenship. In short, there exist both the legal status of a multinational European citizen and official attempts to develop appropriate cultural symbols to strengthen affective loyalties. Nonetheless, such citizenship remains a legal and administrative status that is currently limited to membership within a discrete legal union of nation-states that rank among the wealthiest in the world. This kind of citizenship beyond national borders remains confined within the limits of what the constituent nation states allow. To seek broader forms of transnational citizenship we need to look further afield, for example, to the modern evolution of international law.

International Citizenship

The concept of international citizenship conceives sovereign states as 'citizens' of an international community. In this sense, states operate within a system of common rules and institutional regimes that are bound by transnational values such as international law, justice, human rights and even free trade. Such values may be set out in UN covenants or regional agreements and are intended to guide the international practices of states. 'Good international citizenship' may be understood as fulfilling one's rights and responsibilities as a member of an existing 'international society' of nation-states (see Bull 1977, 25–7; Linklater 1992a). Such membership creates political obligations among states, for example, to carry out the requirements of international law. International citizenship is therefore largely the province of national governments whose activities are constrained by the many international and regional institutions, such as UNESCO and the UNDP, formed under the auspices of organisations such as the United Nations (UN). The key civic actors or 'international citizens' are states as represented by political leaders, diplomats and other government officials.

A state that, like Australia, represents itself as a 'good international citizen' tries to integrate its national interests with a respect for humanity and with its responsibilities to help maintain world order (see Evans 1989; Goldsworthy 1995). It may perform its international civic duty by participating in the establishment of international organisations, in formulating their rules and, where possible, by attempting to implement them both internally and externally. Such states would contribute resources, such as humanitarian aid and military peacekeeping, to the co-operative solution of international problems. A common objective of international citizenship is to establish a good (that is, safe and secure) international community that will protect the interests of states and their national citizens. This form of citizenship is often limited, however, by the perceived interests of the co-operating states and their mutual agreements. Pertinent examples include those international institutions based upon the normative principles of neoclassical economics that are designed to encourage global free trade. Certainly, institutions such as APEC and the General Agreement on Tariffs and Trade and its successor the World Trade Organization are regimes of international co-operation and may be properly understood as instances or expressions of international citizenship. But although the cooperating states may uphold liberal ideals of peace, free trade, international community and cooperation, they will also be constrained by firm realist assumptions about their own interests and what may be possible in a particular political context. Except under the most extreme circumstances, international citizenship is usually limited by mutual respect for the sovereignty of other states.

Global or World Citizenship

The major difference between 'international' and 'global' forms of citizenship lies in the different priorities given to the nation-state and national sovereignty and in assumptions about what is politically possible. In addition, the key civic actors are not states or their officials, but individuals and the voluntary organisations of which they may be members. A global citizenship identity is one in which individuals understand themselves as 'citizens of the world' and act, either co-operatively within transnational organisations or alone, to further cosmopolitan values. The global citizen does not rely upon having a formal legal or administrative status within a nation-state or in the institutions of a global democracy, but may work towards these objectives. In the absence of such reliance, global citizenship recovers the notion of citizenship as an ethico-political practice. Depending upon the circumstance, it can be both inward and outward looking.

Three different concepts of global citizenship are in fact discernible.[3] It can be seen first as a dimension of outward-looking national citizenship, obligating the individual to be actively concerned about government and corporate policies which impact on global society. In this context, global citizenship may entail individual activism to compel governments and corporations to abide by commonly acknowledged international values such as those embodied in the UN Charter, the Universal Declaration of Human Rights, and international law. This type of global citizenship may require pressing governments to honour international treaties and obligations as members of international organisations and opposing government policies detrimental to peace or the global environment. It can also mean an inward-looking citizenship exemplified in campaigning for reforms to certain types of government policy, such as that toward refugees. In this dimension global citizens are individuals who aim to ensure that the actions (internal and external) of national governments and corporations meet acknowledged international principles. Such citizens may act alone or collectively in organisations like the Red Cross or Amnesty International.

This first concept of global citizenship may merge into a second, expressed through membership of, and participation in, voluntary

NGOs and social movements that are less constrained than governments by the formal rules of the inter-state system. Such NGOs may even try to shape that system (Ghils 1992; Korten 1990; Falk 1994). They engage in the whole range of political activities from providing humanitarian aid to engaging in non-violent protest against the policies of their own state or those of other states. These organisations often act well beyond the borders of any particular nation-state in support of universal, humanitarian, ecological or democratic values that may or may not be formally codified. The peace and green movements, for example, engage in struggles against governments and corporations at home and abroad, 'in the interests of the survival of the human and other species' (Burgmann 1993, 187). Such transnational political activism may be understood as fulfilling one's rights and responsibilities as a member of an emerging 'global civil society' (Falk 1995a; Lipschutz 1992). The notion of a global civil society is something larger and more comprehensive than 'international society' (Shaw 1992, 429) (although globalists such as Ghils 1992 may often refer to it as an international society). Here the global citizen typically acts co-operatively with others in transnational movements of protest and social transformation. An ethic of global citizenship would, therefore, often require criticism of international regimes of global free trade that encourage exploitation of developing countries or degradation of the natural environment.

A third concept of global citizenship involves a strategy of seeking more specific legal and institutional frameworks to give substance to citizen rights and duties. This approach may involve examination of the implications of international law for individuals, for example their responsibility for committing war crimes, or the right of citizens to disobey governments that are flouting international law. Cases where citizens have appealed to international law or to UN declarations, and those where national courts have recognised the force of international law, illustrate this evolving concept of global citizenship. Proposals for global democratic institutions such as a second United Nations Assembly Chamber to represent peoples rather than governments (Archibugi and Held 1995; Commission on Global Governance 1995) suggest the future possibility of a political framework for global citizenship. In addition, there are various organisations, such as the Association of World Citizens or the Global Citizens' Association, that seek to establish different forms of world government above the states in international society (Suter 1981, 1995).

For all the idealism of the concept, real practices of global citizenship already exist among the various kinds of international NGOs working for humanitarian purposes, and the social movements seeking social transformation throughout the world. On these grounds we can agree with Habermas (1996, 515) that: 'State citizenship and world citizenship form a continuum whose contours, at least, are already becoming visible.' Having made these relatively benign historical observations, however, we are bound to examine critically a few of the theoretical and practical difficulties with the concept of global citizenship.

Problems in Theory and Practice

One key question is whether we can have global citizenship without global democracy and a world government. Another concerns the dangers inherent in the very idea of world government. Arendt (1968, 81), for example, expressed reservations about the tyrannical and totalitarian possibilities of 'one sovereign force ruling the whole earth'. But proposals for world government constitute only one strand of thinking about global citizenship, and their significance lies primarily in promoting universalist values and perspectives (Oliver and Heater 1994, 205). It appears that a global civil society characterised by a plurality of transnational political institutions and values is already emerging. It is one that does not require the formal institutional structure of a world government.

We must also ask whether, even if there can be few objections in principle to multiple citizenship, any communities or values ought to have precedence over others. Global citizenship discourse alone does not provide explicit answers to such a question. Nevertheless, international human rights, as set out in the UN declaration and its covenants, now provide the predominant standards against which national citizens may assess and appeal their situation. For this reason, multiple citizenship provides an inherent source of political conflict over citizenship claims. It is conceivable, however, that in future such conflicts may be more liable to adjudication and settlement by international judicial institutions such as the International Court of Justice. Although such judgments currently remain advisory, they may begin to carry more moral and judicial force, at least within liberal democracies. Accordingly, in some areas of social and political life, certain kinds of global values may take priority over those of states (see Whitlam 1995).

The question then arises whether there are any firm grounds on which such values can be supported over others so as to counter criticisms that they are simply contemporary expressions of European and masculinist values. Is there, for example, anything that amounts to a doctrine or coherent political theory of global citizenship or is it simply another indeterminate, albeit worthy, altruistic appeal to internationalism? The issue is important because the universalist values and principles that are invoked to give some order and coherence to the experience of globalisation have come under serious challenge. Postmodern and poststructuralist theories, for example, have given normative primacy to difference, diversity, and particularity. Yet, even critics of imperial universalism acknowledge the importance of dual and multiple civic identities that are both local and particular as well as universal. Indigenous peoples, for example, commonly call upon universal values such as that of self-determination in support of their rights to retain their local culture (see e.g. essays in Fletcher 1994; Stokes 1997).

Some feminists (e.g. Young 1989, 251) have criticised the universalist ideal (understood as expressing a general will) because it has 'in practice excluded groups judged not capable of adopting the general point of view' and because it has tended to 'enforce a homogeneity of citizens'. This leads Young and others to advocate a 'politics of difference'. While conceding that universalist thought has often had such consequences, the difficulty remains of determining which differences ought to be respected, tolerated and encouraged and which ought not. Without some qualification, a politics of difference can contribute to the growth of narrow sectarian thinking, exclusivist ethnic nationalism and violence just as easily as can universalism. Anne Phillips argues, however, that a politics of difference does not require the abandonment of all universalist 'pretensions'. Indeed, Phillips (1992, 27) advocates the 'aspiration or impulse to universality' which she describes as:

> a recognition of the partial, and potentially confining nature of all our different and specific identities: a commitment to challenging and transforming the perspectives from which we have previously viewed the world: a politics of greater generality and alliance.

This aspiration fits well within global citizenship discourse and does not rule out a qualified politics of difference that recognises both diversity and human commonalities. Global citizenship may even enhance such a politics where it requires, not only equal respect for individuals and their differences, but also the willingness to recognise, discuss and criticise them (Carter 1996, 49; see also 1997).

This necessarily brief discussion suggests that global citizenship may have to be based upon a minimal universal commitment to communication and mutual dialogue. Although respect for the value of free speech and expression lies at the heart of liberal political theory, a more powerful foundational argument may be found among contemporary critical theorists who argue for the primacy of the values of dialogue, communication and criticism. The notion of a discourse ethic as formulated in the work of Karl-Otto Apel (1980) and Jürgen Habermas (1990) offers the promise of providing suitable philosophical foundations. The discourse ethic defines the meta-principles under which dialogue over substantive moral norms (and moral conflict) ought to occur. It requires, among other things, that no individual or subject be excluded from dialogue beforehand and that only the force of the better argument can prevail. Although we cannot pursue these arguments or criticisms of them here, it is sufficient to note that the discourse ethic encourages the kind of political critique that is essential for the broader project of global citizenship (Linklater 1996, 87). A global citizenship based on an uncompromising and universal commitment to the values of peaceful dialogue, toleration and inclusion would still allow many different ways of living as a citizen of the world.

Conclusion

Just as nationalist ideas rely upon the nation as an 'imagined community', so also global citizenship invokes the image of a moral community whose members share, or ought to share, a number of basic human values. These may include the equal moral worth of each person, mutual respect and tolerance of differences, concern for justice and non-violence. Contemporary global citizenship grows out of a sense of the importance not only of principles, values, and loyalties that transcend the nation state, but also of transnational activism in support of them (Falk 1994). Global citizenship cannot be simply a legal or administrative category; it comprises a political identity that puts great store by active citizenship. Although global citizenship gives broad support to the activity of claiming individual and group rights, perhaps its main political virtues lies in the priority it gives to concern for others and the exercise of civic responsibilities. Such activities necessarily require the capacity to reflect critically upon one's own values and practices. Where this capacity can be fostered, the theory and practice of global citizenship has the potential to reinvigorate and even reform national citizenship. It is arguable therefore that both the theory and practice of global citizenship may assist in understanding and overcoming problems arising from clashes of culture and religion. For this reason, global citizenship is a defensible and necessary complement to an Australian civic identity, based as it already is on multiple forms of citizenship.

For many, however, the notion of a global civic identity and practice may still seem hopelessly utopian. Yet, it is precisely the recovery of utopian thinking that provides a necessary critical perspective upon our communities, civic ideals and practices. Such thinking allows us to imagine what is possible and to see beyond our current comforts, dogmas and assumptions about what is important. Global citizenship is relevant not just to how we treat 'distant others' in poverty or distress *outside* the borders of a nation. It is also vital, for example, in helping us to understand how a particular national civic identity may lack the resources to understand or overcome key problems *within* our communities and nations. In any case, like citizenship within the nation, global citizenship is a provisional and evolving concept that will appear utopian in some circumstances and pragmatic in others. At the very least, it may allow us to recognise more clearly what is valuable and worth protecting in human communities.

Notes

1 Among the Greeks we may note the writings of Zeno and Chrysippus and among the Romans the works of Seneca, and Marcus Aurelius.
2 See, for example, Article 8 of the *Treaty on European Union* signed at Maastricht 7 February 1992, which outlines a number of articles on citizenship within the EU (Clarke 1994, 190).
3 See the more detailed discussion of these categories in Carter (1997, 72).

Further Reading

Davidson, A. (1997). *From Subject to Citizen: Australian Citizenship in the Twentieth Century.* Cambridge: Cambridge University Press.

Heater, D. (1996). *World Citizenship and Government.* Basingstoke: Macmillan.

Held, D. (1995). *Democracy and the Global Order: From the Modern State to Cosmopolitan Governance.* Cambridge: Polity.

Nussbaum, M.C. et al. (1996). *For Love of Country: Debating the Limits of Patriotism.* Ed. J. Cohen. Boston: Beacon Press.

References

Ackerman, B. (1994). 'Rooted Cosmopolitanism.' *Ethics*, 104, 516–35.
Agamben, G. (1993). *The Coming Community*. Minneapolis: Minnesota University Press.
Albo, G. (1994). '"Competitive Austerity" and the Impasse of Capitalist Employment Policy.' In R. Miliband and L. Panitch (eds), *The Socialist Register: Between Globalism and Nationalism*. London: The Merlin Press.
Alston, P. (1995). 'Reform of Treaty-Making Processes.' In P. Alston and M. Chiam (eds), *Treaty-Making and Australia: Globalisation Versus Sovereignty?* Sydney: The Federation Press.
Alston, P. and M. Chiam (eds) (1995). *Treaty-Making and Australia: Globalisation Versus Sovereignty?* Sydney: Federation Press.
Apel, K-O. (1980). *Towards a Transformation of Philosophy*. G. Adey and D. Frisby, trans. London: Routledge.
Archibugi, D. (1995). 'From the United Nations to Cosmopolitan Democracy.' In D. Archibugi and D. Held (eds), *Cosmopolitan Democracy: An Agenda for a New World Order*. London: Polity Press, 121–62.
Archibugi, D. and Held, D. (eds) (1995). *Cosmopolitan Democracy: An Agenda for a New World Order*. London: Polity Press.
Arendt, H. (1958). *The Human Condition*. Chicago: University of Chicago Press.
Arendt, H. (1968). *Men in Dark Times*. New York: Harcourt, Brace and World.
Aristotle (1950). *Aristotle's Constitution of Athens and Related Texts*. K. von Fritz and E. Kapp, eds. New York: Hafner.
Aristotle (1962). *The Politics*. T.A. Sinclair, trans. Harmondsworth: Penguin.
Arnold, J. et al. (1993). *Out of Empire: The British Dominion of Australia*. Port Melbourne: Mandarin.
Aron, R. (1974). 'Is Multinational Citizenship Possible?' *Social Research*, 41(4), 638–56.
Astor, A. (1995). 'The Weight of Silence: Talking about Violence in Family Mediation.' In M. Thornton (ed.), *Public and Private: Feminist Legal Debates*. Melbourne: Oxford University Press.
Australia, House of Representatives (1901). *Debates*, 7 August, 25 September, 26 September.
Australia, House of Representatives (1951). *Debates*, 18 October.

Australia, Parliament, House of Representatives Select Committee on Voting Rights of Aborigines (1961). *Report.* Canberra: Government Printer.
Australia, Parliament, Joint Standing Committee on Migration (1994). *Australians All: Enhancing Australian Citzenship.* Canberra: AGPS.
Australia, Parliament, Senate Legal and Constitutional Committee (1997). *Inquiry into Sexuality Discrimination.* Canberra: Senate.
Australia, Parliament, Senate Committee (1995). *Discussion Paper on a System of National Citizenship Indicators.* Canberra: Senate.
Australia, Parliament, Senate Legal and Constitutional References Committee (1996). *National Well-being: A System of National Citizenship Indicators and Benchmarks.* Canberra: Senate
Australia, Parliament, Senate Standing Committee on Legal and Constitutional Affairs (1993). *Report on Australian Citizenship Amendment Bill 1993.* Canberra: Parliament of the Commonwealth of Australia.
Australian Bureau of Statistics (ABS) (1994). *1992 Unpaid Work in the Australian Economy.* Canberra: ABS.
Australian Bureau of Statistics (ABS) (1997, 1998). *Social Trends.* Canberra: AGPS.
Australian Catholic Social Welfare Commission (ACSWC) (1993). *Citizenship, Rights and Privileges: A Shift in Welfare Policy.* Canberra: ACSWC.
Australian Journal of Political Science (1993). Vol. 28, Special Issue on *Australia's Republican Question.*
Baier, A. (1994). *Moral Prejudices, Essays on Ethics.* Cambridge, Mass.: Harvard University Press.
Baker, C. and B. Janet (1996). *What Does Australian Citizenship Mean Today? A Review of Recent Research and Scholarly Literature.* Commissioned Paper, Curriculum Corporation.
Barbalet, J.M. (1988). *Citizenship.* Milton Keynes, UK: Open University Press.
Barbalet J.M. (1996). 'Developments in Citizenship Theory and Issues in Australian Citizenship.' *Australian Journal of Social Issues,* 31(1), 55–72.
Barber, B. (1984). *Strong Democracy: Participatory Politics for a New Age.* Berkeley: University of California Press.
Barbieri, W.A. (1998). *Ethics of Citizenship: Immigration and Group Rights in Germany.* Durham, NC: Duke University Press.
Bartlett, R.H. (1993). *The Mabo Decision.* Sydney: Butterworths.
Barton, C. (1998). 'The Status of the Precautionary Principle in Australia: Its Emergence in Legislation and as Common Law Doctrine.' *Harvard Environmental Law Review,* 22, 509–58.
Barwick, G. (1995). *A Radical Tory: Garfield Barwick's Reflections and Recollections.* Sydney: Federation Press.
Bauböck, R. (ed.) (1994). *From Aliens to Citizens: Redefining the Status of Immigrants in Europe.* Aldershot: Avebury.
Bauböck, R. (1995). *Transnational Citizenship: Membership and Rights in International Migration.* Aldershot: Edward Elgar.
Bauman, Z. (1989). *Modernity and the Holocaust.* Oxford: Polity Press.
Bauman, Z. (1998). *Globalization.* London: Polity Press.
Bean, C.E., I. McAllister, and J. Warhurst (1990). *The Greening of Australian Politics: The 1990 Federal Election.* Melbourne: Longman Cheshire.
Beck, U., A. Giddens and S. Lash (1994). *Reflexive Modernization – Politics, Tradition and Aesthetics in the Modern Social Order.* Cambridge: Polity Press.
Becker, G. (1975). *Human Capital.* New York: National Bureau of Economic Research.

REFERENCES

Beilharz, P. (1991). 'Welfare and Citizenship in Australia after World War Two: A Parting of Ways.' *The Australian Quarterly*, Spring, 287–93.
Beilharz, P. (1994a). *Transforming Labor – Labour Tradition and the Labor Decade.* Cambridge: Cambridge University Press.
Beilharz, P. (1994b). *Postmodern Socialism-Romanticism, City, State.* Melbourne: Melbourne University Press.
Beilharz, P., M. Considine and R. Watts (1992). *Arguing about the Welfare State: The Australian Experience.* Sydney: Allen & Unwin.
Beiner, R. (ed.) (1995). *Theorising Citizenship.* Albany: State University of New York Press.
Beitz, C.R. (1989). *Political Equality: An Essay in Democratic Theory.* Princeton: Princeton University Press.
Bellah, R. (1996). *Habits of the Heart: Individualism and Commitment in American Life*, rev. edn. Berkeley: University of California Press.
Benedickt, M. (ed.) (1991). *Cyberspace: First Steps.* Cambridge: MIT Press.
Benhabib, S. (1992). *Situating the Self: Gender, Community and Postmodernism in Contemporary Ethics.* Cambridge: Polity Press.
Betts, K. (1995). Multiple Citizenships: Two Reports and Some Implications. *People and Place*, 3(3), 58–62.
Bittman, M. and J. Pixley (1997). *The Double Life of the Family.* Sydney: Allen & Unwin.
Blackshield, T. and G. Williams (1996). *Australian Constitutional Law and Theory: Commentary and Materials.* Sydney: Federation Press.
Blanchot, M. (1988). *The Unavowable Community.* Barrytown, NY: Station Hill Press.
Boardman, R. (1990). *Global Regimes and Nation-States: Environmental Issues in Australian Politics.* Ottawa: Carleton University Press.
Bobbio, N. (1976). *Quale socialismo.* Turin: Einaudi.
Bobbio, N. (1984). *Il futuro della democrazia.* Turin: Einaudi.
Bohman, J. and Rehg, W. (eds) (1997). *Deliberative Democracy. Essays on Reason and Politics.* Cambridge, Mass: The MIT Press.
Bowden, P. (1997). *Caring: Gender-Sensitive Ethics.* London: Routledge.
Braithwaite, J. and P. Pettit (1990). *Not Just Deserts: A Republican Theory of Criminal Justice.* Oxford: Oxford University Press.
Brennan, D. (1994). *The Politics of Australian Child Care.* Cambridge: Cambridge University Press.
Brennan, F. (1994). 'Mabo: Options for Implementation – Statutory Registration and Claims Processes.' In W. Sanders (ed.), *Mabo and Native Title: Origins and Institutional Implications.* Research Monograph 7. Canberra: CAEPR, 31–45.
Brennan, F. (1998). *Legislating Liberty. A Bill of Rights for Australia?* St Lucia: University of Queensland Press, 56–72.
Bridges, T. (1994). *The Culture of Citizenship: Inventing Post-Modern Civic Culture.* Albany: State University of New York Press.
Brossat, A. (1996). *Fêtes sauvages de la démocratie.* Paris: Austral.
Brubaker, R. (1992). *Citizenship and Nationhood in France and Germany.* Cambridge, Mass.: Harvard University Press.
Bryson, L. (1995). 'Two Welfare States: One for Women, One for Men.' In A. Edwards and S. Magarey (eds), *Women in a Restructuring Australia: Work and Welfare.* Sydney: Allen & Unwin.
Buchanan, J. and S. Bearfield (1996). *Reforming Working Time: Alternatives to Unemployment, Casualisation and Excessive Hours.* Fitzroy, Vic.: Brotherhood of St Laurence.

Buchanan, J. and S. Bearfield (1997). *Reforming Working Time. Future of Work Project.* Melbourne: Brotherhood of St Laurence.

Bull, H. (1977). *The Anarchical Society: A Study of World Order in Politics.* London: Macmillan.

Bulmer, M. and A.M. Rees (eds) (1996). *Citizenship Today: The Contemporary Relevance of T.H. Marshall.* London: UCL Press.

Bulmer, M. and A.M. Rees (1996). 'Conclusion: Citizenship in the Twenty-first Century.' In M. Bulmer, and A.M. Rees (eds), *Citizenship Today: The Contemporary Relevance of T.H. Marshall.* London: UCL Press.

Burchell, D. (1995). 'The Attributes of Citizens: Virtue, Manners and the Activity of Citizenship.' *Economy and Society,* 24(4), 540–58.

Burgess, M. and A-G. Gagnon (eds) (1993). *Comparative Federalism and Federation: Completing Traditions and Future Directions.* Toronto: University of Toronto Press.

Burgmann, V. (1993). *Power and Protest: Movements for Change in Australian Society.* Sydney: Allen & Unwin.

Burke, T. (ed.) (1997). *Benchmarking Citizenship.* Hawthorn, Vic.: Swinburne University Press.

Butler, J. (1993). *Bodies That Matter. On the Discursive Limits of 'Sex'.* London and NY: Routledge.

Callan, E. (1997). *Creating Citizens: Political Education and Liberal Democracy.* Oxford: Clarendon Press.

Camilleri, J. A. and J. Falk (1992). *The End of Sovereignty: The Politics of a Shrinking and Fragmenting World.* London: Edward Elgar.

Capling, A., M. Considine and M. Crozier (1998). *Australian Politics in the Global Era.* Melbourne: Longman.

Cappo, P. (1993). *Citizenship and Welfare: Beyond the Republican Debate.* Canberra: Austral an Catholic Welfare Commission.

Cardozo, A. and L. Musto (eds) (1997). *The Battle Over Multiculturalism.* Ottawa: Pearson-Shoyama Institute.

Carney, S. and P. Hanks (1994). *Social Security in Australia.* Oxford: Oxford University Press.

Carney, T. (1996). 'Contractualism, Citizenship and "New Welfare".' *Polemic,* 7(3), 14–19.

Carney, T. (1997). 'Contractual Welfare and Labour Relations in the "Contracting" State.' In A. Frazer, R. McCallum, and P. Ronfeldt (eds), *Individual Contracts and Workplace Relations.* Australian Centre for Industrial Relations Research and Training (ACIRRT) Working Paper No. 50, ACIRRT. Sydney: University of Sydney, 149–80.

Carson, R. (1962). *Silent Spring.* Boston: Houghton Mifflin.

Carter, A. (1996). 'Are Women "Citizens of the World?" Virginia Woolf, War and Nationalism.' *Australian Journal of Politics and History,* 42(1), 39–53.

Carter, A. (1997). 'Nationalism and Global Citizenship.' *Australian Journal of Politics and History,* 43(1), 67–81.

Carter, A. (1998). 'Liberalism and the Obligation to Military Service.' *Political Studies,* 46(1), 68–81.

Cass, B. (1995). 'Overturning the Male Breadwinner Model in the Australian Social Protection System.' In P. Saunders and S. Shaver (eds), *Social Policy and the Challenges of Social Change: Proceedings of the National Social Policy Conference, Sydney, 5–7 July.* Social Policy Research Centre, Sydney: University of New South Wales.

Cass, B. and P. Smyth (eds) (1998). *Contesting the Australian Way: States, Markets and Civil Society.* Cambridge: Cambridge University Press.
Cass, D. and K. Rubenstein (1995). 'Representations of Women in the Australian Constitutional System.' *Adelaide Law Review,* 17, 3.
Castles, F. (1985). *The Working Class and Welfare.* Sydney: Allen & Unwin, with Wellington: Port Nicholson Press.
Castles, F.G. (1996). 'Needs-Based Strategies of Social Protection in Australia and New Zealand.' In G. Esping-Andersen (ed.), *Welfare States in Transition: National Adaptations in Global Economies.* London: Sage.
Castles, S. et al. (1990). *Mistaken Identity. The Demise of Nationalism in Australia.* Sydney: Pluto Press.
Castles, S., B. Cope, M. Kalantzis and M. Morrissey (1992). *Mistaken Identity: Multiculturalism and the Demise of Nationalism in Australia,* 3rd edn. Sydney: Pluto Press.
Centenary of Federation Committee (1994). *2001: A Report from Australia.* Canberra: AGPS.
Cesarani, D. and M. Fulbrook (eds) (1996). *Citizenship, Nationality and Migration in Europe.* London: Routledge.
Chesterman, J. and B. Galligan (1997). *Citizens Without Rights: Aborigines and Australian Citizenship.* Melbourne: University of Melbourne.
Christoff, P. (1994). 'Environmental Politics.' In J. Brett, J. Gillespie, and M. Goot (eds), *Developments in Australian Politics.* Melbourne: Macmillan, 348–67.
Christoff, P. (1996). 'Ecological Citizens and Ecologically Guided Democracy.' In B. Doherty and M. de Gues (eds), *Democracy and Green Politics.* London and New York: Routledge, 151–69.
Christoff, P. (1998). 'From Global Citizen to Renegade State: Australia at Kyoto.' *Arena Journal,* 10, 113–28.
Christoff, P. (1999). 'Regulating the Urban Environment.' In P. Troy (ed.), *Serving the City: The Crisis in Australia's Urban Services.* Sydney: Pluto Press, 34–59.
Civics Expert Group (CEG) (1994). *Whereas the People: Civics and Citizenship Education.* Canberra: AGPS.
Clarke, P. (ed.) (1994). *Citizenship.* London: Pluto Press.
Clarke, P.B. (1996). *Deep Citizenship.* London: Pluto Press.
Cohen, M. (1991). 'Exports, Unemployment and Regional Inequality: Economic Policy and Trade Theory.' In D. Drache and D. Gertler (eds), *The New Era of Global Competition.* Montreal and Kingston: McGill-Queen's University Press.
Cohen, M. (1992). 'Rooted Cosmopolitanism'. *Dissent,* 39, 478–83.
Cohen, P. and M. Somerville (1990). *Ingelba and the Five Black Matriarchs.* Sydney: Allen & Unwin.
Commission on Global Governance (1995). *Our Global Neighbourhood.* Oxford: Oxford University Press.
Commonwealth Immigration Advisory Council (1949), Tenth Meeting, 24 November, Agenda Item 21.
Connolly, W. (1983). 'Discipline, Politics and Ambiguity', *Political Theory* 11, 325–41.
Connolly, W. (1988). *Political Theory and Modernity.* Oxford: Basil Blackwell.
Coombs, H.C. (1994). 'From Curtin to Keating: The 1945 and 1994 White Papers on Employment: A Better Environment for Human and Economic

Diversity?' *A Discussion Paper*, North Australia Research Unit, Australian National University, Darwin.
Cope, B., M. Kalantzis and N. Solomon (1994). *Diversity Makes Good Business. A Report to the Human Rights Commission*. Canberra: AGPS.
Corlett, W. (1989). *Community Without Unity: A Politics of Derridarian Extravagance*. Durham, NC: Duke University Press.
Cox, E. (1995). 'A Truly Civil Society.' *1995 Boyer Lectures*. Sydney: ABC Books.
Crawford, M (1993). *The Roman Republic*. 2nd edn. Cambridge, Mass.: Harvard University Press.
Dabscheck, B. (1997). 'Human Rights and Industrial Relations.' *Labour and Industry*, 7(3), 1–27.
Dagger, R. (1997). *Civic Virtues: Rights, Citizenship, and Republican Liberalism*. New York: Oxford University Press.
Dahl, R.A. (1989). *Democracy and its Critics*. New Haven and London: Yale University Press.
Dahl, R. and E. Tufte (1973). *Size and Democracy*. Stanford: Stanford University Press.
Dahlgreen, T. and C. Sparks (1991). *Communication and Citizenship*. London: Routledge.
Davidson, A. (1991). *The Invisible State: The Formation of the Australian State, 1788–1901*. Cambridge: Cambridge University Press.
Davidson, A (1995). 'Consumer Sovereignty and the Citizen'. *Consumer Future Summit and Conference Background Papers, 29 August 1995, Parliament House*. Canberra: Australian Consumer Council.
Davidson, A. (1996). 'Expansionary Citizenship: The European Experience.' Paper at the *Conference on Globalisation and Citizenship*. Swinburne University of Technology/UNRISD Geneva (December).
Davidson, A (1997a). *From Subject to Citizen: Australian Citizenship in the Twentieth Century*. Cambridge: Cambridge University Press.
Davidson, A. (1997b). 'Globalism, The Regional Citizen and Democracy.' In B. Galligan and C. Sampford (eds), *Rethinking Human Rights*. Sydney: Federation Press.
Davis, S.R. (ed.) (1996). *Citizenship in Australia: Democracy, Law and Society*. Carlton, Vic.: Constitutional Centenary Foundation.
Dean, H. (1996). *Welfare, Law and Citizenship*. London: Prentice Hall.
Dean, M. and B. Hindess (eds) (1998). *Governing Australia. Studies in Contemporary Rationalities of Government*. Cambridge: Cambridge University Press.
Departmen of Defence (1991–92). *Defence Report*. Canberra: AGPS.
Departmen of Employment, Education, Training, and Youth Affairs (DEETYA) (1997). *Discovering Democracy Civics and Citizenship Education: A Ministerial Statement*. Canberra: Department of Employment, Education, Training and Youth Affairs.
Derrida, J. (1994). *Specters of Marx: The State of Debt, the Work of Mourning and the New International*. Peggy Kamuf, trans. New York: Routledge.
Detmold, M. J. (1994). 'The New Constitutional Law.' *Sydney Law Review*, 16, 228.
Dewey, J. (1964 [1916]). *Democracy and Education*. New York: Macmillan.
Dewey, J. (1927). *The Public and Its Problems*. New York: The Swallow Press.
Dietrich, D (1997). '(Re)-Fashioning the Techno-Erotic Woman: Gender and Textuality in the Cybercultural Matrix.' In S. Jones (ed.), *Virtual Culture: Identity and Communication in Cybersociety*. London: Sage.
Dixon, O. (1965). *Jesting Pilate*. Sydney: Law Book.

Doyle, J. (1993). 'Constitutional Law: "At the Eye of the Storm."' *Western Australia Law Review*, 23, 15.
Dunne, M. and T. Bonazzi (eds) (1995). *Citizenship and Rights in Multicultural Societies*. Keele, England: Keele University Press.
Duschesne, S. (1997). *Cityonneté à la française*. Paris: Science Po.
Dworkin, R. (1978). 'Liberalism.' In S. Hampshire (ed.), *Public and Private Morality*. Cambridge: Cambridge University Press, 113–43.
Eade, J. (ed.) (1997). *Living the Global City: Globalisation as a Local Process*. London and NY: Routledge.
Eardley, T. (1997). *New Relations of Welfare in the Contracting State: The Marketisation of Services for the Unemployed in Australia*. Social Policy Research Centre Discussion Paper No. 79, Social Policy Research Centre. Sydney: University of New South Wales.
Eckersley, R. (1999). 'Generation Wrecked.' *Age*, 19 March, 14.
Eckersley, R. (ed.) (1998). *Measuring Progress: Is Life Getting Better?* Melbourne: CSIRO Publishing.
Einhorn, B., M. Kaldor, and Z. Kavan (eds) (1996). *Citizenship and Democratic Control in Contemporary Europe*. London: Edward Elgar.
Eisenstein, H. (1996). *Inside Agitators: Australian Femocrats and the State*. Sydney: Allen & Unwin.
Elshtain, J.B. (1987). *Women and War*. New York: Basic Books.
Emirbayer, M. and A. Mische (1998). 'What is Human Agency.' *American Journal of Sociology*, 103(4) (January), 962–1023.
Emy, H. V. (1993). *Remaking Australia: The State, The Market and Australia's Future*. Sydney: Allen & Unwin.
Emy, H.V. and P. James (1996). 'Debating the State.' In P. James (ed.), *The State in Question: Transformations of the Australian State*. Sydney: Allen & Unwin.
Esping-Andersen, G. (1985). *Politics Against Markets: The Social Democratic Road to Power*. Princeton, NJ: Princeton University Press.
Esping-Andersen, G. (1990). *The Three Worlds of Welfare Capitalism*. Cambridge: Polity Press.
Etzioni, A. (1995). *Rights and the Common Good: The Communitarian Perspective*. New York: St Martin's Press.
Etzioni, A. (1996). *The New Golden Rule: Morality and Community in a Democratic Society*. New York: Basic Books.
Evans, D.T. (1993). *Sexual Citizenship. The Material Construction of Sexualities*. London: Routledge.
Evans, G. (1989). 'Australian Foreign Policy: Priorities in a Changing World.' *Australian Outlook*, 43(2), 1–15.
Falk, R. (1992). *Explorations at the Edge of Time: The Prospects for World Order*. Philadelphia: Temple University Press.
Falk, R.A. (1994). 'The Making of Global Citizenship.' In B. van Steenbergen (ed.), *The Condition of Citizenship*. Thousand Oaks, CA: Sage, 127–40.
Falk, R.A. (1995a). 'The World Order between Inter-State Law and the Law of Humanity: The Role of Civil Society Institutions.' In Archibugi and Held (eds), *Cosmopolitan Democracy*, 163–79.
Falk, R.A. (1995b). *On Human Governance: towards a New Global Politics*. Cambridge: Polity.
Ferrajoli, L. (1991). 'Beyond Sovereignty and Citizenship: A Global Constitutionalism.' In B. Barry (ed.), *Democracy and Power: Essays in Political Theory*, vol. I. Oxford: Oxford University Press.

Fincher, R. and J. Nieuwenhuysen (eds) (1998). *Australian Poverty: Then and Now.* Melbourne: Melbourne University Press.
Fingleton, J. (1996). *Final Report: Review of the Aboriginal Councils and Associations Act.* Vol. 1: Main text; vol. 2: Case study reports. Canberra: Australian Institute of Aboriginal and Torres Strait Islander Studies.
Finney, C. (1993). *Paradise Revealed: Natural History in Nineteenth-Century Australia.* Melbourne: Museum of Victoria.
Fisse, B. and J. Braithwaite (1993). *Corporations, Crime and Accountability.* Cambridge: Cambridge University Press.
Fletcher, C. (ed.) (1994). *Aboriginal Self-Determination in Australia.* Canberra: Aboriginal Studies Press.
Foucault, M. (1981). 'Omnes et Singulatim: Towards a Criticism of "Political Reason".' In S. McMurrin (ed.), *The Tanner Lectures on Human Values,* II. Salt Lake City: University of Utah Press.
Foucault, M. (1983). 'Why Study Power?'. In Dreyfus, H. and Rabinow P. (eds), *Michel Foucault: Beyond Structuralism and Hermeneutics.* Chicago: University of Chicago Press.
Foucault, M. (1984 [1976]). *The History of Sexuality. Vol. 1: An Introduction.* London: Penguin/Peregrine.
Fraser, J.M. (1981). Multiculturalism: Australia's Unique Achievement: Inaugural Address to the Australian Institute of Multicultural Affairs. Melbourne, 30 November.
Frazer, E. and N. Lacey (1993). *The Politics of Community: A Feminist Critique of the Liberal-Communitarian Debate.* Toronto: University of Toronto Press.
Funder, K. (ed.) (1996). *Citizen Child: Australian Law and Children's Rights.* Melbourne: Australian Institute of Family Studies.
Galbally, F. et al. (1978). *Review of Post-Arrival Programs and Services.* Canberra: AGPS.
Galligan, B. (1995). *A Federal Republic. Australia's Constitutional System of Government.* Cambridge: Cambridge University Press.
Galligan, B. (1998). 'Reconstructing Australian Citizenship.' *Quadrant* 42(11) (Nov.), 11–18.
Gatens, M. (1991). *Feminism and Philosophy: Perspectives on Difference and Equality.* Cambridge: Polity Press.
Gates, B. (1995). *The Road Ahead.* Harmondsworth: Viking Penguin.
Gauchet, M. (1989). *La révolution des droits de l'homme.* Paris: Gallimard.
Gersuny, C. (1994). 'Industrial Rights: A Neglected Facet of Citizenship Theory.' *Economic and Industrial Democracy,* 15, 211–26.
Ghils, P. (1992). 'International Civil Society: International Non-Governmental Organizations in the International System.' *International Social Science Journal* XLIV(3), 417–31.
Giddens, A. (1998). *The Third Way: The Renewal of Social Democracy.* Cambridge: Polity Press.
Gil, D. (1992). *Unravelling Social Policy.* Rochester, Vermont: Schenkman.
Gilligan, C. (1982). *In a Different Voice.* Cambridge, Mass.: Harvard University Press.
Glazer, N. (1997). *We Are All Multiculturalists Now.* Cambridge, Mass.: Harvard University Press.
Goldsworthy, D. (1995). 'Australia and Good International Citizenship.' In S. Lawson (ed.) *The New Agenda: Cooperating for Peace and Beyond.* Sydney: Allen & Unwin, 171–87.

Goodall, H. (1993). 'Border Wars: The Shifting Meanings of Boundaries in Aboriginal/Coloniser Relations in South Eastern Australia.' *Communal/Plural*, 2, 47–64.
Goodall, H. (1996). *Invasion to Embassy: Land in Aboriginal Politics in New South Wales. 1770–1972*. Sydney: Allen & Unwin.
Goodwin, C.S. (1995). *A Resurrection of the Republican Ideal*. Lanham, MD: University Press of America.
Goot, M. and T. Rowse (1991). 'The "backlash" Hypothesis and the Land Rights Option.' *Australian Aboriginal Studies*, 1, 3–12.
Gordon, D. (1994). *Citizens Without Sovereignty: Equality and Sociability in French Thought*. Princeton, NJ: Princeton University Press.
Gordon, D.M. (1994). 'Twixt the Cup and the Lip: Mainstream Economics and the Formulation of Economic Policy.' *Social Research*, 61(1), 1–33.
Grassby, A.J. (1973). Official Statement by Mr A.J. Grassby, 11 October. *Australian Foreign Affairs Record*.
Gray, J. (1995). *Liberalism*, 2nd edn. Buckingham: Open University Press.
Graycar, R. (1996). 'Telling Tales: Legal Stories About Violence Against Women.' *Australian Feminist Law Journal*, 7, 79.
Green, L.C. (1987). 'Is World Citizenship A Legal Practicality?' *Canadian Yearbook of International Law* 25, 151–85.
Gullett, W. (1997). 'Environmental Protection and the "Precautionary Principle": A Response to Scientific Uncertainty in Environmental Management.' *Environmental and Planning Law Journal*, February, 14(1), 52–69.
Gunningham, N. and A. Cornwall (1994). 'Legislating the Right to Know.' *Environmental and Planning Law Journal*, August, 11(4), 274–88.
Gutmann, A. (1985). 'Communitarian Critics of Liberalism.' *Philosophy and Public Affairs*, 14(3) (Summer), 308–22.
Gutmann, A. (1987). *Democratic Education*. Princeton, NJ: Princeton University Press.
Gutmann, A. (ed.) (1992). *Multiculturalism and the 'Politics of Recognition'*. Princeton: Princeton University Press.
Habermas, J. (1990). *Moral Consciousness and Communicative Action*. S. Lenhardt and S.W. Nicholsen, trans. Cambridge: Polity.
Habermas, J. (1991). 'Citizenship and National Identity: Some reflections on the future of Europe.' *Praxis International*, 12(1) (April), 1–19.
Habermas, J. (1994). The Asylum Debate (Paris Lecture, 14 January 1993). *The Past As Future*. Lincoln and London: University of Nebraska Press, 121–42.
Habermas, J. (1996). *Between Facts and Norms*. W. Rehg, trans. Cambridge: Polity.
Hain, P. (1983). *The Democratic Alternative: A Socialist Response to Britain's Crisis*. Harmondsworth: Penguin.
Hammar, T. (1990). *Democracy and the Nation State: Aliens, Denizens and Citizens in a World of International Migration*. Aldershot: Avebury.
Hampson, I. (1996). 'The Accord: A Post-Mortem.' *Labour and Industry*, 7(2): 55–77.
Hartsock, N. (1982). 'The Barracks Community in Western Political Thought: Prolegomena to a Feminist Critique of War and Politics,' *Women's Studies International Forum*, 5, 283–6.
Hasluck, P.M.C. (1959). Are Our Aborigines Neglected? Unpublished address given at the Pleasant Sunday Afternoon service, Lyceum, Sydney, 12 July 1959. Box 80 item 294, Elkin Papers, Fisher Library, University of Sydney.
Hasluck, P.M.C. (1965). 'The Problem of Administration.' In R. and C. Berndt (eds), *Aboriginal Man in Australia*. Sydney: Angus & Robertson, 435–52.

Hasluck, P.M.C. (1988). *Shades of Darkness*. Melbourne: Melbourne University Press.
Heater, D. (1990). *Citizenship: The Civic Ideal in World History, Politics and Education*. London: Longman.
Heater, D. (1996). *World Citizenship and Government*. Basingstoke: Macmillan.
Held, D. (1993). 'Democracy: From City-States to Cosmopolitan Order.' In D. Held (ed.), *Prospects for Democracy*. Cambridge: Polity, 13–52.
Held, D. (1995). *Democracy and the Global Order: From the Modern State to Cosmopolitan Governance*. Cambridge: Polity.
Herman, E.S. and R.W. McChesney (1997). *The Global Media: The New Missionaries of Global Capitalism*. London: Cassell.
Heywood, A. (1994). *Rights, Obligations and Citizenship*. Melbourne: Macmillan.
Higgins, W. (1994). 'Industry Policy.' In J. Brett, J. Gillespie and M. Goot (eds), *Developments in Australian Politics*. Melbourne: Macmillan.
Hill, B. (1986). *The First English Feminist: Reflections upon Marriage and Other Writings by Mary Astell*. Aldershot: Gower.
Hindess, B. (1993). 'Citizenship in the Modern West.' In B.S. Turner (ed.) Citizenship and Social Theory. Thousand Oaks CA: Sage, 19–35.
Hindess, B. (1994). 'The world we have lost.' *Australian and New Zealand Journal of Sociology*, 30(3), 234–9.
Hindess, B. (1996). *Discourses of Power: From Hobbes to Foucault*. Oxford: Blackwell.
Hindess, B. (1998). 'Neo-liberalism and the National Economy.' In M. Dean and B. Hindess (eds), *Governing Australia*. Cambridge: Cambridge University Press.
Hirsch, G.C. and H. Hirsch (1990). 'Learning to Live Together: Political Socialization and the Formation of International Identity.' *International Journal of Group Tensions*, 20(4), 369–90.
Hirschman, A.O. (1970). *Exit, Voice, and Loyalty*. Cambridge, MA: Harvard University Press.
Hirst, P. (1993). 'Associational Democracy'. In D. Held (ed.), *Prospects for Democracy: North, South, East, West*. Cambridge: Polity Press.
Hirst, P. (1994). *Associative Democracy: New Forms of Economic and Social Governance*. Cambridge: Polity Press.
Hirst, P. and G. Thompson (1996). *Globalization in Question: The International Economy and the Possibilities of Governance*. Cambridge: Polity.
Hogan, D. (1996).'The Liberty of the Moderns: Interests, Justice and Civic Education.' *Melbourne Studies in Education*, 37(1) (May), 57–88.
Hogan, D. (1997a). 'Framing Civics.' In *Men and Women of Australia: Report of a National Professional Development Project on Informed Citizenship*. Hobart: Faculty of Education.
Hogan, D. (1997b). 'The Logic of Protection: Citizenship, Justice and Political Community.' In K. Kennedy (ed.), *Civics Education and the Modern State*. London: Falmer.
Hogan, D. (1997c). 'Understanding Citizenship.' In *Men and Women of Australia: Report of a National Professional Development Project on Informed Citizenship*. Hobart: Faculty of Education.
Hogan, D., M. Fearnley-Sander, and S. Lamb (1996). 'From Civics to Citizenship: *Whereas the People* and Civic Education.' In Australian Curriculum Studies Association, *Occasional Papers*.
Hogan, M. and K. Dempsey (eds) (1995). *Equity and Citizenship Under Keating*. Sydney: Public Affairs Research Centre, University of Sydney.

Holland, K.M., F.L. Morton, and B. Galligan (eds) (1996). *Federalism and the Environment: Environmental Policymaking in Australia, Canada and the United States.* Westport, Connecticut, and London: Greenwood Press.

Honneth, A. (1995). *The Struggle for Recognition: the Moral Grammar of Social Conflicts.* J. Anderson, trans. Cambridge: Polity Press.

Hornblower, S. (1993). 'Creation and Development of Democratic Institutions in Ancient Greece.' In J. Dunn (ed.), *Democracy: The Unfinished Journey 508 BC to AD 1993.* Oxford: Oxford University Press, 1–16.

Horne, D. (1989). *Ideas for a Nation.* Sydney: Pan Books.

Horne, D. (ed.) (1994). *Teaching Young Australians to Be Australian Citizens.* Melbourne: National Centre for Australian Studies, Monash University.

Horner, J. and M. Langton (1987). 'The Day of Mourning.' In B. Gammage and P. Spearritt (eds), *Australians 1938.* Sydney: Fairfax, Syme, Weldon, 29–35.

Horsman, M. and A. Marshall (1994). *After the Nation State: Citizens, Tribalism and the New World Disorder.* London: Harper Collins.

Hudson, W. (1998). 'Citizenship and Multiple Identities.' *Southern Review*, 31(1), 54–63.

Hudson, W. and G. Bolton (eds) (1997). *Creating Australia: Changing Australian History*, Sydney: Allen & Unwin.

Hudson, W. and D. Carter (eds) (1993). *The Republicanism Debate.* Sydney: New South Wales University Press.

Hufton, O. (1992). *Women and the Limits of Citizenship in the French Revolution.* Toronto: University of Toronto Press.

Human Rights and Equal Opportunity Commission (HREOC) (1997a). *Human Rights for Australia's Gays and Lesbians.* Canberra: HREOC.

Human Rights and Equal Opportunity Commission (HREOC) (1997b) *Bringing Them Home: National Enquiry into the Separation of Aboriginal and Torres Strait Islander Children From Their Families.* Canberra: HREOC.

Humana, C. (1992). *World Human Rights Guide*, 3rd edn. New York: Oxford University Press.

Hutton, D. and L. Connors (1999). *A History of the Australian Environment Movement.* Cambridge and Melbourne: Cambridge University Press.

Hyland, N. (1995). *Citizenship of the European Union.* Dublin: Dublin: Institute of European Affairs.

Ideas for Australia (1994). *How to be Australian.* Melbourne: Monash University.

Institute of Social Research, Swinburne University of Technology (1999). 'International Index of Social and Civic Health: A Comparison of Data from UNDP, World Bank, OECD and other international sources' (mimeo). Hawthorn, Vic.: Swinburne University of Technology.

Irving, H. (1993). 'Citizens and Not-Quite Citizens.' *Constitutional Centenary*, October, 9.

Irving, H. (1997). *To Constitute a Nation: A Cultural History of Australia's Constitution.* Cambridge: Cambridge University Press.

Jacobson, D. (1997). *Rights Across Borders: Immigration and the Decline of Citizenship.* Baltimore and London: The Johns Hopkins University Press.

Jagose, A. (1996). *Queer Theory.* Melbourne: Melbourne University Press.

Janoski, T. (1998). *Citizenship and Civil Society. A Framework of Rights and Obligations in Liberal, Traditional and Social Democratic Regimes.* Cambridge: Cambridge University Press.

Jansen, S.C. (1989). 'Gender and the Information Society: A Socially Structured Silence.' *Journal of Communication*, 39(3), 196–213.

Jayasuriya, L. (1994). 'Citizens.' In R. Nile (ed.), *Australian Civilisation*. Melbourne: Oxford University Press.
Jellin, E. and E. Hershberg (eds) (1996). *Constructing Democracy: Human Rights, Citizenship and Society in Latin America*. Boulder, Col.: Westview Press.
Johnson, C. (1998). 'Keating, Howard, Gates and the Politics of Cyberfutures.' *Proceedings of the Joint Conference of the Australasian Political Science Association and European Union Studies Association of New Zealand*, 1, 393–405.
Joint Standing Committee on Migration, Parliament of the Commonwealth of Australia (1994). *Australians All: Enhancing Australian Citizenship*. Canberra: AGPS.
Jones, K.B. (1990). 'Citizenship in a Woman-Friendly Polity.' *Signs: Journal of Women in Culture and Society*, 15, 781.
Jones, K.B. (1993). *Compassionate Authority: Democracy and the Representation of Women*. London: Routledge.
Jordens, A-M. (1995). *Redefining Australian Immigration, Citizenship and National Identity*. Sydney: Hale and Iremonger.
Jupp, J. et al. (1986). *Don't Settle for Less*. Canberra: AGPS.
Kalantzis, M (1995). 'Centres and Peripheries.' *RePublica*, 3. Sydney: Harper Collins, 205–19.
Kalantzis, M and B. Cope (1993). 'Republicanism and Cultural Diversity.' In W. Hudson and D. Carter (eds), *The Republicanism Debate*. Sydney: University of New South Wales Press, 118–44.
Kaplan, A. (1997). 'Was Democracy Just a Moment?' *Atlantic Monthly*, December, 55–80.
Keane, J. (1992). 'The Modern Democratic Revolution: Reflections on Lyotard's *The Pos-modern Condition*.' In D. Benjamin (ed.), *Judging Lyotard*. London: Routledge: 81–98.
Keane, J. and J. Owens (1986). *After Full Employment*. London: Hutchinson.
Keating, P. (1992). Speech by Prime Minister Keating, Redfern, 10 December.
Keating, P. (1993a). Speech by Prime Minister Keating, Sydney, 28 April.
Keating, P. (1993b). 'New Visions for Australia.' *Australian Quarterly*, LXV, 1.
Keating, P. (1994). Speech by Prime Minister Keating, Citizenship Promotion Launch, Sydney Town Hall, 4 November.
Kelly, P. (1992). *The End of Certainty*. Sydney: Allen & Unwin.
Kelsen, H. 1945). *A General Theory of Law and the State*. Cambridge, Mass.: Harvard University Press.
Kennett, G. (1994). 'Individual Rights, The High Court and the Constitution.' *Melbourne University Law Review*, 19, 581.
Kenny, S. (1997). 'Citizenship and Welfare, the Welfare State?'. In Swinburne University of Technology Centre for Urban and Social Research, *Benchmarking Citizenship: an Introduction to Standard-Setting for Democracy and Social Well-Being in Australia*. Citizenship in Australian Series no. 1. Melbourne: Centre for Urban and Social Research, Swinburne University of Technology.
Klusmeyer, D. (1996). *Between Consent and Descent: Conceptions of Democratic Citizenship*. New York: Carnegie Endowment for International Peace.
Korpi, W. and J. Palme (1996). The Paradox of Redistribution and the Strategy of Equality: On the Role of Welfare Institutions for Inequality and Poverty in Western Countries. A paper presented at the RC19 Conference, Canberra, August.
Korten, D.C. (1990). *Getting to the 21st Century: Voluntary Action and the Global Agenda*. West Hartford, CT: Kumarian Press.

Kuhnle, S. (1987). 'Citizenship.' *Blackwell Encyclopedia of Political Institutions.* Oxford: Blackwell.
Kukathas, C. (1993).'Multiculturalism and the Idea of an Australian Identity.' In C. Kukathas (ed.), *Multicultural Citizens: The Philosophy and Politics of Identity.* Sydney: The Centre for Independent Studies.
Kukathas, C. (1997). 'Cultural Toleration'. In I. Shapiro and W. Kymlicka (eds), *NOMOS XXXIX: Ethnicity and Group Rights.* New York: New York University Press.
Kymlicka, W. (1991). *Liberalism, Community and Culture.* Oxford: Clarendon Press.
Kymlicka, W. (1995). *Multicultural Citizenship: A Liberal Theory of Minority Rights.* Oxford: Clarendon Press.
Kymlicka, W. and W. Norman (1994).'Return of the Citizen: A Survey of Recent Work on Citizenship Theory.' *Ethics*, 104, 369–77.
Laclau, E. and C. Mouffe (1985). *Hegemony and Socialist Strategy: Towards a Radical Democratic Politics.* New York: Verso.
Lake, M. (1994). 'Personality, Individuality, Nationality: Feminist Conceptions of Citizenship 1902–1940.' *Australian Feminist Studies*, 19, 25.
Lake, M. et al. (1994). *Creating a Nation.* Melbourne: McPhee Gribble.
Lang, J.D. (1870). *The Coming Event, or, Freedom and Independence for the Seven United Provinces of Australia.* Sydney: John Sherriff.
Langmore, J. and J. Quiggin (1994). *Work for All: Full Employment in the Nineties.* Melbourne: Melbourne University Press.
Latham, M. (1998). *Civilising Global Capital: New Thinking for Australian Labor.* Sydney: Allen & Unwin.
Lekachman, R. (1957). 'The Non-Economic Assumptions of John Maynard Keynes.' In M. Komarovsky (ed.), *Common Frontiers of the Social Sciences.* Glencoe, Ill.: The Free Press.
Lesbian and Gay Legal Rights Service (1994). *The Bride Wore Pink. Legal Recognition of Our Relationships. A Discussion Paper*, 2nd edn. Darlinghurst, NSW: Lesbian and Gay Legal Rights Service.
Lewis, J. (1994). 'Gender, the Family and Women's Agency in the Building of Welfare States.' *Social History*, 19(1): 37–55.
Lingis, A. (1994). *The Community of Those Who Have Nothing in Common.* Bloomington: Indiana University Press.
Linklater, A. (1992a). 'What Is Good International Citizenship?' In P. Keal (ed.), *Ethics and Foreign Policy.* Sydney: Allen & Unwin, 21–43.
Linklater, A. (1992b). *Men and Citizens.* London: Macmillan.
Linklater, A. (1996). 'Citizenship and Sovereignty in the Post-Westphalian State.' *European Journal of International Relations*, 2(1), 77–103.
Lipschutz, R.D. (1992). 'Reconstructing World Politics: The Emergence of Global Civil Society.' *Millennium* 21(30), 389–420.
Lipschutz, R.D., with J. Mayer (1996). *Global Civil Society and Global Environmental Governance.* New York: State University of New York Press.
Lister, R. (1997). *Citizenship: Feminist Perspectives.* London: Macmillan Press.
Locke, J. (1955 [1690]). *Two Treatises of Civil Government.* London: Dent (Everyman).
Luhmann, N. (1998). *Observations on Modernity.* W. Whobrey, trans. Stanford, CA: Stanford University Press.
Lyon, D. (1988). *The Information Society.* London: Polity Press.
Lyotard, J-F. (1977). *Instructions païennes.* Paris: Galilée.
Lyotard, J-F. (1985). *Just Gaming.* W. Godzich, trans. Manchester: Manchester University Press.

Macedo, S. (1988). 'Capitalism, Citizenship and Community.' *Social Philosophy and Policy*, 6, 113–39. Reproduced in B.S. Turner and P. Hamilton (eds), *Citizenship: Critical Concepts*. London: Routledge, 111–34.

Macedo, S. (1991). *Liberal Virtues: Citizenship, Virtue and Community in Liberal Constitutionalism*. Oxford: Clarendon Press.

McGrath, A. (1993). '"Beneath the Skin": Australian Citizenship, Rights and Aboriginal Women.' *Journal of Australian Studies*, 37, 99.

McGregor, R. (1993). 'Protest and Progress: Aboriginal Activism in the 1930s.' *Australian Historical Studies*, 25(101) (October), 555–68.

Machiavelli, N. (1969). *The Discourses*. B. Crick, ed. Harmondsworth: Penguin.

MacIntyre, A. (1984). *After Virtue*, 2nd edn. Notre Dame, Indiana: University of Notre Dame Press.

Macintyre, S. (1991). *A Colonial Liberalism: The Lost World of Three Victorian Visionaries*. Melbourne: Oxford University Press.

McKenna, M. (1996). *The Captive Republic: A History of Republicanism in Australia 1788–1996*. Cambridge: Cambridge University Press

McNeill, W.H. (1986). *Polyethnicity and National Units in World History*. Toronto: University of Toronto Press.

Macphee, I.M. (1982). *Australian Citizenship: Ministerial Statement*. 6 May.

Mamdani, M. (1996). *Citizenship and Subject: Contemporary Africa and the Late Colonial Legacy*. Princeton, NJ: Princeton University Press.

Manville, P.B. (1991). *The Origins of Citizenship in Ancient Athens*. Princeton, NJ: Princeton University Press.

Marginson, S. (1997). *Educating Australia: Government, Economy and Citizen Since 1960*. Cambridge: Cambridge University Press.

Markus, A. (ed.) (1988). *Blood from a Stone: William Cooper and the Australian Aborigines' League*. Sydney: Allen & Unwin.

Marsh, I. (1995a). *Beyond the Two Party System: Political Representation, Economic Competitiveness and Australian Politics*. Cambridge: Cambridge University Press.

Marshall, T.H. (1950). *Citizenship and Social Class and Other Essays*. Cambridge: Cambridge University Press.

Marshall, T.H. (1963). 'Citizenship and Social Class.' In T.H. Marshall (ed.), *Sociology at the Crossroads, and Other Essays*. London: Heinemann.

Marshall, T.H. (1965). *Class, Citizenship and Social Development*. New York: Anchor.

Martin, D.F. and J.D. Finlayson (1996). 'Linking Accountability and Self-Determination in Aboriginal Organisations.' CAEPR Discussion Paper no. 116. Canberra: Australian National University.

Marx, K. (1977). 'Towards a Critique of Hegel's Philosophy of Right. Introduction.' In D. McLellan (ed.), *Selected Writings*. Oxford: Oxford University Press.

Meadows, D.H, D.L. Meadows, J. Randers, and W.W. Behrens (1970). *The Limits to Growth*. London and Sydney: Pan Books.

Meadows, M. and C. Morris (1998). 'Into the New Millennium: The Role of Indigenous Media in Australia.' *Media International Australia*, 88, 67–78.

Meehan, E. (1993a). *Citizenship and the European Community*. London: Sage.

Meehan, E. (1993b). 'Citizenship and the European Community.' *Political Quarterly*, 64(2), 172–86.

Meehan, E. (1994). 'Equality, Difference and Democracy.' In D. Miliband (ed.), *Reinventing the Left*. Cambridge: Polity.

Melleuish, G. (1995). *Cultural Liberalism in Australia*. Cambridge: Cambridge University Press.

Meredyth, D. and D. Tyler (eds) (1993). *Child and Citizen: Genealogies of Schooling and Subjectivity*. Brisbane: Institute for Cultural Policy Studies, Griffith University.
Meyer, W.J. (1998). 'The Politics of Differentiated Citizenship'. In K. Slawner and M.E. Denham (eds), *Citizenship after Liberalism*. New York: Peter Lang Publishing.
Milburn, C. (1995). 'Complaint Lodged Over Ok Tedi Ads.' *Age*, 19 October, 28.
Mill, J.S. (1958 [1861]). *Considerations on Representative Government*. New York: Bobbs-Merrill.
Mill, J.S. (1963). *Collected Works of John Stuart Mill*. Toronto: Toronto University Press, vols 16, 17 and 21.
Mill, J.S. (1989 [1859]). *On Liberty and Other Writings*. S. Collini, ed. Cambridge: Cambridge University Press.
Miller, C. (1999). 'Legal Threat to Save Snowy River Species.' *Age*, 31 July, 7.
Miller, D. (1992). 'Community and Citizenship.' In S. Avineri and A. De-Shalit (eds), *Communitarianism and Individualism*. Oxford: Oxford University Press.
Minson, J.P. (1993). *Questions of Conduct: Sexual Harassment, Citizenship, Government*. London: MacMillan.
Mishra, R. (1984). *The Welfare State in Crisis*. Brighton: Wheatsheaf Books.
Molnar, H. (1998). 'National Convergence or Localism? Rural and Remote Communications.' *Media International Australia*, 88, 5–9.
Montesquieu, C. de S. (1977 [1748]). *The Spirit of Laws*. D.W. Carrithers, ed.; Thomas Nugent, trans. Berkeley and London: University of California Press.
Montesquieu, C. de S. (1989 [1748]). *The Spirit of the Laws*. A.M. Cohler, B.C. Miller and H.S. Stone, trans. and eds. Cambridge: Cambridge University Press.
More, E. (1998). 'Management Challenges for South-East Asia in a Deregulated and/or Privatised Telecommunications Environment.' *Australian Journal of Communication*, 25(2), 115–41.
Morgan, W. (1995). 'Still in the Closet: The Heterosexism of Equal Opportunity Law.' *Critical Inquiries* 1(2), 119–46.
Mouffe, C. (1993). *The Return of the Political*. London, New York.
Moyal, A. (1986). *A Bright and Savage Land: Scientists in Colonial Australia*. Sydney: Collins.
Muir, K. (1993). *Arms and the Woman*. London: Hodder and Stoughton.
Nair, S. (1997). *Contre les lois Pasqua*. Paris: Arlea.
Naisbitt, J. (1994). *Global Paradox*. Sydney: Allen & Unwin.
Nancy, J-L. (1991). *The Inoperative Community*. Minneapolis: Minnesota University Press.
Nicolet, C. (1990). *The World of the Citizen in Republican Rome*. London: Batsford.
Nie, N., J. Junn and K. Stehlik-Barry (1996). *Education and Democratic Citizenship in America*. Chicago: University of Chicago Press.
Nielsen, J.S. (ed.) (1993). *Religion and Citizenship in Europe and the Arab World*. London: Grey Seal Books.
Norman, R. (1992). 'Citizenship, Politics and Autonomy.' In D. Milligan and W.W. Miller (eds), *Liberalism, Citizenship and Autonomy*. Aldershot: Avebury.
Novak, M. (1982). 'The Communitarian Individual in America'. *The Public Interest*, 68, 3–20.
Nozick, R. (1974). *Anarchy, State and Utopia*. Oxford: Blackwell.
Nussbaum, M.C. et al. (1996). *For Love of Country: Debating the Limits of Patriotism*. J. Cohen, ed. Boston: Beacon Press.

Offe, C. (1985). *Disorganized Capitalism: Contemporary Transformations of Work and Politics.* J. Keane, ed. Cambridge: Polity Press.

Office of Multicultural Affairs (1989). Department of the Prime Minister and Cabinet, National Agenda for a Multicultural Australia. *Sharing Our Future.* Canberra: Australian Government Publishing Service, vii.

Office of Multicultural Affairs, Department of the Prime Minister and Cabinet (1993). *Productive Diversity in Business,* Canberra: OMA.

Office of the Status of Women, Australian Government (1988). *Community Attitudes towards Domestic Violence in Australia,* Canberra: Public Policy Research Centre.

Oldfield, A. (1990a). 'Citizenship: An Unnatural Practice?' *The Political Quarterly,* 61, 177–87.

Oldfield, A. (1990b). *Citizenship and Community: Civic Republicanism and the Modern World.* London: Routledge.

Oliver, D. and D. Heater (1994). *The Foundations of Citizenship.* Hemel Hempstead: Harvester Wheatsheaf.

Ormerod, P. (1994). *The Death of Economics.* London: Faber and Faber.

Ormerod, P. (1996). 'A New Social Contract? Unemployment in Europe.' *EUI Working Paper,* no. 96/39. Florence: European University Institute.

Osborne, D.E. and T. Gaebler (1993). *Reinventing Government: How the Entrepreneurial Spirit Is Transforming the Public Sector.* Ringwood: Penguin.

Pain, N. (1989). 'Third Party Rights Public Participation under the Environmental Planning and Assessment Act 1979 (NSW): Do the floodgates need opening?' *Environmental and Planning Law Journal,* 5(1) (March), 26–35.

Painter, M. (1996). 'Economic Policy and Market Liberalism.' *Australian Journal of Political Science,* 31(3), 287–99.

Painter, M. (1998). *Collaborative Federalism: Economic Reform in Australia in the 1990s.* Cambridge: Cambridge University Press.

Paley, W. (1825). *The Principles of Moral and Political Philosophy,* vol. 4. Collected Works. London: C. and J. Rivington

Panitch, L. (1994). 'Changing Gears: Democratising the Welfare State.' In A.F. Johnson, S. McBride and P.J. Smith (eds), *Continuities and Discontinuities: The Political Economy of Social Welfare and Labour Market Policy.* Toronto: University of Toronto Press.

Papadakis, E. (1993). *Politics and the Environment, The Australian Experience.* Sydney: Allen & Unwin.

Papadakis, E. (1996). *Environmental Politics and Institutional Change.* Cambridge: Cambridge University Press.

Pateman, C. (1988). *The Sexual Contract.* Cambridge: Polity.

Pateman, C. (1992). 'Citizen Male.' *Australian Left Review,* 137, 30–3.

Patterson, O. (1991). *Freedom in the Making of Western Culture.* New York: Basic Books.

Pavlik, J. (1998). *New Media Technology: Cultural and Commercial Perspectives.* Boston: Allyn and Bacon.

Pearson, D.E. (1995). 'Community and Sociology.' *Society,* 32(5) (July/August), 45–52.

Pearson, N. (1993). 'Reconciliation: To Be Or Not to Be – Nationhood, Self-Determination or Self-Government.' *Aboriginal Law Bulletin,* 3(61), 14–17.

Peters, T.J. and R.H. Waterman (1982). *In Search of Excellence: Lessons From America's Best-Run Companies.* New York: Harper and Row.

Peterson, N. and W. Sanders (eds) (1998). *Citizenship and Indigenous Australians: Changing Conceptions and Possibilities.* New York: Cambridge University Press.

Petre, D. and D. Harrington (1996). *The Clever Country? Australia's Digital Future.* Sydney: Lansdowne.
Pettit, P. (1996). 'Our Republican Heritage.' *Eureka Street*, 6(6), 41–5.
Pettit, P. (1997). *Republicanism: A Theory of Freedom and Government.* Oxford: Clarendon Press.
Pettit, P. (1998) Review of M. Sandel, *Democracy's Discontent: America in Search of a Public Philosophy. Journal of Philosophy*, vol. xcv, no. 2 (February), 73–96.
Phillips, A. (1991). *Engendering Democracy.* Cambridge: Polity Press.
Phillips, A. (1992). 'Universal Pretensions in Political Thought.' In M. Barrett and A. Phillips (eds), *Destabilizing Theory: Contemporary Feminist Debates.* Stanford: Stanford University Press, 10–30.
Phillips, A. (1993). *Democracy and Difference.* London: Polity Press.
Phillips, D.L. (1993). *Looking Backward: A Critical Appraisal of Communitarian Thought.* Princeton, NJ: Princeton University Press.
Pixley, J.F. (1993). *Citizenship and Employment: Investigating Post-Industrial Options.* Cambridge: Cambridge University Press.
Pixley, J.F. (1995). 'Combining Work and Welfare: Against Basic Income.' *Just Policy VCOSS*, 4, 17–25.
Pixley, J.F. (1996). 'Economic Democracy: Beyond Wage Earners Welfare.' In J. Wilson et al. (eds), *The Australian Welfare State.* Melbourne: Macmillan.
Pixley, J.F. (1997). 'Employment and Social Identity.' In M. Roche and R. van Berkel (eds), *European Citizenship and Social Exclusion.* Aldershot: Ashgate.
Plant, R. (1988). *Citizenship, Rights and Socialism.* London: Fabian Society.
Plant, R. (1991). 'Social rights and the construction of welfare.' In G. Andrews (ed.), *Citizenship.* London: Laurence and Wishhart.
Plant. R. (1992). 'Citizenship, Rights and Welfare.' In A. Coote (ed.), *The Welfare of Citizens.* London: Institute of Public Policy Research/Rivers Oram Press.
Plummer, K. (1995). *Telling Sexual Stories.* London: Routledge.
Pocock, B. (ed.) (1997). *Strife: Sex and Politics in Labour Unions.* Sydney: Allen & Unwin.
Pocock, J.G.A. (1975). *The Machiavellian Moment: Florentine Political Thought and the Atlantic Tradition.* Princeton, NJ: Princeton University Press.
Pocock, J.G.A. (1998). 'The Ideal of Citizenship since Classic Times.' In G. Shafir (ed.), *The Citizenship Debates: A Reader.* Minneapolis: University of Minnesota Press, 31–41.
Polanyi, K. (1944). *The Great Transformation: The Political and Economic Origins of Our Time.* Boston: Beacon Press.
Poster, M. (1995). *The Second Media Age.* Cambridge: Polity Press.
Price, R. (1991). *Political Writings.* D.O. Thomas, ed. Cambridge: Cambridge University Press.
Pringle, R. (1992). 'Absolute Sex? Unpacking the Sexuality/Gender Relationship.' In R.W. Connell and G.W. Dowsett (eds), *Rethinking Sex. Social Theory and Sexuality Research.* Melbourne: Melbourne University Press, 76–101.
Pryles, M. (1981). *Australian Citizenship Law.* Sydney: Law Book.
Pusey, M. (1991). *Economic Rationalism in Canberra: A Nation-building State Changes its Mind.* Cambridge: Cambridge University Press.
Putnam, R.D. (1993). *Making Democracy Work: Civic Traditions in Modern Italy.* Princeton, NJ: Princeton University Press.
Quick, J. and R.R. Garran (1976 [1901]). *The Annotated Constitution of the Australian Commonwealth.* Sydney: Legal Books.
Quiggin, J. (1996). *Great Expectations: Microeconomic Reform and Australia.* Sydney: Allen & Unwin.

Rahe, P.A. (1992). *Republics Ancient and Modern: Classical Republicanism and the American Revolution*. Chapel Hill: University of North Carolina Press.
Rawls, J. (1972). *A Theory of Justice*. Cambridge, MA: Belknap Press.
Rawls, J. (1973). *A Theory of Justice*. Oxford: Oxford University Press.
Rawls, J. (1993). *Political Liberalism*. New York: Columbia University Press.
Raz, J. (1986). *The Morality of Freedom*. Oxford: Clarendon Press.
Raz, J. (1994). 'Multiculturalism: A Liberal Perspective.' In *Ethics in the Public Domain: Essays in the Morality of Law and Politics*. Oxford: Clarendon Press.
Rees, S. and G. Rodley (eds) (1995). *The Human Costs of Managerialism*. Sydney: Pluto Press.
Rees, S., G. Rodley and F. Stilwell (eds) (1993). *Beyond the Market: Alternatives to Economic Rationalism*. Sydney: Pluto Press.
Reich, R. (1992). *The Work of Nations*. New York: Vintage.
Reynolds, H. (1987). *The Law of the Land*. Ringwood: Penguin.
Reynolds, H. (1996). *Aboriginal Sovereignty: Three Nations, One Australia?* Sydney: Allen & Unwin.
Rheingold, H. (1993). *The Virtual Community: Homesteading on the Electronic Frontier*. Reading, Mass.: Addison-Wesley.
Richardson, D. (1998). 'Sexuality and Citizenship.' *Sociology*, 32(1), 83–100.
Richmond, A.H. (1994). 'Ethnic Nationalism and Postindustrialism.' In J. Hutchinson and A.D. Smith (eds), *Nationalism*. Oxford: Oxford University Press, 289–300.
Riesenberg, P. (1992). *Citizenship in the Western Tradition: Plato to Rousseau*. Chapel Hill: University of North Carolina Press.
Robinson, D. (1993). 'Public Participation in Environmental Decision-Making.' *Environmental and Planning Law Journal*, October, 10(5), 320–40.
Robinson, D. (1996). 'The Environmental Defender's Office NSW, 1985–1995.' *Environmental and Planning Law Journal*, June, 13(3), 155–78.
Roche, M. (1992). *Rethinking Citizenship: Welfare, Ideology and Change in Modern Society*. Cambridge: Polity Press.
Roche, M. (1995). 'Citizenship and Modernity.' *British Journal of Sociology*, 46(4), 715–33.
Roche, M. and R. van Berkel (eds) (1997). *European Citizenship and Social Exclusion*. Aldershot: Ashgate.
Rogers, J. and W. Streeck (1994). 'Productive Solidarities: Economic Strategies and Left Politics.' In D. Miliband (ed.), *Reinventing the Left*. Cambridge: Polity.
Rorty, R. (1989). *Contingency, Irony and Solidarity*. Cambridge: Cambridge University Press.
Rosenau, J.N. and J. Der Derian (eds) (1993). *Global Voices: Dialogues in International Relations*. Boulder, CO: Westview Press.
Rousseau, J-J. (1967 [1762]). *The Social Contract*. In *The Social Contract and Discourse on Inequality*. L. Crocker, ed. New York: Pocket Books.
Rousseau, J-J. (1986). *The First and Second Discourses With the Replies to Critics and Essay on the Origin of Languages*. V. Gourevich, trans. New York: Harper and Row.
Rousseau, J-J. (1977). *The Social Contract and the Discourses*. London: Dent.
Rowley, C. D. (1971). *Outcasts in White Australia*. Ringwood, Vic.: Penguin.
Rowse, T. (1998). *White Flour White Power: From Rations to Citizenship in Central Australia*. Cambridge: Cambridge University Press.

Rubenstein, K. (1995). 'Citizenship in Australia: Unscrambling Its Meaning.' *Melbourne University Law Review*, 20, 503.
Rubin, G. (1984). 'Thinking Sex: Notes for a Radical Theory of the Politics of Sexuality.' In C.S. Vance (ed.), *Pleasure and Danger. Exploring Female Sexuality*. New York: Routledge and Kegan Paul.
Sainsbury, D. (1996). *Gender, Equality and Welfare States*. Cambridge: Cambridge University Press.
Sandel, M. (1982). *Liberalism and the Limits of Justice*. Cambridge; Cambridge University Press.
Sardar, Z. (1996). 'alt.civilizations.faq: Cyberspace as the Darker Side of the West.' In Z. Sardar and J.R. Ravetz (eds), *Cyberfutures: Culture and Politics on the Information Superhighway*. New York: New York University Press.
Saul, J.R. (1997). *The Unconscious Civilization*. New York: Free Press.
Saunders, P. (1994). *Welfare and Inequality: National and International Perspectives on the Australian Welfare State*. Cambridge: Cambridge University Press.
Sawer, M. (1990). *Sisters in Suits, Women and Public Policy in Australia*. Sydney: Allen & Unwin.
Sawer, M. (1995). Review of Brennan, *Australian Journal of Political Science*, 30(2), 377–8.
Sawer, M. and M. Simms (1993). *A Woman's Place: Women and Politics in Australia*, 2nd edn. Sydney: Allen & Unwin.
Scates, B. (1997). *A New Australia: Citizenship, Radicalism and the First Republic*. Cambridge: Cambridge University Press.
Schmid, G. (1995). *Är full sysselsättning fortfarande möjlig?* (Is full employment still possible?) Stockholm: PM Bäckström Förlag.
School of Social Science and Policy (1997). *Report on Police Attitudes to Domestic Violence*. Sydney: School of Social Science and Policy, University of New South Wales.
Schultz, J. (1994). 'Media Convergence and the Fourth Estate.' In J. Schultz (ed.), *Not Just Another Business: Journalists, Citizens and the Media*, 35–52. Leichhardt: Pluto Press.
Schultz, J. (ed.) (1994). *Not Just Another Business: Journalists, Citizens and the Media*. Leichhardt: Pluto Press.
Schumpeter, J. (1947). *Capitalism, Socialism and Democracy*. New York: Harper and Row.
Seccombe, W. (1993). 'Democracy and Ecology.' In G. Albo, D. Langille and L. Panitch (eds), *A Different Kind of State? Popular Power and Democratic Administration*. Toronto: Oxford University Press.
Sedgwick, E.K. (1990). *Epistemology of the Closet*. London: Penguin.
Senge, P. (1991). *The Fifth Discipline, the Art and Practice of the Learning Organization*. New York: Doubleday.
Shafritz, J. (ed.) (2000). *The International Encyclopedia of Public Policy and Administration*. Boulder, CO: Westview Press.
Sharp, N. (1996). *No Ordinary Judgment*. Canberra: Aboriginal Studies Press.
Shaver, S. (1995).'Women, Employment and Social Security.' In A. Edwards and S. Magarey (eds), *Women in a Restructuring Australia: Work and Welfare*. Sydney: Allen & Unwin.
Shaw, M. (1992). 'Global Society and Global Responsibility: The Theoretical, Historical and Political Limits of "International Society."' *Millennium*, 21(3), 421–34.

Shelton, D. (1991). Human Rights, Environmental Rights, and the Right to Environment. *Stanford Journal of International Law*, 28, 103–38.

Singh, M.G. (1996). *Citizenship in Australia's Multicultural Society*. Curriculum Corporation.

Skates, B. (1997). *A New Australia: Citizenship and the First Republic*. Cambridge: Cambridge University Press.

Skinner, Q. (1990). 'The republican ideal of political liberty.' In G. Bock, Q. Skinner and M. Viroli (eds), *Machiavelli and Republicanism*. Cambridge: Cambridge University Press.

Skocpol, T. (1992). *Protecting Soldiers and Mothers, the Political Origins of Social Policy in the United States*. Cambridge, MA: Belknap at Harvard.

Slawner, K. and M.E. Denham (eds) (1998). *Citizenship After Liberalism*. New York: Peter Lang.

Smith, D.E. (1995). 'Representative Politics and the New Wave of Native Title Organisations.' In J. Finlayson and D.E. Smith (eds), *Native Title: Emerging Issues for Research, Policy and Practice*. CAEPR Research Monograph 10, Canberra: Australian National University, 59–74.

Smith, M.J. (1998). *Ecologism: Towards Ecological Citizenship. Concepts in the Social Sciences*. Open University Press.

Smith, R. (1997). *Civic Ideals: Conflicting Visions of Citizenship in US History*. New Haven, CT: Yale University Press.

Smith, T. (1994). 'The Power of Business' *Human Rights: The New Consensus*. United Nations High Commissioner for Refugees. London: Regency Press.

Smyth, P. (1994). *Australian Social Policy: The Keynesian Chapter*. Sydney: University of New South Wales Press.

Soysal, Y.N. (1994). *Limits of Citizenship: Migrants and Postnational Membership in Europe*. Chicago and London: University of Chicago.

Speck, C. (1996). 'Women's War Memorials and Citizenship.' *Australian Feminist Studies*, 23, 129–45.

Spender, D. (1995). *Nattering on the Net: Women, Power and Cyberspace*. North Melbourne: Spinifex.

Springborg, L. (1993). 'An Historical Note on Republicanism.' In W. Hudson and D. Carter (eds), *The Republicanism Debate*. Kensington, NSW: New South Wales University Press, 201–7.

Spurgeon, C. (1998). 'National Culture, Communications and the Information Economy.' *Media International Australia*, 87, 23–34.

Stacey, M. (1973). 'The Myth of Community Studies'. In C. Bell and H. Newby (eds), *Community Studies: An Introduction to the Sociology of the Local Community*. New York: Praeger.

Stein, P. (1996). 'Comment.' *Environmental and Planning Law Journal*, June, 13(3), 179–85.

Stephen, Sir Ninian (1993). 'Issues in Citizenship.' Deakin Lecture 1993.

Stier, M. (1998). 'How Much of Communitarianism is Left (and Right)?'. In P.E. Lawler and D. McConkey (eds), *Community and Political Thought Today*. Westport CT: Praeger.

Stilwell, F. (1993). *Economic Inequality: Who Gets What in Australia*. Sydney: Pluto Press.

Stokes, G. (1997). 'Citizenship and Aboriginality: Two Conceptions of Identity in Aboriginal Political Thought.' In G. Stokes (ed.), *The Politics of Identity in Australia*. Cambridge: Cambridge University Press, 158–71.

Strange, S. (1996). *The Retreat of the State: The Diffusion of Power in the World Economy*. Cambridge: Cambridge University Press.

Strasbourg Consensus (1983). *The Strasbourg Consensus.* Strasbourg: Council of Europe.
Stretton, H. and Orchard, L. (1994). *Public Goods, Public Enterprise, Public Choice: Theoretical Foundations of the Contemporary Attack on Government.* New York: St Martin's Press.
Sullivan, B. (1997). *The Politics of Sex. Prostitution and Pornography in Australia.* Cambridge: Cambridge University Press.
Sullivan, P. (1996). *All Free Man Now: Culture, Community and Politics in the Kimberley Region, North-West Australia.* Canberra: Australian Institute of Aboriginal and Torres Strait Islanders Studies.
Suter, K. (1981). *A New International Order: Proposals for Making A Better World.* Sydney: World Association of World Federalists.
Suter, K. (1995). 'Towards a Federal World State.' In M. Salla, W. Tonetto and E. Martinez (eds), *Essays on Peace.* Rockhampton: Central University of Queensland Press, 197–212.
Sydney, A. (1990). *Discourses Concerning Government.* T.G. West, ed. Indianapolis: Liberty Classics.
Sykes, R. (1997). *Snake Cradle.* Sydney: Allen & Unwin.
Sylvan, L. (1995). 'Global Trade, Influence and Power.' In P. Alston and M. Chiam (eds), *Treaty-Making and Australia: Globalisation Versus Sovereignty?* Sydney: Federation Press.
Taberner, J., N. Brunton, and L. Mather (1996). 'The Development of Public Participation in Environmental Protection and Planning Law in Australia.' *Environmental and Planning Law Journal,* 13(4) (August): 260–68.
Takaki, R. (1993) *A Different Mirror: A History of Multicultural America.* New York: Little Brown.
Taylor, C. (1977). 'What is Human Agency?'. In T. Mischel (ed.), *The Self.* London: Blackwell, 103–38.
Taylor, C. (1992). *Multiculturalism and the Politics of Recognition.* Princeton: Princeton University Press.
Taylor, C. (1994). 'The Politics of Recognition.' In A. Gutmann (ed.), *Multiculturalism.* Princeton, NJ: Princeton University Press.
Thomas, J. (1993). 'Citizenship and Historical Sensibility.' *Australian Historical Studies,* 25(100), 383–93.
Thomas, J. (1994). 'The History of Civics Education in Australia' (Appendix 4.1) In Civics Expert Group (ed.), *Whereas the People: Civics and Citizenship Education,* Canberra: AGPS.
Thompson, E. (1994). *Fair Enough: Egalitarianism in Australia.* Sydney: UNSW Press.
Thornton, M. (1991). 'Feminism and the Contradictions of Law Reform.' *International Journal of the Sociology of Law,* 19, 453.
Thornton, M. (1995). 'Embodying the Citizen.' In M. Thornton (ed.), *Public and Private: Feminist Legal Debates.* Melbourne: Oxford University Press.
Thornton, M. (1996). 'Historicising Citizenship: Remembering Broken Promises.' *Melbourne University Law Review,* 20, 1072.
Thornton, M. (1997). 'The Judicial Gendering of Citizenship: A Look at Property Interests During Marriage.' *Journal of Law and Society,* 24, 486.
Tiffen, R. (1994). 'The Media and Democracy: Reclaiming an Intellectual Agenda.' In J. Schultz (ed.), *Not Just Another Business: Journalists, Citizens and the Media.* Leichhardt: Pluto Press.

Tinder, G. (1986). 'Should All Peoples Be United in a Single Global Society?' In *Political Thinking: The Perennial Questions*. Glenview IL: Scott, Foresman and Company, 41–5.
Toyne, P. (1994). *The Reluctant Nation: Environment, Law and Politics in Australia*. Sydney: ABC Books.
Tully, J. (1995). *Strange Multiplicity: Constitutionalism in an Age of Diversity*. New York: Cambridge.
Turner, B.S. (1986). *Citizenship and Capitalism: The Debate Over Reformism*. London: Allen & Unwin.
Turner, B.S. (1993). 'Outline of a Theory of Human Rights.' In B.S. Turner (ed.), *Citizenship and Social Theory*. Thousand Oaks CA: Sage, 162–90.
Turner, B. and P. Hamilton (eds) (1994). *Citizenship: Critical Concepts*, 2 vols. London: Routledge.
Turner, G. (1994). *Making It National*. Sydney: Allen & Unwin.
Twine, F. (1994). *Citizenship and Social Rights: The Interdependence of Self and Society*. London: Sage.
United Nations Development Programme (UNDP) (1990, 1998). *Human Development Report*. New York: Oxford University Press.
Valverde, M. (1996). '"Despotism" and Ethical Liberal Governance.' *Economy and Society*, 25(3) (August), 357–72.
Van Berkel, R. and M. Roche (1997). *European Citizenship and Social Exclusion*. Brookfield, VT: Ashgate.
van Gunsteren, H. (1994). 'Four conceptions of citizenship.' In B. van Steenbergen (ed.), *The Condition of Citizenship*. London: Sage, 36–48.
van Gunsteren, H.R. (1998). *A Theory of Citizenship: Organizing Plurality in Contemporary Democracies*. Boulder, Colorado: Westview Press.
van Steenbergen, B. (ed.) (1994). *The Condition of Citizenship*. London: Sage.
Verba, S., K. Schlozman and H. Brady (1995). *Voice and Equality*. Cambridge, MA: Harvard University Press.
Voet, R. (1994). 'Women As Citizens: A Feminist Debate.' *Australian Feminist Studies*, 19, 61–77.
Vogel, U. and M. Moran (1991). *The Frontiers of Citizenship*. New York: St Martin's.
Wajcman, J. (1991). *Feminism Confronts Technology*. Cambridge: Polity Press.
Waks, L.J. (1996). 'Environmental Claims and Citizen Rights.' *Environmental Ethics*, Summer, 18(2), 133–48.
Walby, S. (1994). 'Is Citizenship Gendered?' *Sociology*, 28(2), 379–95.
Walker, R.B. (1991). 'Fauna and Flora Protection In New South Wales, 1866–1948.' *Journal of Australian Studies*, 28 (March), 17–28.
Walter, J. (1996). *What Does Australian Citizenship Mean Today?* Curriculum Corporation commissioned paper.
Walzer, M. (1983). *Spheres of Justice*. New York: Basic Books.
Walzer, M. (1991). 'The Civil Society Argument.' *Dissent* (Spring): 293–304.
Ward, I. (1995). *The Politics of the Media*. Melbourne: Macmillan.
Warnick, B. (1998). 'Appearance Or Reality? Political Parody on the Web in Campaign '96.' *Critical Studies in Mass Communication*, 15, 306–24.
Warrington, J. (ed. & trans.) (1959). *Aristotle – Politics*. Everyman's Library. London: JM Dent & Sons.
Weale, A. (1991). 'Citizenship Beyond Borders.' In U. Vogel and M. Moran (eds), *The Frontiers of Citizenship*. London: Macmillan, 155–65.
Webb, L.J., D. Whitelock and J. Le Gay Brereton (eds) (1969). *The Last of Lands: Conservation in Australia*. Brisbane: The Jacaranda Press.
Webb, S. and B. (1902). *Industrial Democracy*. Printed by the authors for the Trade Unionists of the United Kingdom: London.

Weeks, J. (1998). 'The Sexual Citizen.' *Theory, Culture and Society,* 15(3–4), 35–52.
Weiss, L. (1998). *The Myth of the Powerless State: Governing the Economy in a Global Era.* London: Polity Press.
Weiss, L. and J.L. Hobson (1995). *States and Economic Development.* Cambridge: Polity.
Wells, C. (1995). *Law and Citizenship in Early Modern France.* Baltimore, MD: The Johns Hopkins University Press.
Whitlam, G. (1995). 'States Rights v World Values.' *University of Western Australia Law Review,* 25(1), 1–20.
Willcox, M. (1996). 'Comment.' *Environmental and Planning Law Journal,* 13(3) (June), 151–54.
Wills, S. (1995). 'Sexual Equity.' In M. Hogan and K. Dempsey (eds), *Equity and Citizenship Under Keating.* Sydney: Public Affairs Research Centre, Dept of Government and Public Administration, University of Sydney.
Wirszubski, C. (1968). *Libertas as a Political Idea at Rome.* Oxford: Oxford University Press.
Wiseman, J. (1998). *Global Nation? Australia and the Politics of Globalisation.* Cambridge and Melbourne: Cambridge University Press.
Wishart, D. (1986). 'Allegiance and Citizenship As Concepts in Constitutional Law.' *Melbourne University Law Review,* 15, 662.
Wittgenstein, L. (1997 [1953]). *Philosophical Investigation.* G.E.M. Anscombe, trans. 2nd edn. Cambridge, Mass.: Blackwell.
Woodward, A.E. (1974). *Aboriginal Land Rights Commisson: Second Report April 1974.* Canberra: AGPS.
Yeatman, A. (1994). *Postmodern Revisionings of the Political.* London: Routledge.
Yeatman, A. (1995) 'Interpreting Contemporary Contractualism.' In J. Boston (ed.), *The State Under Contract.* Wellington: Bridget Williams Books, 124–39.
Yeatman, A. (1996). *Democratic Theory and the Subject of Citizenship. Culture and Citizenship.* Brisbane: Australian Key Centre for Cultural and Media Policy.
Yeatman, A. (1997). 'Contract, Status and Personhood.' In G. Davis, B. Sullivan and A. Yeatman (eds), *The New Contractualism?* Nathan, Qld: Centre for Australian Public Sector Management, Griffith University, 39–56.
Yeatman, A. (1998). 'Interpreting Contemporary Contractualism.' In M. Dean and B. Hindess (eds), *Governing Australia: Studies in Contemporary Rationalities of Government.* Cambridge: Cambridge University Press, 227–41.
Young, I.M. (1987). 'Impartiality and the Civic Public: Some Implications of Feminist Critiques of Moral and Political Theory.' In Seyla Benhabib and Drucilla Cornell (eds), *Feminism as Critique.* Oxford/Minneapolis: Polity/University of Minnesota Press.
Young, I.M. (1989). 'Polity and Group Difference: A Critique of the Ideal of Universal Citizenship.' *Ethics* 99, 250–74.
Young, I. M. (1990). *Justice and the Politics of Difference.* Princeton, NJ: Princeton University Press.
Young, I.M. (1997). 'Deferring Group Representation'. In I. Shapiro and W. Kymlicka (eds), *NOMOS XXXIX: Ethnicity and Group Rights.* New York: New York University Press, 349–76.
Zolo, D. (1992). *Democracy and Complexity: A Realist Approach.* Cambridge: Polity.
Zolo, D. (1997). *Cosmopolis: Prospects for World Government.* Cambridge: Polity.
Zwiebach, B. (1975). *Civility and Disobedience.* Cambridge: Cambridge University Press.

Index

Aboriginal Councils and Associations Act 92
Aboriginals Land Trust Act 95
Aboriginals Ordinance (Northern Territory) 88
Aborigines 9, 86–98, 117, 118
 as British subjects 3
 communal traditions 92, 94
 genocide 47
 institutions 92, 95–6
access 106, 108, 192–7
accountability 67, 71, 72, 73, 130
Ackerman, B. 233
Albo, G. 128
Alston, P. 124
Alston, R. 195
American Revolution 176
Amnesty International 233, 237
Angell, N. 178
APEC 106, 236
Apel, K-O. 240
arbitrary interference 31, 32, 90
Archibugi, D. 202, 238
Arendt, Hannah 62, 114, 232
Aristotle, 38, 66, 77, 114, 222
Arnold, J. 19
Aron, R. 235
assimilation 83–92, 94, 101–3, 108, 110
Association of World Citizens 238
Astell, M. 33
Athens 37, 39
 see also Greece
Atkinson, M. 3
Augustine 17
Australian Aboriginal Progressive Association 87
Australian Citizenship Act 3, 80, 104, 114, 116–17

Australian Conservation Foundation 207
Australian Greens 208
Australian Industries Greenhouse Network 211
autonomy 38, 43, 66, 138–40, 159–63, 171–2, 219, 220–1, 223

Baier, A. 62, 63
Banks, J. 207
Barbalet, J.M. 5, 77, 122, 123, 128
Barber, B. 176, 177, 219
Barbieri, W.A. 1
Barton, C. 210
Barton, E. 102, 106
Bauböck, R. 7
Bauman, Z. 143, 202
Bavin, T.R. 19
Bean, C.E. 208
Bearfield, S. 147
Beck, U. 18
Becker, G. 219
Beilharz, P. 3, 9, 37–44, 80, 81
Beiner, R. 7
Beitz, C. 167–8
Bellah, R. 219
Bellamy, D. 211
belonging 223, 227, 228
'benchmark men' 111, 117–19
Benhabib, S. 62, 138, 141, 142
Bentham, J. 33, 161, 162, 163, 178
Berlin, I. 161
Betts, K. 235
bill of rights 24, 48, 212
Blackburn, Justice 94
Blackstone, W. 27
Bland, F.A. 48
Boardman, R. 211

266

Bobbio, N. 51, 233
Body Shop, The 130
Bonazzi, T. 7
Bowden, P. 60, 61
Brady, H. 167
Braithwaite, J. 27, 130
Brennan, J. 78, 113, 156
Brennan, F. 24
Bridges, T. 6
Brossat, A. 51
Brubaker, R. 1
Brunton, N. 210
Bryson, L. 144
Buchanan, J. 147
Bull, H. 236
Bulmer, M. 6, 138
Burchell, D. 8
Burgess, M. 4
Burgmann, V. 238
Butler, J. 151, 152

Camilieri, J.A. 7
capacities 16, 86, 88, 165, 168, 223–4
　of Indigenous people 88–9, 91, 93, 97
capitalism 146, 183
Cappo, P. 81
Cardozo, A. 7
care 56, 59, 60, 63, 64
Carney, S. 143
Carney, T. 140
Carson, R. 207
Carter, A. 10, 174–84, 240
Carter, D. 23
Cass, B. 144
Cass, D. 118
Castan, R. 94
Castles, F. 142, 144, 147
Castles, S. 4, 103, 143
Cesarani, D. 1
Chalmers, T. 20
Chesterman, J. 2, 3, 89
Christoff, P. 10, 189, 200–14
Cicero 27, 171
citizen-soldier 175–7, 181, 183
citizenship 5–7, 16, 78
　active 168, 189, 201, 223–26
　Australian 4, 18, 19, 45–7, 48, 57, 67, 78, 142–3
　capacity for 16, 86, 93, 97 165, 168, 223, 224
　claims to 38
　communitarian 10
　consumer 81, 126, 130, 131
　corporate 129, 130, 191, 195, 223
　democracy and 45–55
　differential 15–25

　differentiated 15, 180–1, 183
　discourse 1, 2, 68, 73
　domain of 8, 9, 16
　dual 106, 113, 115, 235
　ecological 10, 200, 206, 209, 211, 212
　economic 29, 121–35, 223
　educational 158–73
　environmental 200–14, 223, 224
　exclusion from 16, 18, 79, 101, 102, 108, 111, 122, 138, 141, 143, 180, 227
　feminist critiques 60, 61
　global 123, 224, 231–42
　'good' 17, 18, 114
　Indigenous 86–98
　industrial 126, 128, 129, 131
　international 66, 232, 236
　intimate 152, 153
　legal 111–120
　liberal conception of 5, 6, 171
　limits to 66–74
　meaning of 115
　media 185–199
　military 223
　and military service 174–84
　moral 67, 83, 224, 225, 228
　multicultural 223
　and multiculturalism 99–110
　multinational 232, 235
　multiple 16, 18–22, 234, 239
　object of 8, 9, 10
　political 23, 77–85
　practice of 16, 40, 61
　protective 165–6, 169–70
　religious 17
　republican 15, 23, 24, 174
　sexual 150–7, 223
　social 127, 136–49
　subject of 8, 9
　transnational 232, 235–9
　world 237–9
citizenship acts, Australian 2, 3, 80, 89, 104, 114, 115–17
civic virtue 158, 159, 171, 225
civics education 3, 45, 54, 55
Civics Expert Group 41, 45, 78
civil society 9, 61, 64, 84, 219
Clarke, P. 8
Cohen, M. 128, 233
Cohen, P. 92
Commission on Global Governance 238
common good 170, 171
commonwealth 126
Commonwealth Electoral Act 115
communal traditions, of Aborigines 92, 94
communications, global 187, 188, 198
　see also technological innovation

Communist Party of Australia 87
communitarianism 34, 35, 136, 140, 142, 170, 171, 215–30
    strong 224
community 72, 78, 140, 220
    cyberspace 194
    of fate 67
    of learning 165
    moral 7, 67, 221, 241
    political 202
    in political theory 219–21
    shared 179, 180
    thin or thick 224–6
    transnational 205
    value of 226–7
    virtual 202
    voluntary 222
Conference on Humans and the Environment 211
Connolly, W. 220, 221
Connors, L. 207
conscription 176, 178, 182
Considine, M. 3, 39, 80, 81
constitution 27, 48, 49, 100, 106
    French 49
    US 27
Constitution, Australian 79, 80, 83, 106, 111–15, 215
consumers 81, 125, 126
contractualism 139–41
Coombs, H.C. 127
Cooper, W. 87
Cope, B. 103, 107, 143
Corlett, W. 220, 223
Cornwall, A. 210
corporate citizenship 129, 130, 191, 195, 223
cosmopolitan ideas 232, 233, 234
Council for Aboriginal Affairs 92
Council of Europe 50
Cox, E. 6, 9, 56–65, 219
Crawford, M. 26
customary law 91–4

Dabscheck, B. 128
Dagger, R. 1, 161
Dahl, R. 69, 77, 160
Dahlgreen, T. 187
Davidson, A. 2, 9, 18, 45–55, 77, 81
Dawson, J. 113
Day of Mourning 86, 87, 89
Dean, M. 8
Deane, J. 113
defence 174, 177, 179
democracy 35, 36, 77, 126, 128, 131 138, 141, 142, 164, 191, 203, 212, 219, 239
    and citizenship 45–55

Denham, M.E. 6
Der Derian, J. 202
deregulation, 42, 43, 69, 123, 146
Dewey, J. 165, 172
Dietrich, D. 193
differential citizenship 15–25
differentiated citizenship 180–1, 183
Diogenes the Cynic 232
Discovering Democracy 45–52, 54
discrimination 150, 154, 156, 180
Dixon, O. 113
domain of citizenship 8, 9, 16
Domestic Relations Act of 1994 (ACT) 154
Dunne, M. 7
Durkheim, E. 122
Duschesne, S. 48

Eade, J. 52
Eardley, T. 140
Earth Summit 211
ecological citizenship 10, 200, 206, 209, 211–12
ecologically sustainable development 106, 208, 210
economic citizenship 29, 121–35, 223
economic rationalism 71, 81, 83, 84
economics 124, 126, 131
economy 70, 71, 125, 143
education 9, 81
    and citizenship 158–73
efficiency, economic 105
egalitarianism 79
Ehrlich, P. 211
Einhorn, B. 1
Eisenstein, H. 58
Elshtain, J.B. 182
employment 117–28, 133, 140, 147
    see also work
Emy, H.V. 132
Environment Protection Act 1969 (US) 211
environmental citizenship 200–14, 223, 224
Environmental Defenders' Offices 210
environmental movement 125, 126, 136, 202, 203, 206, 207, 208, 210, 211, 212, 233, 238
Environmental Protection (Impact of Proposals) Act 1974 210
Equal Opportunity Act 1995 (Victoria) 156
equality 77, 82, 137, 138, 140, 142, 171, 218
    gender 143, 144, 148, 151
    political 167–8
equity 106, 108
Esping-Andersen, G. 142, 143, 147
ethic, discourse 16, 240, 241
ethnic cleansing 67, 218

Etzioni, A. 52, 176, 219, 221, 225
European Union 53, 235
Evans, D.T. 117, 152, 153, 236
Evans, G. 95, 96
exclusion 16, 18, 79, 111, 122, 138, 140, 180
  nationalism of 101, 102, 108

Falk, J. 7
Falk, R. 202, 233, 238, 241
federation 2, 4, 57, 101, 106, 109, 112, 234–5
feminism 117, 125, 126
  and citizenship 4, 6, 56–65, 144, 176, 206
  and media 193
  and military service 191, 182
  and sexuality 150–1
Ferguson, W. 87
Ferrijoli, L. 7
Field Naturalists' Clubs (NSW and Victoria) 207
Findlayson, J.D. 97
Fingleton, J. 97
Finney, C. 207
Fisse, B. 130
Fletcher, C. 240
foreign power, citizen of 112–14
Foucault, M. 71, 72, 152, 220
Fraser government 92, 104
Frazer, E. 136
freedom 30–4, 50, 128, 178
  negative 138
  as non-domination 28–9, 31–2, 35, 161
  as non-interference 33
  republican 27–30
French Revolution 37–8, 49, 176
Friends of the Earth 233
Fulbrook, M. 1

Gaebler, T. 8
Gagnon, A.-G. 4
Galbally Report 104, 105
Galligan, B. 2, 3, 4, 89, 227
Game Protection Act (NSW) 209
Garran, R.R. 112
Gatens, M. 117
Gates, Bill 190, 191, 196
Gauchet, M. 51
Gaudron, J. 113, 114
general will 169, 170, 240
genocide 47, 143
George, J. 148
Gersuny, C. 122, 128
Ghils, P. 238
Giddens, A. 18, 219
Gilligan, C. 60

Glazer, N, 7
Global Citizens' Association 238
global citizenship 232–4
globalisation 40–3, 52, 106, 200–1, 211, 218, 232–4
  and immigration 100
Goldstein, V. 47
Goldsworthy, D. 236
good, common 170, 171, 225
Goodall, Heather, 87, 88
Goodwin, C.S. 1
Goot, M. 97
Gould, J. 207
government 69, 70, 73, 109, 110, 158
  local 53, 106
  national 71–3
  world 239
Grassby, A. 103–4
Gray, J. 136
Greece 67, 175, 176
Green, L.C. 233
Green, T.H. 3
Greenpeace 207, 211, 233
Gullett, W. 210
Gunningham, N. 210
Gutmann, A. 7, 8, 159, 163, 172, 221

Habermas, J. 7, 81, 201, 239, 240
Hain, P. 220
Hamilton, P. 8
Hammar, T. 7
Hampson, 146
Hanks, P. 143
Hanson, P. 52, 54, 132
Harrington, D. 189
Harrington, J. 27, 175
Hartstock, N. 176
Hasluck, P. 88–91, 102, 103
Hawke government 105
Heater, D. 7, 15, 77, 114, 232, 233, 239
Held, D. 202, 233, 234, 238
heritage, Indigenous 87
Herman, E.S. 191, 192
Hersberg, E. 6
heterogeneity 141, 217
Heywood, A. 226
Higgins, W. 10, 136–49
High Court (Australia) 93–5, 97, 111, 112–14, 118
Hill, B. 33
Hindess, B. 7, 10, 15, 66–74, 179, 180
Hindmarsh Island 118
Hirsch, G.C. and H. 233
Hirst, P. 136, 220
Hobbes, T. 161
Hobson, J.L. 128

Hogan, D. 9, 158–73
homogeneity 33, 34, 102, 141, 201, 217
homosexuality, laws against 154
Honneth, A. 218
Hornblower, S. 175
Horne, D. 4, 172
Horner, J. 86
'householding' 124
Howard government 96, 97, 132
Howard, J. 195, 215, 216
Hudson, W. 1–11, 15–25
Human Rights (Sexual Conduct) Act 154, 155
Human Rights and Equal Opportunity Commission 154, 155
Hutton, D. 207
Hyland, N. 1

identity 38, 39, 100, 105, 194, 197, 223
  civic 231, 241
  multiple 42
  national 108, 182
immigration 102, 103, 106, 116, 201
imperialism 42
inclusion 137, 218, 223, 227
incorporation 92, 95
Indigenous citizenship 86–98
Indigenous people 9, 79, 86–98, 101, 117, 118
  and new media 194
individualism, liberal 219, 225
information, distribution of 169, 185, 191
  information poor 193
  information rich 192
'infotainment' 193
innovation, technological 186–92, 197, 201
insitutions 31, 32, 84, 132, 142, 235
  and citizenship 22–4
  international 200, 202, 238
  post-liberal 148
integration 103, 108, 140
Inter-Governmental Agreement on the Environment 210
interaction 140, 190, 194
interests 168, 174
  common 171
  framing of 163–4
  protection of 165
  theory of 159–63
interference 31, 32, 90
International Court of Justice 239
International Labour Organization 125
International Red Cross 233, 237
internationalism 5, 231
interpretation, constitutional 113
  judicial 115

intersubjectivism 136–7
Irving, H. 2, 19, 57, 58, 114

Jacobson, D. 1
James, P. 132
Janoski, T. 6
Jansen, S.C. 193
Jayasuriya, L. 80
Jefferson, T. 176
Jellin, E. 6
Johnson, C. 195
Jones, K.B. 117, 118
Jordens, A.-M. 2
Junn, J. 164, 169
Jupp Report 105
justice 60, 63, 78, 138, 140, 142, 162, 219
  international 183, 236
  social 105

Kalantzis, M. 9, 99–110, 143
Kaldor, M. 1
Kane, J. 1–11, 215–30
Kant, I. 37, 38, 161, 162, 163, 177, 233
Kaplan, A. 51
Kardamitsis, 113, 114, 117
Kavan, Z. 1
Keane, J. 124
Keating, P. 53, 105, 106, 182, 195
Keating government 95
Kelsen, H. 47
Kemp, D. 45–8, 52
Kenny, S. 142
Kernot, C. 96
Keynes, J.M. 125
  Keynesianism 127, 131
Klusmeyer, D. 5
Korpi, W. 143, 145, 146
Korten, D.C. 238
Kukathas, C. 172
Kymlicka, W. 1, 40, 77, 83, 7, 160, 161, 171, 176, 220

labour 124, 128
  market 123, 144, 149
  movement 125, 126, 148
Lacey, N. 136
Lake, M. 3, 39, 117
Land and Environment Court (NSW) 210
land rights 93, 94, 96
land trusts 96
Lang, J.D. 19–22
Langton, M. 86
language, of citizenship 68, 73
Lash, S. 18
Latham, M. 219

law, environmental 208, 209, 210
  international 197, 234, 236, 238
  rule of 29, 35, 110
Le Pen, J. 52
Lesbian and Gay Legal Rights Service 156
Levi-Strauss 130
Lewis, J. 138
liberalism 26, 33, 35, 64, 136, 139–41, 148, 179, 183, 212, 225, 226
  and community 217, 218
  criticism of 138, 215–16, 219–20, 223
  economic 144, 145, 149
  market 121, 125
  and military service 178, 179
  welfare 225
liberty 26, 60, 158, 160, 163, 172
  as non-domination 9, 161
  republican 159, 160, 161, 162, 163
  see also freedom
Linklater, A. 232, 233, 236, 241
Linnean Society 207
Lipschutz, R.D. 205
Lister, R. 151
Locke, J. 166, 178
Lovelock, Bill 91, 92
Luhmann, N. 18
Lyon, D. 192

Mabo decision 93, 95, 105, 118
McAllister, I. 208
McChesney, R.W. 191, 192
McGrath, A. 118
McGregor, R. 88
McHugh, J. 113
MacIntyre, A. 219
MacKellar, M. 104
Macphee, I.M. 104, 105
Macedo, S. 140, 166
Machiavelli, N. 27, 175
Mamdani, M. 1
manufacturing sector 145
Marginson, S. 3
Maritime Union of Australia 51
market 83, 122, 142, 145, 147
Markus, A. 87
Marshall, T.H. 5, 6, 39, 41, 78, 122, 127–8, 138, 153, 179, 204, 222
Martin, D.F. 97
Marxism 125, 131
Mason, C.J. 113
mateship 216
Mather, L. 210
Meadows, D.H. et al. 207
Meadows, M. 194
media 185–99
  see also technological innovation

Medicare 81
Meehan, 1, 7, 235
Meriam land claim 93, 95, 105
Meyer, W.J. 217
military service, citizenship and 174–84
Mill, J.S. 86, 160, 162, 163, 168, 179, 217
Miller, D. 136
Miller, C. 208
minority groups 117
  sexual 150, 153
Minson, J.P. 7
modernism 40, 43
Molnar, H. 193
Montaigne, M. de 233
Montesquieu, C. de 27, 28, 32, 158, 159
Moran, M. 6
More, E. 188
Morgan, W. 155, 156
Morris, C. 194
Morrissey, M. 103, 143
Mouffe, C. 172
Mountain Trails Clubs 207
Moyal, A. 207
Moynihan, Justice 94, 95
Muir, K. 181
multiculturalism 7, 9, 39, 52, 79, 104, 108, 109, 141, 220, 227
Multilateral Agreement on Investment 124
multinational citizenship 232, 235
Murdoch, R. 195
Murray Island 94
Murray, L. 116
Musto, L. 7

Nair, S. 52
nation-state 7, 15, 39–40, 45, 49, 52–3, 100–1, 174, 201, 202, 218, 222, 231, 234, 237
National Agenda for a Multicultural Australia 105
National Organization for Women 182
nationalism 4, 5, 101–3, 107–9, 121, 123, 183, 217, 231
  of exclusion 101, 102, 108
Nationality and Citizenship Act 2, 89, 116
Native Title Act 95, 96
Natural History Association 207
naturalisation 114, 115, 206
NGOs 233, 237, 238
Nie, N. 164, 169
Nielsen, J.S. 1
non-domination, freedom as 9, 28–9, 31–2, 35, 161
non-interference, freedom as 30, 31, 33
Norman, R. 122, 132
Norman, W. 40, 77, 83, 176

norms, sexual 152, 157
Novak, M. 219
Nozick, R. 219
Nussbaum, M.C. 233

O'Dowd, B. 47
object of citizenship 8, 9, 10
obligations 63, 116
Offe, C. 207
Ok Tedi 130
Oldfield, A. 8, 222
Oliver, D. 239
One Nation 132
opportunity, equal 181
organisations, popular 147–9
Ormerod, P. 85
Osborne, D.E. 3
Our Common Future 211
Owens, J. 124
ownership, of media 186, 195

Packer, K. 195
Pain, N. 210
Painter, M. 125
Paley, W. 33, 34
Palme, J. 143, 145, 146
Panitch, L. 131
Papadakis, E. 208
Papua New Guinea 130
participation 51, 53, 108, 138, 140, 200, 202, 223–4, 228
  in mass media 187
Pateman, C. 6, 60, 117, 141, 151
Patten, C. 87
Patterson, O. 58
peace movement 238
Pearson, N. 95, 221
Petre, D. 189
Pettit, 4, 9, 23, 26–36, 51, 161, 171
Phillips, A. 117, 118, 240
Phillips, D.L. 221
Pixley, J. 6, 9, 17, 121–35, 139, 144
Plant, R. 83, 121
Plummer, K. 152, 153
pluralism 67, 71–2, 226
  civic 99–101, 105, 106–9, 110
Pocock, B. 144
Pocock, J.G.A. 175
Polanyi, K. 142
policy, economic 125, 127
  foreign 177
  industry 143–5
  labour market 143, 145–6
  post-liberal 148
  welfare 143, 145, 146
political citizenship 77–85

politics of difference 220, 240
Poster, M. 190
postmodernism 5, 69, 220
  and citizenship 37–44
power 50, 63, 64, 117, 132
  arbitrary 28, 31, 32, 90, 141, 178
preamble to Australian constitution 215–16
Price, R. 30
privatisation 82
property 43, 117, 128
prostitution 154, 155
Prostitution Control Act (Victoria) 154
Pryles, M. 116
public good 225
  life 56
  reason 166
  space 187, 198
Pusey, M. 144
Putnam, R.D. 219

Quick, J. 112
Quiggin, J. 127

Racial Discrimination Act 1975 118
racism 102, 118
Rahe, P.A. 176
Rainbow Warrior 211
Ramia, G. 10, 136–49
rationality 63, 164, 136
Rawls, J. 141, 160, 162–4, 171, 179, 180, 219
Raz, J. 160, 162, 163, 171, 220
reconciliation 79, 106
Rees, A.M. 6, 138
regulation 144, 145, 147, 148
Reich, R. 41, 42, 70
republic, Australian 83, 84, 106
republicanism 35, 36, 136, 158, 177, 182
  Australian 19, 20
  and citizenship 4, 26–36
Resource Assessment Commission 208
respect 220
responsibility 89, 117, 223, 224, 228
Reynolds, H. 93
Rheingold, H. 196
Richardson, D. 152
Richmond, A.H. 234
Riesenberg, P. 222
rights 6, 7, 34, 35, 50, 63, 64, 80, 84, 112, 116, 117, 174, 181, 204, 210, 220
  to bear arms 176, 179
  citizenship 86, 223
  civil 24, 127, 128, 132
  consumer 121, 132
  ecological 203, 204, 205, 206

economic 225, 228
environmental 203–6
of gays, lesbians and queers 155
human 53, 130, 205, 236
Indigenous 97
industrial 121, 128, 129, 132
international human 239
land 88, 92, 94, 95, 96, 97
political 127, 132
property 210
social 100, 122, 123, 132, 139, 203–6, 225, 228
of women 56, 148
Robinson, D. 210
Roche, M. 1, 5, 77, 122
Rogers, J. 127
Rome 67, 175, 176
Rorty, R. 41
Rosenau, J.N. 202
Rousseau, J-J. 47, 48, 51, 168, 169, 170, 175
Rowley, C.D. 92
Rowse, T. 3, 9, 86–98
Royal Societies 207
Rubenstein, K. 115, 118
Rubin, G. 151, 152
rule of law 29, 35, 110

Salvaris, M. 9, 77–85
same-sex relationships, legal status of 156
Sandel, M. 219
Sardar, Z. 191, 194
Saul, J.R. 77, 84
Saunders, P. 143
Sawer, M. 59, 118
Scandinavia 146–7, 148
Schlozman, K. 167
Schmid, G. 146–7
Schneider, S. 211
Schultz, J. 186
Schumpeter, J. 142, 166
Scott, E. 19
Second World War 182, 183
security, economic 123, 133
social 127, 140
Sedgwick, E.K. 151
self-determination 77, 92, 94, 105, 109, 161–2, 172
sensationalism in media 186
sex workers 154
see also prostitution
sexual practices 151–2, 157
Sharp, N. 94
Shaver, S. 144
Shelton, D. 205
Simms, M. 118
Singh, M.J. 7

Skinner, Q. 171
Skocpol, T. 39
slavery, 28, 30
Slawner, K. 6
Smith, D.E. 97
Smith, M.F. 4
Smith, T. 130
social capital 57, 61–3, 64, 219
social citizenship 136–49
social contract 60
social protection 142, 156–6, 169–70
social services 81, 82
Solomon, N. 107
Somerville, M. 128, 233
South Africa 130
sovereignty 124, 130, 169
Indigenous 93
national 42, 49, 203, 218, 237
Soysal, Y.N. 7
Sparks, C. 187
Speck, C. 182
Spender, D. 193
Springborg, P. 175, 176
Spurgeon, C. 195
Stacey, M. 221
state 30, 59, 64, 67
see also nation-state
Statute of Westminster Adoption Act (1942) 2
Stehlik-Barry, K. 164, 169
Stein, P. 210
Steir, M. 221
Stephen, N. 78, 80
Stoics 161, 232, 233
Stokes, G. 3, 9, 88, 231–42
Stolen Children 118
Strasbourg Consensus 50, 53
Streeck, W. 127
subject of citizenship 8, 9
subjecthood 18, 112, 136
British 116
Sullivan, B. 9, 97, 150–7
Suter, K. 238
Suzuki, D. 211
Switzerland 176
Sydney, A. 30
Sykes, R. 118
Sykes v. Cleary 113–15

Taberner, J. 210
Takaki, R. 103
Taylor, C. 160, 161, 218, 219, 220, 226
technological innovation 186–92, 197, 201
technology transfer 201
telecommunications 195
The Body Shop 130
Thornton, M. 9, 111–20

Tiffen, R. 186
tolerance 220, 226
Toohey, J. 113
Toyne, P. 210
transnational citizenship 232, 235–9
transnational corporations 130
trust 61–4
Tufte, E. 77
Tully, J. 7, 138, 141
Turner, B. 8, 23, 77, 122, 147
Turner, G. 81, 233
Twine, F. 5

UN Charter 237
UNDP 236
UNESCO 236
United Nations 236, 238
Universal Declaration of Human Rights 128, 237
utilitarianism 161–2
utopia, technological 188–91
utopian thinking 241

Valverde, M. 86
van Acker, E. 9, 185–99
Van Berkel, R. 1
van Gunsteren, H. 3, 206
van Steenbergen, B. 3, 205
Verba, S. 167
Victorian Land Conservation Council 208
virtue, civic, 158, 159, 171, 225
Voet, R. 176
Vogel, U. 6
von Mueller, F. 207
vote, equal 47, 58, 167

Wajcman, J. 193
Waks, L.J. 204
Walby, S. 6, 122
Walker, R.B. 209
Walter, J. 22, 24
Walzer, M. 8, 52, 219
war, 178–9
Ward, I. 193

Warhurst, J. 208
Warrington, J. 114
watchdog, role of media 185
Watts, R. 3, 39, 80, 81
Weale, A. 233
Webb, S. and B. 128–9
Weeks, J. 152–3
Weiss, L. 128
welfare state 5, 42, 53, 81, 143, 144, 146, 149
White Australia Policy 79, 101, 102, 112, 143
Whitlam, G. 239
Whitlam government, 47, 58, 81
Wik decision, 51, 93, 118
Wilderness Society 207
Wildlife Preservation Society of Australia 207
Willcox, M. 210
Wills, S. 154
Wirszubski, C. 26
Wishart, D. 112
Wittgenstein, L. 221
women 57, 58, 117
    as soldiers 181–2
    see also feminism
Woodward, Justice 95, 96
work 127–9, 133
    integration with welfare 146–7
    paid 124–5, 140
    unpaid 56, 59, 121, 124, 133, 140
    see also employment
Workers' Educational Association 3
world citizenship 237–9
World Conservation Strategy 211
World Trade Organization 107, 122, 236

Yeatman, A. 4, 6, 7, 141
Yolugu case 94
Young, I.M. 34, 60, 151, 180, 218, 240

Zolo, D. 51
Zoological Society 207
Zwiebach, B. 114